RYNR

BELOW THE BELT

BELOW THE BELT

Novelty, Subterfuge and Surprise in Naval Warfare

John Winton

CONWAY MARITIME PRESS

© John Winton 1981
First published in Great Britain 1981 by
Conway Maritime Press Ltd,
2 Nelson Road, Greenwich,
London SE10 9JB

ISBN 0 85177 236 6

Typesetting by Computacomp (UK) Ltd, Fort William, Scotland
Printed and bound in Great Britain by Butler & Tanner Ltd, Frome

CONTENTS

LIST OF ILLUSTRATIONS

with which he put the Danish fleet to flight in Kiel harbour, in 1850. After 36 years on the bottom it was raised and put on display at the Naval Museum, Berlin. (Author's Collection)

Early photograph of Robert Whitehead with a trials torpedo, somewhat battered. (RNAD Museum, Gosport)

Page 80
Launch of Royal Navy's first submarine *Holland I* at Vickers Son & Maxim Ltd, Barrow-in-Furness, 2 November 1901. (Author's Collection)

Interior of an early submarine (possibly Holland's third boat, built at Delameter Iron Works, New York, 1881). 1. Captain's seat 2. Steering wheel 3. Fore-planes 4. Aft planes 5. Depth gauge 6. Air bottles. (Author's Collection)

Page 95
Popular pre-1914 idea of the fate of submarines in the next war: *Hermione* running down *B3*. (From *Trafalgar Refought* (1905) by Sir W Laird Clowes and Alan Burgoyne)

The reality of submarine attack: HMS *Aboukir* sinking after torpedo attack by *U9*, 22 September 1914. (Picture by Charles Dixon)

Page 96
Machine vessels at Antwerp, 1585. (Willem Baudart)

Lieutenant R D Sandford RN winning the VC by driving the old submarine *C3*, loaded with explosives, against the Mole at Zeebrugge. He and his crew can be seen escaping in their dinghy before the submarine blew up. (Author's Collection)

Page 116
HMS *Campbeltown* in the lock gates at St Nazaire. (Imperial War Museum)

55-foot Coastal Motor-Boat of the type which attacked Kronstadt harbour in 1919. (Imperial War Museum)

Page 135
Cdr Antonio Pellegrini's *Grillo* ('Cricket'), the curious boom-climbing 'tank' used in an attack on Pola harbour, 13 May 1918. (Author's Collection)

An Italian MAS boat with two torpedoes loaded. (Imperial War Museum)

Page 136
Cdr Luigi Rizzo attacking the Austrian dreadnought *Svent Istvan* on the night of 9/10 June 1918. (Author's Collection)

Below the Belt

One of the 'Sleeping Beauties' tried out by the Cockleshell Heroes: Quentin Reeves' Motorised Submersible Canoe, seen here sinking slowly to make the last stage of its stealthy approach to the target. (Author's Collection)

Page 153
A Welman craft on launchway with detachable warhead (left) being prepared for fitting. (Royal Navy Submarine Museum)

A 'T' class submarine, with Mk I Chariots and two containers, mounted aft, alongside a depot ship. (Author's Collection)

Page 154
A British Mark I Chariot being hoisted out for trials. (Imperial War Museum)

German explosive motor-boats found at Flushing, 1945. (Author's Collection)

Page 174
German 'Linse' explosive motor-boats in harbour. (Imperial War Museum)

A German 'Neger' human torpedo being readied for action. (Conway Picture Library)

Page 175
Captured German 'Seehund' midget submarines in the bomb-proof factory where they were being built, 1945. (Author's Collection)

German 'Biber' one-man midget submarine beached ashore. (Imperial War Museum)

Page 176
XE-craft midget submarine on the surface in Sydney Harbour, 1945. (Imperial War Museum)

Two Japanese suicide motor-boats, captured by US Marines on Okinawa, April 1945. Chalked on the nearest boat is the warning: 'Danger. These boats are booby-trapped.' (Author's Collection)

CHAPTER 1

'It was new – it was singular – it was simple!' Nelson wrote to Lady Hamilton. 'When I came to explain to them the Nelson touch, it was like an electric shock.' Nelson had rejoined his flagship *Victory* on the evening of 28 September 1805 and had called his captains, his band of brothers, on board to brief them. Afterwards, in this letter of 1 October, Nelson succinctly expressed, in a few striking phrases, the perennial aims of every successful naval commander: to confuse and confound his enemy with some new weapon or new tactic, to make some move which was unexpected, unusual and even unfair. He succeeded in carrying his subordinate commanders with him; a plan was useless unless those who were to carry it out understood and had faith in it. From admirals downwards, Nelson said, it was repeated: 'It must succeed, if ever they will allow us to get at them.'

The plans Nelson explained to his captains before Trafalgar were indeed revolutionary in terms of naval tactics of the time. For a hundred years before Nelson, fleets had fought in formal lines of battle, manoeuvring in rigid formation until they came within range of each other. Once within hitting range, the tactic was to press alongside and stay alongside pouring in fire 'as fast as she could suck it' until, as every English sailor confidently expected (and with good reason), the enemy struck his flag.

Close quarter fighting was still Nelson's intention but he intended a more flexible, original approach. He would have his fleet in three divisions. One, of sixteen ships, he would lead himself; Collingwood would lead another. There would also be an advance squadron of eight of the fastest ships lying up to windward. Collingwood would aim to cut the enemy's battle line twelve ships from its rear. Nelson himself would go for the centre, where he expected his adversary Villeneuve to be. Those enemy ships not attacked at first, in the leading section of their fleet, would need time to turn and come back. In the meantime, Nelson and Collingwood would defeat their opponents in detail.

As Nelson said, 'Nothing is certain in a sea fight', and in the event he had less ships than he expected and thus had no windward

9

squadron. The rest of the plan, however, worked as Nelson had hoped and prayed it would.

Nelson's plan was all the more startling (some of his captains wept when they heard it) because the age of sail offered a commander few opportunities for innovation or guile, apart from disguise or decoy, or bluffing or misleading his opponent. Tactically, the need to gain and hold the weather gauge was paramount. In this sense the wind imposed a kind of tactical simplicity. Technological advance in weapons was so slow over the centuries that *Victory* herself, with some improvements in gun mountings and navigational instruments, was still essentially the same weapon of war as *Sovereign of the Seas*, launched in 1637.

Yet, within the limitations of his time, Nelson was following a tradition which goes back in recorded western naval history to the Greek admirals of the Peloponnesian War. The Greeks of the fifth century BC had an attitude to naval warfare which survives today. The most successful of their commanders did not consider naval engagements as mere land battles fought on board ships. They knew there was a science of the sea, and they had navies largely manned by citizens who were quite capable of understanding subtle psychological debating points about their adversaries.

The Athenians entered the Peloponnesian War in 431 BC with the best navy in the known world at the time and a confidence born of the crushing strategic naval victory over the Persian fleet at Salamis, which was still within living memory. The Greeks had, in fact, prepared the way for their victory at Salamis with a trick which was just as effective in the Second World War: the delivery into the enemy's councils of false or misleading information about one's own intentions. Xerxes had 1207 ships (according to Aeschylus) against Themistocles' 310. The Greeks had somehow to lure the Persians into the narrow waters off Salamis where the restricted space would nullify the advantage of numbers. Just as the body of a Royal Marine officer bearing false information about the next Allied landing in the Mediterranean was allowed to fall into German hands, so Themistocles dispatched the famous messenger Sicinnus, by night, to Xerxes' camp with false intelligence: the Greeks were demoralised, contemplating flight, and on the morrow would either make no resistance or fight amongst themselves. Sicinnus was believed, just as 'The Man Who Never Was' was believed, and the Persian ships were lured into the narrows.

The Greeks were adept at psychological warfare, both to demoralise opponents and to hearten their own side. They were ever resourceful in devising tactic, and counter-tactic, ploy and counter-ploy. In a sense the Greeks could be said to have constructed the historical framework for any study of unusual or unorthodox fighting at sea.

The standard Greek warship of the line was the trireme, manned by 5 officers, 25 deck-hands or boatswains, and 170 oarsmen (ranged and rowing in a manner which is still a matter of debate amongst naval historians). Although marines were often embarked for boarding an enemy, or as additional weapon-throwers, the trireme's main weapon was the ram. The two most important offensive manoeuvres were the *diekplous*, in which one fleet endeavoured to break through its opponent's line, then wheel about and ram the enemy's unprotected sides, or the *periplous*, in which one fleet attempted to row around the ends of its opponent's line and take its ships in the rear. Both manoeuvres required a high degree of training and seamanship.

A typical action, fought and won by Phormio, one of the best admirals of the ancient world, took place in the Gulf of Patras one night late in the summer of 429 BC. Phormio was leading a fleet of 20 Athenian triremes across the Gulf when he sighted a formation of some 47 ships of the Peloponnesian alliance, Corinthians and Spartans. It was actually an invasion fleet, drawn up in an unusual way, being formed in a circle each ship with its bows projecting outwards, and just close enough to its neighbour to prevent a *diekplous*. This was, in fact, the very formation used successfully by the Athenians themselves in an action off Cape Artemisius two months before Salamis. In the centre of the Peloponnesian circle were some light, troop-carrying craft, with 5 of the fastest and best-equipped warships, ready to go and reinforce any threatened sector of the circle.

The action took place midway in the Gulf, off the town of Patras. Phormio at first made no attempt to attack, and forbade his ships to do so. Instead, the Athenian triremes rowed steadily round and round the perimeter of the Peloponnesian circle, forcing it inwards, as though they were sheepdogs herding a flock of ewes. Phormio expected his opponents to lose their tight, careful formation and to break up as they were crowded in upon each other. He also knew that as they rounded the nearest point of land, a wind would very probably begin to blow up from the Gulf, as it almost always did about dawn.

So it came about. At dawn, the wind got up sharply, the water grew choppy, and the Peloponnesians, already compressed too close for comfort, had to try and deal simultaneously with the wind and sea and with their own small craft, which were getting in the way. As Phormio watched from without, the Peloponnesians collapsed into confusion. Ships collided, entangled their oars, and their captains

11

blamed each other. The crews were too fully occupied in fending off their friends to bother about their enemy. As Thucydides described it, 'what with the shouting and swearing and yelling, nobody could hear what the captains were saying or the orders given by the boatswains.'

Phormio now gave the signal to attack. The Athenians promptly sank one admiral's ship and then went on to destroy every ship they engaged. The Peloponnesians broke away in confusion and fled back to Patras. The Athenians pursued them, captured 12 of their ships, and made their crews prisoners.

It was a tremendous victory, and a humiliation which the Spartans in particular felt very deeply. A nation of soldiers, unused to battles at sea, the Spartans did not appreciate the huge difference in expertise between the Athenian and the Peloponnesian sailors. The Spartans put the defeat down to cowardice. Angrily, they collected together a new fleet of 77 ships, at a harbour called Panormus, on the southern shore of the Gulf of Patras. Phormio meanwhile still had his 20 ships at Rhium, on the northern shore.

Nothing happened for nearly a week. The Peloponnesians did not want to come out because they remembered what had happened last time. Phormio hesitated to go in, because he felt that a restricted space would favour his opponents. Both sides took the chance to do some training, and to harangue their ship's companies.

Cnemus and Brasidias, the Peloponnesian commanders, pointed out to their fleet that they now had many more ships than last time, when they had been caught off guard, and unprepared for what had happened. Nobody could be blamed for that. But, they said, we must learn from past errors. Every man must now do his best. The brave would be rewarded. Cowards, they ended ominously, would be punished.

For his part, Phormio could see that some of his ship's companies, experienced though they were, were understandably a little depressed by the strength of the enemy they could see ranged against them. The reason the Peloponnesians have gathered such a great force, Phormio told his men, was because they had been beaten once and were afraid of being beaten again. They believed, in their ignorance of sea affairs, that they could behave at sea just as they did on land. They are frightened, he said, and convinced we would not be here unless we were going to inflict upon them something worthy of the occasion. When one side is greatly out-numbered and *still* takes up the challenge, Phormio explained, it must mean they have something (as Thucydides reported it) 'to fall back on that is very great indeed'.

Interestingly, Phormio was instilling in his men's minds the suggestion that some unusual device or manoeuvre would equalise the difference in numbers, although there is no evidence that he had any such device in mind at the time. Phormio reassured his men he would not fight in the Gulf of Corinth, or venture into it. There would be little room for ramming, and the battle would soon become just like a land engagement, where the enemy would have the advantage of numbers. Trust in discipline and silence, Phormio said. In any battle these two counted for a great deal, and especially in a naval engagement. You have beaten these men once, he reminded them, and beaten men never have quite the same resolution when they come up against the same opponents a second time.

That was true enough, and no doubt the Athenians were encouraged by that thought. Nevertheless, the Peloponnesians did succeed in luring Phormio into the Gulf. They put to sea at dawn in four columns, sailing along the coast line, with their best 20 ships on their right wing. Seeing his base at Naupactus threatened, Phormio reluctantly put to sea himself, to cover the Peloponnesian advance.

At a signal, the Peloponnesian right wing wheeled and attacked Phormio's fleet, cutting off 9 of his ships and capturing or driving them ashore. The remaining 11 escaped and 10 of them reached Naupactus where they formed up in the harbour entrance, prows pointing to seaward and the enemy, and prepared to defend themselves. The delighted Peloponnesians pursued them, singing paeans of anticipated victory as they sailed along.

At this point came the manoeuvre which turned the battle. The eleventh and remaining Athenian ship was being pursued by a ship from Leucas (a Greek offshore island). There happened to be a merchantman anchored in the roads just ahead. The Athenians might have been fleeing, but their ship-handling was still immaculate. The Athenian rowed right round the merchantman and rammed the ship from Leucas amidships and sank it.

This, as Thucydides says, was an unexpected and unlikely action and it threw the rest of the pursuing Peloponnesians into confusion. The whole momentum of their pursuit dropped away. Some stopped rowing altogether, losing way and waiting for the rest to catch up. This was a very dangerous thing to do, with the Athenians in such close attendance and ever ready to counter-attack.

Phormio saw his chance and sallied out again. His men gave a great shout and fell upon the enemy who, in their state of disorder and uncertainty, put up only a feeble resistance. In their ignorance of the coast-line, some of the Peloponnesians ran aground.

The tables were completely turned. The Athenians retrieved all 9 ships they had lost and captured 6 more. The captain of the ship from Leucas, a Spartan called Timocrates, committed suicide.

After an inconclusive truce which began in 421 BC, the war

moved in 415 BC to Syracuse in Sicily, where the Athenians dispatched a huge invasion fleet of 134 ships, and an army of some 27,000 men. The Athenians had the overwhelming confidence that the possession of an incomparable navy brings. They had the ships, they had the men and the weapons, they had the will and the means to win.

So it seemed, and certainly the first naval actions inside the Great Harbour of Syracuse went to Athens. Poor station-keeping and discipline robbed the Syracusans of victory from a promising tactical situation, when they had forced the Athenians to retreat. When the Syracusans tried to barricade themselves behind a boom of stakes driven into the sea-bed, the Athenians brought up a ship of 10,000 talents (10 talents was about 600 pounds) fitted with towers and screened bulwarks; men in small boats fastened ropes to the stakes which were led to windlasses on the protected decks of the great ship. The stakes were dragged up or broken off short.

Meanwhile, in the spring of 413 BC, a minor and inconclusive naval action was fought in a narrow, crescent-shaped bay in the Gulf of Corinth which had the most ominous implications for the Athenian Navy. The Athenians had 33 ships at Naupactus, Phormio's old base. The Corinthians had a squadron stationed almost opposite, to protect the convoys of merchant ships bound for Sicily.

Both sides were about equal in numbers. When the Athenians under Diphilus sortied out for battle, the Corinthians under Polyanthus attacked first, ramming with specially strengthened bows. Space was so restricted that the Athenians were forced to ram head on, a tactic they always disliked. The Corinthians eventually lost 3 ships; 7 Athenian ships were disabled. There was no pursuit. No prisoners were taken by either side. The wrecks drifted out to sea on the wind, and the Athenians recovered them. Technically, it was an Athenian victory, but the Corinthians commemorated their non-defeat with victory trophies, while the Athenians did not celebrate. Their non-victory was a defeat. As Thucydides says, anticipating by some 2000 years a similar state of affairs between the English and the French navies in the Napoleonic Wars, 'For the Corinthians counted it a victory if they were not thoroughly defeated, and the Athenians considered that they had lost if they did not win easily.'

So, the Athenian navy was not invincible after all, and the Syracusan was just the navy to take encouragement. The Syracusans were themselves Greeks, who had settled and colonised that part of Sicily. They had a city state, like Athens, and a ruling democracy, like the Athenians. They were every bit as ready as the Athenians to match invention with invention, guile with guile. It was in every way a case of Greek meeting Greek.

The Syracusans learned lessons from the earlier actions and made technical improvements to their ships. They shortened their prows, to make them more solid. They reinforced with stout struts the outriggers – structures projecting from the sides of the triremes to enable the most forward rowers, sitting where the hull began to narrow towards the bows, to have a proper fulcrum for their oars.

The Syracusans launched coordinated assaults by land and sea, and gained an initial advantage. The Athenians thought they were being attacked only by land. At first, some Athenians deployed to repel the land assault. Then others hastily manned the ships. Eventually the Athenians mustered some 75 ships against the Syracusans' 80.

It was very soon clear that this battle in the Great Harbour was not going to be the fast-moving, free-ranging succession of skilled manoeuvres at which the Athenians excelled. This was no rapier play, but a hard slogging match. When they were forced to retreat, the Athenians could only back-water towards a small stretch of the Harbour shore, because the Syracusans held most of it. The Athenians were pressed back into an ever-decreasing, cramped space, whilst the Syracusans could make for the open sea, and could also bring in reinforcements.

On the first day, both sides cautiously tried each other's strengths. The Syracusans rammed and sank one or two Athenians, but otherwise there was little activity. Nicias the Athenian commander could see there was little to choose between the two sides and expected another attack on the second day. Overnight he had his damaged vessels repaired and placed a line of merchant ships, about 200 feet apart, in front of the defensive stockade. These ships also had what Thucydides calls 'dolphins' suspended from beams to guard the passages between the ships. The 'dolphins' were very probably heavy weights, which could be dropped through the bottom of any ship which tried to pass by.

Next day, earlier than before, but still with the same broad plan, the Syracusans again attacked, and again, for much of the day, there was little to choose between the two sides. The battle now swung decisively, on a simple trick.

Triremes had very little stowage room on board. The crew, of some 200 men, always went ashore after action, to prepare and eat their meals. Ariston, the best helmsman in the Syracusan fleet, now persuaded the Syracusan commanders to send a message to the city, ordering the food market to be moved down to the harbour shore, and ordering everyone who had provisions to sell to bring them near the ships. The plan was to get the Syracusan sailors ashore, have their meal quickly, and go into action again. This was done. The Syracusan fleet backed-water towards the city, and the crews disembarked.

To the Athenians, this was a very welcome sight. Clearly, the Syracusans had had enough for one day. Thinking their work was over until the next morning, the Athenian sailors leisurely disembarked, to stretch their legs on shore, prepare and eat their meal, examine their ships and gear for damage and generally to get ready in an unhurried way for the morrow's action. Suddenly, to their dismay, they saw the whole Syracusan fleet putting out into the Harbour again.

The Athenians re-embarked in a state of tremendous confusion. Most of them had not yet eaten. None of them were mentally prepared for battle. For some time, the two fleets watched each other. The Syracusans could afford to wait. Their sailors were refreshed and had full stomachs. Finally, the Athenians tired of waiting and, cheering each other on, attacked all along the line.

Now, to their discomfort, the Athenians discovered that this was to be a different kind of battle. They, with their lightly-built ships, abhorred head-on encounters, scorning them as the sure sign of a poor helmsman. But the Syracusans, having so massively reinforced their ships' bows, now actively sought prow-to-prow collisions and began to inflict terrible damage upon their lighter opponents. To this tremendous structural damage to the ships was added the casualties amongst the crews caused by the javelin throwers the Syracusans had packed on their upper decks. The Syracusans also used flotillas of small craft who sneaked in close under the Athenian oars and hurled weapons onto the Athenian decks.

In the end, the Athenians were badly beaten. They retreated through their line of defensive merchant ships. But they were still dangerous. When two of the pursuing Syracusans came too close, one ship was captured and the other destroyed. Seven Athenian ships were captured in the battle and many more destroyed. Their crews were made prisoner or summarily put to death. The Syracusans put up victory trophies, and grew ever more confident of winning, by sea as well as by land.

In Syracuse, as always in military history, events on land and sea went together. Land forces could be supported or frustrated by sea power. In the end, sea power needed a final resolution on land to make it meaningful. Before the Syracusans could take any further action to follow up their success, the Athenians were reinforced by the arrival of about 70 ships carrying 5000 hoplites (heavy infantry), javelin throwers, slingers and archers, commanded by Demosthenes and Eurymedon. But the advantage of the reinforcements was soon dissipated in a heavy defeat for the Athenians in the night battle of Epipolae, which caused widespread despondency amongst the

Athenian army. Demosthenes, coming with a fresh eye to the campaign, suggested that the Athenians consider the possibility of withdrawal to another part of Sicily. Nicias refused. He believed that the Syracusans were in just as precarious a position, and it would not do to advertise the Athenians' predicament.

Demosthenes' advice was underlined by yet another Syracusan victory, with the debut of yet another new tactic. The Athenian fleet of 76 ships under Eurymedon was comprehensively defeated by a Syracusan fleet of 86 ships. Eurymedon himself was killed. Not satisfied with merely driving the Athenian ships ashore, the Syracusans filled an old merchant ship with faggots and pine logs and set it adrift, hoping it would burn the Athenian ships they had not been able to capture. The Athenians managed to put out the flames before the ship could come near their ships.

This primitive form of fire-ship had failed, but nevertheless it had been another great naval victory for Syracuse. Their ships now began to sail about the Great Harbour much as they pleased, whilst the Athenians were utterly disheartened. They could hardly believe what had happened to them. The skilful use of new tactics and manoeuvres by the Syracusans, together with hard unrelenting fighting whenever it was necessary, reduced the Athenians to the state where they decided they must risk everything in one final confrontation. When they saw the Syracusans busy blocking the mile-wide entrance to the Great Harbour with a line of triremes, merchant ships and other craft, anchored broadside on, the Athenians realised that unless they acted quickly their only escape route to the sea would be sealed.

The Athenian difficulties were increased because they had finally decided to break out across country to Catana and had already sent the bulk of their stores and provisions there. It was decided to set up a smaller camp perimeter, with the sick and wounded guarded by a small garrison. The rest, everybody who was of military age and capability, would be embarked in every ship that could be made available, whether she was properly sea-worthy or not, for one great (in modern parlance) 'show-down'.

The Athenians eventually managed to muster 110 ships, manned by hoplites, archers, and javelin-throwers. Nicias, whose uncertain handling of the campaign was in some measure responsible for the Athenians' plight, addressed his ships' companies before they set out. He could see they were out of spirits because they had been so thoroughly and so unexpectedly defeated. Because they were short of food, they wanted to fight it out at once. You are all experienced campaigners, he said, and are not the sort of people who think that having lost a battle once you will always be frightened of losing again (this was, in fact, precisely what the Athenians were thinking).

Nicias went on to explain an important change in Athenian tactics. This time, their decks would be packed with armed men and, very unusually for the Athenians, the ships had been fitted with grappling irons to seize the enemy ships and allow the hoplites to board. This was a resort to the very kind of toe-to-toe slugging matches which the Athenians had always disdained. The greatest navy of its time had been reduced to a state where, as Nicias admitted, it was going to try and fight a land battle at sea.

Nicias artfully pitched his speech to impress the different elements in his command. Serving with the native-born Athenians were a number of other peoples, men from the Greek coastal cities, allies and colonists of Athens, enemies of the Syracusans, people who paid tribute to Athens and people from the Greek offshore islands who were more or less bound to throw in their lots with Athens. These 'who were not really Athenians' Nicias pointedly reminded that they had always shared the spoils of empire. You have always been treated with great respect, he told them, precisely because you were seen to be part of the Athenian empire. You must now look down on the Corinthians whom you have often beaten, and the Sicilians who would not have dreamed of standing up to us in our prime.

To the native Athenians, Nicias was even more blunt. He pointed out the brutal truth that if these ships were lost, there were no more. If these troops failed, there were no reserves. If this action was not a victory, the enemy would sail for Athens at once.

The Syracusans had an excellent intelligence service and knew of the grappling irons. They stretched slippery hides over their ships' bows so that the grapnels would slide off. Gylippus and the other Syracusan commanders also addressed their men. Their speeches are given, with Nicias', by Thucydides. It is very rare to have such a complete, word-for-word, blow-by-blow account of any naval campaign, ancient or modern, with the thoughts, tactics, plans and devices of both sides.

The Athenians, Gylippus said, have come here to enslave us. They have the greatest empire any Hellenes, past or present, have ever had. But *you* were the first to stand up to their navy, on which all their successes depend. *You* have defeated them already and you will defeat them again. When people think they are especially good at something, and then they are beaten at that very thing, they change their whole opinion of themselves. They become far less confident than if they had never believed in their own superiority in the first place. The surprise of their failure to come up to their own opinion of themselves makes them much more likely to give in, even though they actually had ample strength to win. This is very probably what is happening to the Athenians now. Now, they are trying to copy *our* methods of fighting. We know all about those and how to counter them. They are filling their ships with archers and javelin-throwers, all *landlubbers*, who have no idea how to fight in ships. They have not even bothered to think how they are going to throw their javelins from a sitting position! They have greater numbers, true, but this harbour is a very confined space and many of their ships will be slow in carrying out manoeuvres. Besides we have good intelligence information that they are desperate and are now trusting more to luck than good management (this was certainly true enough of the Athenian state of mind). Remember, they want to enslave you and your families. They are not just *ordinary* enemies. They are the most deadly enemies we have ever had. You are fighting for the liberty of Sicily.

Nicias seems to have had forebodings about the battle. He went round and spoke personally to every captain, reminding him of his family and his past exploits. 'He said other things, too, the things that men can be expected to say when they are actually on the edge of the event and do not bother to avoid giving the impression of using conventional language; instead they bring forward the kind of appeals that can generally be used on all occasions: wives, children, gods of the native land; yet still they cry out these names aloud, since, in the terror of the moment, they believe that they will help.'

On the day, it was even worse than Nicias had feared. The battle was the hardest yet. The Athenians fought with the fury of desperation, the Syracusans under the spectre of slavery. The Athenians frantically attacked the boom, trying to reach the open sea and safety. The Syracusans placed their ships all round the Harbour and closed upon the Athenians from all sides, flinging them backwards. The battle became a general mêlée, with ships ramming and being rammed at the same time, and helmsmen had to think simultaneously of attack and defence. Javelins, arrows and stones were hurled from ship to ship. The din of battle was not only terrifying in itself but made it impossible for orders to be heard. If any ship backed away, her captain was hailed by name and asked, if Athenian, was he going to try and land where the Syracusans were already supreme, and, if Syracusan, was he running away from a beaten enemy?

For, as the day wore on, it became clear that the Athenians were beaten. On shore, their soldiers had been watching the struggle, shouting that here they were winning, there they were holding on. But, towards the end, the shouts died away. The Athenian ships were driven back, and further back, until they grounded, where they were

19

beached and abandoned. The Syracusans came later and burned or dragged the ships away, just as they pleased.

Defeat at sea was followed inevitably by defeat on land. The Athenian army, such of it as had survived, was harried and ambushed on the march. Finally, the Athenians were all killed or captured, to the last man. Demosthenes and Nicias were put to death. For the Athenians, as a memorable passage of Thucydides records, it was 'the most calamitous of defeats; for they were utterly and entirely defeated; their sufferings were on an enormous scale; their losses were, as they say, total; army, navy, everything was destroyed, and, out of many, only few returned. So ended the events in Sicily.'

Yet, the Athenians were an extraordinarily resourceful and resilient people. They still had a fleet at home and in 406 BC, seven years after the disaster in Sicily an Athenian fleet of 150 ships, with Samians and other allies, defeated a Spartan fleet of 120 ships, under Callicrates the Spartan. The battle, to raise the siege of Mytilene, took place amongst the Argusinae islands, off the coast of Asia Minor. The Greeks made cunning use of small islets, disposing their ships between them effectively to extend their battle line and prevent the Spartans' *periplous*. As Xenophon, who took up the story of the Peloponnesian War where Thucydides left off, explains in his *Hellenica*, the Athenians were inferior seamen but the Spartans were frustrated and Callicrates himself was lost overboard when his flagship rammed another vessel.

But the final defeat of the Athenians came about in the following year, once again by a successful trick, successful because the Athenians were still over-confident in their fleet victualling arrangements.

In September 405 BC the entire Athenian fleet of 180 vessels sailed for the Dardanelles, to protect the passage of grain ships from south Russia, which were being threatened by a strong Spartan fleet under Lysander. The Spartans stormed and captured a wealthy city, full of wine and grain, called Lampsacus, on the southern shore of the strait. The Athenians, following the Spartans up the strait, stopped for provisions at a town called Sestus, on the northern shore, and then anchored 2 miles away, at the mouth of Aegospotami (river of goats), which was opposite Lampsacus. The strait, at this point, is about a mile and a half wide.

Just before dawn, the next day, Lysander's men embarked in their ships, and rigged side screens along the bulwarks, normally used as protection from missiles but here used for concealment. The Athenians, expecting action, formed up in battle line at the river mouth. But the Spartans, on Lysander's orders, did not come out. The Athenians waited until late in the day and then, when nothing happened, put back into Aegospotami. The crews went ashore, to get food. At once Lysander dispatched scout-ships to see what the Athenians were doing and not until the scouts had returned did he allow his men to disembark.

The same thing happened for four days. The Athenians formed up in battle order and waited. Lysander's ships were manned, but stayed in harbour. The Athenians waited, and then disembarked. The crews, growing over-confident, scattered further and further afield every everning. They even began to pour scorn on the Spartans for not giving battle. But the great Alcibiades, living in semi-exile in his castle nearby, saw what was happening and took the trouble to visit the Athenian base. He advised them to shift their camp to Sestus, where they would have a base and a harbour. But the Athenian admirals told him to be gone. They were now in command, not he.

On the fifth day, when the Athenians had, once again, formed up, waited and then disembarked, Lysander told his scouting ship to hoist a shield when in mid-channel, to signal that the Athenians had all scattered ashore. When he saw the signal, Lysander at once put to sea with his whole fleet, descended upon the mostly deserted Athenian ships drawn up on the beach and captured them all – except 8, and those only escaped through the alertness of Conon, the best of the Athenian admirals. Some of the other ships had only two rows of oars manned, some none at all, but Conon's 8 triremes were fully manned, and, with the Paralus, the 'state trireme' used for public missions and as a dispatch boat, managed to get away. Except for these 9 ships, the whole Athenian fleet was captured, with most of their crews.

On his way, Conon cheekily raided Lampsacus and captured Lysander's 'cruising sails' preventing a proper pursuit. Nevertheless, the loss of 171 ships meant the effective end of the Athenian navy. Without a fleet, Athens was starved into submission and the war ended the next year.

In about 398 BC Dionysius I of Sicily, a most inventive naval designer, launched the first warships propelled not, as in the triremes, by one man to an oar, but by four or five men manning long sweeps. The problem had been simply one of skilled manpower. A trireme required 170 rowers ranged (although no dogmatic assertions can be made about the design or manning of ships of the ancient world) very probably in three ranks, one above the other, with the top row of oarsmen seated on some form of outrigger, built upon the bulwarks. The trireme rower had to be a skilled oarsman, capable of keeping time with the others in his rank and those above or below him, as well as being able to stop rowing or to back-water as ordered, without 'catching a crab' or entangling his oar with his neighbours.

In the new quadriremes and quinqueremes, as they were called, four or five men pulled at one oar, but only one of the men needed to be a skilled oarsman. The others merely provided added muscle power, taking their time and stroke from the master-oar.

Dionysius I began what would now be called an 'arms race' on a stupendous scale for his time, engaging thousands of skilled workers to work in 160 'ship-sheds' most of which could hold two ships, built all around the Great Harbour of Syracuse. He was probably the first man in history to put naval rearmament upon an organised basis, and with the 200 ships he built and the further 110 he refitted, he won himself an empire which embraced nearly all of Sicily and much of southern Italy.

After the death of Alexander the Great his empire decayed and was cut up by his former generals and chiefs of staff, in particular Antigonus Monopthalmos (the 'One-Eyed') of Macedon, and Ptolemy, satrap and later king of Egypt. It was Antigonus' son Demetrius who could almost be called the father of naval gunnery. He had always been interested in siege weapons, catapults and *ballistae* (his nickname was 'Poliorcetes' – Besieger of Cities) and he mounted throwing weapons in his ships capable of hurling 21-inch long darts for distances of up to 400 yards, giving them a tremendous advantage in the early stages of an engagement.

From quadriremes and quinqueremes, the 'fours' and 'fives', Demetrius Poliorcetes progressed to 'sixes' and 'sevens' built for him in Phoenician yards. By 310 BC he had gone up to 'eights', 'nines', 'tens', an 'eleven' and even a 'thirteen' which required 1800 men to row it. Ten years later he was building 'fifteens' and 'sixteens'. His son, Antigonus Gonatas, went further and built an 'eighteen'. Ptolemy's son had a 'twenty' and two giant 'thirties'. Ptolemy IV built a 'forty' which was over 400 feet long and required 4000 rowers.

The exact arrangement of the oars in these ships is still debatable. Clearly a ship with forty banks of oars would be a geometric impossibility. The ships may have been basic triremes with the 'number' referring to the number of men in each rowing unit. Thus, a 'fifteen' might have had 8 rowers in the upper and 7 in the lower bank. The colossal 'forty' might even have been a trireme, greatly enlarged, with 40 men disposed between a section of three banks of oars, with 14 men pulling the top oar, 13 the middle, and 13 the lower. But even this is conjecture.

The 'forty' saw no action, but the smaller ships certainly did, in a series of naval engagements between Demetrius and Ptolemy, or between their respective sons, who carried on their fathers' campaigns. In 306 BC Demetrius and Ptolemy met in an important sea battle at Salamis – not the Greek city of the former battle, but a city on the southern coast of Cyprus. Both sides had about 150 warships, mostly quadriremes and quinqueremes, but Demetrius also had some 'sixes' and some Phoenician 'sevens', with catapults and throwing machines mounted on the fo'c'sles of some of his ships.

Demetrius tried a variation on the time-honoured *diekplous* and *periplous*. The two fleets were drawn up facing each other and at right angles to the shore. Demetrius purposely weighted his left-hand, seaward, wing with 7 Phoenician 'sevens' and 30 Athenian quadriremes, backed up by a second line of 'sixes' and more quadriremes. At the same time he deliberately weakened his right-hand, shore, wing, hoping to turn the enemy fleet, like a great door pivoting on a hinge.

When the fleets had closed to a third of a mile apart, Demetrius gave the signal to engage – a gilded shield flashed in the sunlight – which was repeated from ship to ship along his line. After a shower of missiles which did great execution, the two lines clashed together. Demetrius himself, according to Diodorus Siculus, fought brilliantly, standing in the stern of his flagship, a 'seven', which must have been boarded in the later stages, for Diodorus recounts Demetrius repulsing a crowd of men who rushed upon him with javelins and spears. Of the many missiles hurled at him, Demetrius avoided most and the rest fell upon his defensive armour.

Furthermore, just as Demetrius had planned, Ptolemy's seaward wing was driven back and the whole line began to pivot, so that a part of Ptolemy's fleet was in danger of being cut off and pinned against the shore. Ptolemy saw the danger and broke off the action, but Demetrius captured 40 ships and their crews, and later towed in another 80 which had capsized and were full of water. Like the other battle of the same name, this was a great strategic victory and sea power passed to the victors.

The best example in the ancient world of a new naval weapon to meet a particular tactical situation was developed by the Romans, a nation of landlubbers who in spite of their many successes never really took the sea to their hearts. Given the choice, a true Roman would always much rather hire someone else to go to sea in his stead. But in the third century BC the Romans realised that the only way to defeat their greatest enemies, the Carthaginians, was by sea.

The Carthaginians had a large and well-trained navy, mostly armed with quinqueremes. Rome had no navy at all. So the Romans built a navy from scratch. They borrowed naval architects and shipwrights from the peoples of the Greek coastal cities of Italy, and from Syracuse, who had not lost their naval expertise. They also had a captured Carthaginian warship to use as a model.

With their national energy, and the confidence of ignorance, the Romans pressed the work forward and built their own quinqueremes 'from the tree' to the final rigging-out, in 60 days. The Roman ships were bigger, slower, less handy, than the Carthaginians, but they had ample space for carrying marines. Oarsmen for the triremes were recruited from the Greek cities, and for the quinqueremes from the other Latin tribes of the Italian peninsula. The Senate refused to allow Roman citizens to serve on the rowing benches.

But though they had the ships, the Romans still had a basic tactical problem. They could not hope to match the Carthaginian seamanship and ship-handling. All the naval niceties of *diekplous* and *periplous*, all the tackings and backings of oared ship warfare, were quite beyond the average Roman and his allies. The Romans therefore needed some means of getting to grips with their enemy firmly, so that he could not get away, whilst the marines boarded and did the deadly job of execution which the Roman legionaries knew so well.

In June 260 BC, the quickly-built and hurriedly-manned Roman fleet sailed from Ostia to Syracuse where the solution may have been found. It might even have been the handiwork of Archimedes, then 27 years old and quite possibly living in Syracuse at the time. The device was called the 'raven', *corvus* in Latin, *corax* in Greek. It is not often that a war-winning naval invention of the ancient world is described in detail, and Polybius' account is worth giving in full:

A round pole stood on the prow, 4 fathoms (10.80 metres) long and 3 palms (0.23 metres) in diameter. That pole had a tackle at the top; round it was put a ladder, on which cross-planks had been nailed so that the result was a gangway, 4 feet wide and 6 fathoms long. The aperture in the planking was oblong and it went round the pole right after the first 2 fathoms of the ladder. The gangway had also a railing along each of its long sides, as high as a man's knee. At its end something like a pointed pestle was attached, made of iron, at the upper end of which there was a ring, so that the whole looked like the machines used in the working of corn. To that ring was fastened a rope, with which, as soon as the ships charged, they raised the ravens by means of the tackle-block on the pole and dropped them on the deck of the enemy ship, sometimes forward, sometimes bringing them round to meet flank-attacks. As soon as the ravens were fixed in the planks of the decks and joined the ships together, if they met side to side, they sprang on board from all sides, but if they met prow to prow, they made their attack over the raven itself, two abreast. The men who led the way protected the front by holding up their shields, and those who followed covered the flanks by resting the rims of their shields on the railing.

In August that year of 260 BC the two fleets met for the first time at Mylae, off the northern coast of Sicily. The Romans had 140 ships under a new but very capable admiral, Caius Diulius. The Carthaginians had slightly fewer ships, but they were well worked-up and experienced quinqueremes, with a 'seven' as flagship.

The Carthaginians saw at once the curious-looking structures of the ravens, cocked up at an odd angle in the bows of the Roman ships. They seemed unseamanlike and faintly ridiculous. Whatever they were, they could hardly be weapons of war, and so, the Romans rowed towards the Carthaginians while the Carthaginians confidently allowed them to approach.

When the ships drove in alongside each other, down came the ravens, embedding their heavy iron spikes deep in the Carthaginian decks. While the Roman oarsmen wrestled to keep their ships alongside and prevent the Carthaginians pressing past and thus wrenching the spikes out, the legionaries put up their shields and ran across the gangways, swarming over the waists and rowing benches of the Carthaginians, stabbing and thrusting with sword and javelin.

The Romans captured 31 Carthaginian ships, including the flagship, in the first encounter. Realising for the first time that they had a new and respectable foe against them, the Carthaginians skilfully regrouped and went straight in to the old and well-tried manoeuvre of the *diekplous*. But Caius Diulius, who now had a 3-to-1 advantage in numbers after the first encounter, knew the counter-move and had kept back a reserve of ships – the standard defence, in fact, against the *diekplous*. When the Carthaginians had completed the *diekplous* and emerged on the far side of the Roman line, Caius Diulius' reserves rowed forward to meet them. Down crashed their ravens, and the Carthaginians met the same fate as the others. In all, the Carthaginians lost 44 ships and more than 10,000 men.

The Romans went on to build more ships and in every action of the First Punic War which now followed, they had more ships then their opponents. The continued success of the ravens, their superiority in numbers, coupled with fortunately fine weather and compounded by deteriorating seamanship on the Carthaginian side, gave the Romans more victories at Ecnomus in 256 BC, off Cape Hermaeum in 255, and finally in the conclusive victory off the Aegetes Islands in 241 which brought the first Punic War to an end. By that time, the positions of the two navies had been completely reversed. It was the Romans who had experienced crews fighting in new ships, with new tactics and the confidence of several victories and the Carthaginians whose raw crews fought in old ships with the knowledge of heavy recent defeats. The Romans continued to maintain a fleet for the Second Punic War and were prepared to use it. But that war was fought almost entirely upon land. The Carthaginians had no navy.

Archimedes may or may not have been concerned with the *corvus* but he certainly took part in the war in 212 BC when Syracuse, having defected to the side of Carthage in the Second Punic War, was attacked by Marcus Marcellus. First, he designed an extraordinary machine which, as described by Polybius, grasped Roman barges, hauled them out of the water and, after raising them to the height of the walls of Syracuse, hurled them down, men and all, into the sea. In the face of this daunting weapon, Marcellus moved his barges further off, but Archimedes countered with another machine which made it possible for the Syracusans to lift stones the size of waggons and throw them, one at a time, to sink the Roman barges.

Not surprisingly, Marcellus moved his barges even further away, as far as an arrow could fly, in fact. But Archimedes was equal to that. He arranged several hexagonal mirrors and at an appropriate distance from them set small quadrangular mirrors of the same type which were adjustable by metal plates and small hinges. The effect of this contraption was to act like an enormous magnifying glass, which concentrated the rays of the sun at noon and, focused on Marcellus' barges, reduced them all to ashes, even at the distance of an arrow flight.

Fire was the last great tactical weapon to be developed by the navies of the centuries before Christ. It was the imaginative use of fire at sea which led to the discovery of gunpowder and is, in a sense, the clearest link between the navies of the ancients and those of the medieval and modern worlds.

Above: Bas relief found on the Acropolis, Athens, of the midships section of a trireme, dating approximately to the time of the Peloponnesian War. Known as the Lenormant relief, its arrangement of rowers is still hotly debated by naval historians. (Author's Collection)

Below: An eighteenth century version of the corvus *'boarding bridge'* of the Roman Navy described by Polybius, used against the Carthaginians in the First Punic War in 260 BC. (From M de Folard's *Histoire de Polybe*, Vol 1, 1753)

Above: A Byzantine warship of the fleet of the Emperor Michael II (AD 820–829) attacking an enemy with 'Greek Fire'. (From an illustration in a fourteenth century MS of 'Sinopsis Historiarum' by Ioannes Scylitzes in the Biblioteca Nacional, Madrid)

Below: Seventeenth century Dutch fire-ships with (right) a sail fitted to prevent it yawing on the way to the target. The secret was in the compartment C described in a Latin caption above it as a 'Chamber with hidden iron and marble, balls and chains, and millstones packed together'. (Author's Collection)

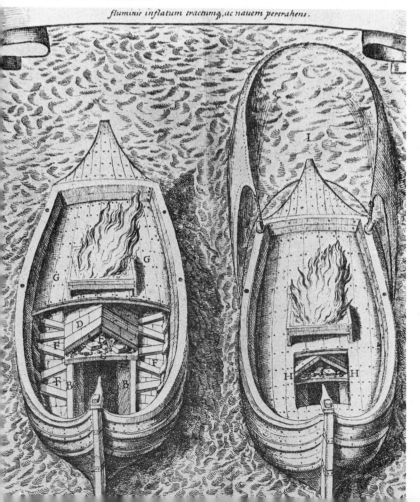

fluminis inflatum tractumq, ac nauem pertrahens.

Chapter 2

'It made such a noise in coming,' said the Crusaders, of Greek fire, 'that it seemed like thunder.' The terrifying sound, like an explosion, which accompanied the discharge seems to suggest that by the time of the Crusaders Greek fire had indeed become some primitive form of explosive. Certainly the early attempts to direct, control and aim fire, as a tactical weapon at sea, did lead eventually to the invention of gunpowder and the coming of the naval gun.

The Syracusans in the Great Harbour had improvised a fire-ship. A much better organised and more determined attempt was made by the Tyrians in 333 BC when the city of Tyre was besieged by Alexander. The Tyrians were hard-pressed. Alexander had built a causeway, which was steadily being lengthened, from the shore to the island-city, protected by towers and war machines. The Tyrians filled a cattle-boat with dry brushwood and other timber which would burn well, raised the bulwarks so that the vessel would hold as much pitch, sulphur and other inflammable material as possible. In the bows they set up a gantry, of two masts, with a yard across them which was double the usual length. Cauldrons full of more inflammable materials were slung from the yard. The stern was ballasted, to lift the bows as far as possible out of the water.

On a fair wind, and towed by several hawsers slung from triremes, the fire-ship was taken stern-first to the mole, and the fires were lit. Before she struck, her crew leaped overboard and swam to safety. The fire soon caught the towers on the mole and set them ablaze, while the crews of the triremes lying off fired arrows to prevent any of Alexander's men coming up to extinguish the fires. Once the towers were well alight, more Tyrians from the city jumped into boats, landed on the mole where they pulled down a protective palisade and set fire to all the war engines.

The operation was a complete success, but it had an ominous result for the city. It taught Alexander that without sea power he could never take Tyre. He went away to Sidon to collect a fleet, and he was joined by the navies of other nations. This was the turning point of the siege.

Below the Belt

The navy of Rhodes, in the second century BC, was very probably the first to use fire as a tactical weapon. The Rhodian navy, one of the finest of the ancient world, was a small service, normally with not more than about 40 major warships, and it was select: the Rhodians never used slaves, or criminals, or tributary peoples, colonials and citizens of the lower classes to man their fleet. On the contrary, to the Rhodians the navy was the senior service and it was manned by citizens of proper degree who looked upon the navy almost as a vocation, and certainly as a career for life. For almost a century Rhodes used her navy to preserve the balance of power and to keep the freedom of the seas for all in their part of the eastern Mediterranean, rather as the British used the Royal Navy hundreds of years later.

In 197 BC the Rhodian navy assisted Rome to defeat Philip V of Macedon and almost at once Rome began another war, against Antiochus III, King of Syria, also with the help of the Rhodian navy. The Syrians' admiral was Polyxenidas, a Rhodian, who for some reason had been banished from his home city, and who secretly tried to do a deal with Pausistratus, the Rhodian admiral. If his banishment could be lifted, Polyxenidas would betray the whole of the fleet of Antioch. After some negotiations, to and fro, Pausistratus was lulled into a state of over-confidence, in which he believed that the pact with Polyxenidas relieved him of the necessity of taking any other action. He grew careless and was consequently trapped in a narrow, land-locked bay by Polyxendias, who had also landed troops ashore and thus had Pausistratus caught by sea and by land.

Nearly all of Pausistratus' fleet of 36 ships were captured or sunk. Pausistratus himself was killed. But 5 Rhodian ships, and 2 from the island of Cos, managed to escape by, as Livy explains it, 'making a passage for themselves through the thick of the enemy by the terror of the blazing flames; for they carried on before them on two poles projecting from their prow a great quantity of fire contained in iron vessels'. The mere threat of fire at sea was a potent weapon.

Later that same year fire-pots were used in a fleet action for the first time. It was in September, at Cape Myonnesus, on the coast of Asia Minor, when Polyxenidas, with 89 ships, met a combined Roman, Rhodian and Pergamum fleet of 80 ships led by Eudamus, one of the best Rhodian admirals. It was Eudamus, in July or August of that year, off Side in the Gulf of Adalia, who had defeated a fleet of Phoenician ships, Antiochus' allies, under the redoubtable Hannibal himself with one of the best executed *diekplous* in naval history; half Hannibal's fleet had been put out of action and thus he was not able to assist Polyxenidas at Myonnesus.

The supreme commander of the fleet was Lucius Aemilius Regillus, a Roman and one of the stupidest admirals of all time. He had already depleted his fleet by unnecessarily sending ships up to the Dardanelles. Having thus given Polyxenidas numerical superiority, he then went on almost to make him a present of the battle. Regillus placed himself at the head of the line, where his ships were actually outnumbered by Polyxenidas and ordered Eudamus to take station in the rear. Happily, Eudamus disobeyed his orders, or rather modified them (the comparison between Hyde Parker and Nelson at Copenhagen is inescapable) by keeping 22 of his best quadriremes, some of them armed with the fire-pots, available for an instant counter-attack when, as he feared, Polyxenidas began to roll up Regillus' seaward wing.

Events turned out as Eudamus anticipated. Polyxenidas broke Regillus' line and began to defeat his ships one by one. Eudamus' ships then rowed quickly forward, threatening with their fire-pots. When Polyxenidas' ships turned away, they exposed their midships to ramming. The battle was over and Polyxenidas' ships retreated to Ephesus, where they remained until the war ended in the following year.

Very probably, Eudamus' fire-pots contained a variety of Greek fire or 'sea fire'. A form of it was certainly known by then. Describing the siege of Plateae in Sicily in 429 BC, Thucydides says that the besiegers 'also threw fire with sulphur and pitch which soon caught the wood'. Aeneas Tacticus, writing about a hundred years after Thucydides, gave a recipe for 'an unextinguishable fire': 'Take pitch, sulphur, tow, manna, incense and the scrapings of gummy woods from which torches are made, light the mixture and throw it against the object you wish to reduce to cinders'.

Greek fire of some kind was used in the later stages at Actium, the naval action in the Ionian Sea off the west coast of Greece, in which Octavian decisively defeated Mark Antony and effectively settled the course of history in the western world. Octavian's successful naval commander, Marcus Vipsanius Agrippa, was a victorious general on land and was also, arguably, the best admiral of the ancient world. Agrippa was quick to see and to seize the strategic possibilities of sea power and to employ the latest tactical weapons. Four years earlier he had defeated Pompey's son Sextus in a sea-fight off Naulochus, a few miles along the coast from Mylae in Sicily, largely due to the success of his own invention: a grapnel attached to a length of stout pole which was catapulted on to the enemy's decks. The grapnel caught in a ship's side and the pole resisted the enemy's attempts to hack through it in the time while Agrippa's ships were hauling themselves alongside.

In the summer months of 31 BC, leading up to Actium, Agrippa out-fought and out-manoeuvred Mark Antony. By 2 September, when the battle took place, Antony had been forced to choose a confrontation by sea, instead of on land, although his crews were ill-trained, badly-fed, ravaged by sickness, and mostly pressed men – as Plutarch says, they were 'every description of men, common travellers and ass-drivers, harvest labourers and boys'. His ships, badly manned and badly rowed, were large (Antony's flagships was a 'ten') and slow. They were slowed even more by cumbersome, squared pieces of timber bolted to the bows to prevent damage by ramming. (Pliny also suggests that Antony's galley was even further hindered by a 'ship-detaining' worm or *remora*, fastened leech-like to the bottom of the hull.)

Antony's ships were 'richly ornamented as if they were meant for a triumph' whereas, as Plutarch says in a passage reminiscent of contemporary accounts of the Spanish Armada, Caesar 'had ships that were built not for size or show, but for service, not pompous galleys but light, swift and perfectly manned'. Many of Caesar's galleys were Liburnians, crewed by superb seamen from the country of Liburnia, on the northern coast of the Adriatic.

In the early stages, the station-keeping of some of Antony's fleet was somewhat ragged. The Egyptian ships tended to hold back, allowing Agrippa's ships to get in amongst them; several of Antony's ponderous giants were surrounded by three or four Liburnians. Antony's soldiers embarked fought off the attacks by showering arrows and fiery missiles from wooden towers which served as fighting tops. After the celebrated departure of Antony and Cleopatra (which had almost certainly been most carefully planned beforehand) their remaining ships were outnumbered and the battle turned Agrippa's way. His men came in close to hew at the oars and snap off the rudders of Antony's ships. Some climbed up the sides and boarded, capturing the ships and driving their crews into the sea.

At this point, according to the historian Dio Cassius, Caesar sent for fire from his camp ashore. Javelins with torches tied to them were hurled on board Antony's ships, whilst archers shot arrows with blazing tow bound round their shafts. Rafts laden with burning materials were set adrift and, worst of all, 'engines would throw from a distance pots full of charcoal and pitch'.

When a ship caught fire, the crews first used their drinking water to try and douse the flames. If that did not succeed, they used sea-water which they collected in buckets. But the buckets were few and small and many of them were hoisted up only half full. This made matters worse for, according to Dio Cassius, 'salt water poured on a fire in small quantities makes it burn vigorously'. The crews then tried to smother the fires with their heavy mantles and, finally, with the corpses of their ship-mates. But as the wind increased (the very wind which was taking Cleopatra off to safety) the flames took hold, and the mantles and bodies themselves became added fuel.

The battle, which had begun about noon, ended shortly after 4 o'clock with total victory for Agrippa and Octavian. Those of Antony's ships which had not been burned were run aground or surrendered. Only the 60 ships with Cleopatra escaped.

The precise recipe for Greek fire has been lost, but there were probably several ways of making it. Its basic ingredient was what the ancients called 'naphtha', a crude oil which actually oozed out of the ground in many areas of the Near and Middle East, with sulphur, pitch, or even quick-lime, added to it. If some oxygen carrier such as saltpetre were also added, the mixture was capable of spontaneous combustion. Thus the ingredients, and the method of manufacture, of a form of gunpowder were all present.

The manufacture of Greek fire was such a closely guarded 'state' secret that its inventor's name has been lost. The Emperor Constantine is said to have had the recipe revealed to him by an angel and he commanded his successors to keep the secret. One high official who was bribed to betray the recipe to a foreigner was entering church one day when, most appropriately, a flame descended from heaven and incinerated him. In another version of the tale, the secret was brought to Constantinople in 672 AD by one Callinicus, an engineer, who had been driven out of his native town by the Arabs who were then attacking the Byzantine empire.

The Byzantines had a good navy, whose chief warships were called dromons; they were a large type of bireme, with 100 oars, disposed in two banks of 25 on each side. They had rams, and two or three masts, with sails for running before the wind. They often had a high tower forward, from which marines could hurl missiles, and more structures projecting out over the bulwarks amidships, from which heavy weights could be dropped upon a vessel attempting to come alongside. Also up forward were the flame-throwers, and catapults and throwing machines. Some of the largest dromons had extra flame-throwers amidships and in the stern.

Greek fire was either catapulted in clay pots onto an enemy's decks, where it burst and spread like a primitive form of incendiary shell, or actually directed through an early development of the rocket. This was a bronze tube, which contained a reed filled with Greek fire, with its ends stoppered. The tube was aimed and a fuse lit. The reed ignited, the gases released drove it out of the tube and a streak of flame leaped out towards the enemy. For close quarters, the Byzantines used a tube of wood lined with bronze, with its inboard end connected to an air pump. The tube was loaded with Greek fire. When this was lit, air from the pump provided oxygen and blew a stream of fire outwards. There were also hand-held flame-throwers, which the marines concealed behind their shields until they were close enough to their opponents to use them.

The Arabs, who also had a fleet of dromons, mounted a series of raids on the Byzantine empire from their island base at Cyzicus, in the Black Sea. In AD 673, the Byzantines counter-attacked, using Greek fire, and decisively defeated the Arabs, thus preserving their empire for the time being.

According to ancient writers, Greek fire could only be extinguished with sand, vinegar, or urine. Wet hides or sheets of felt, soaked in vinegar or sour wine, were often stretched over decks as a defence against Greek fire. The great Saracen ship which was attempting to lift the siege of Acre, attacked by Richard Coeur de Lion's ships off Beirut on 1 June 1191, had green-painted hides stretched over her forecastle for this very purpose.

She was an enormous ship, bigger than anything the English had ever seen, with three tall masts, and streaks of red and yellow painted on her sides. A contemporary account called her 'a marvellous ship! a ship than which, except Noah's Ark, none greater was ever read of!' King Richard, who was in his own galley *Trench-the-Mer*, sent Peter de Barres to challenge the stranger, who said that she was French, on her way from Antioch to Acre. But she flew no French flag, and none of her crew could speak French.

One man in Richard's ship said that he had seen this vessel in Beirut, being loaded with 100 camel-loads of arms, slings, bows, darts and arrows. She also had on board 7 Saracen admirals and 80 chosen Turks, besides a great quantity of provisions, more than any man could count. She also had a large amount of Greek fire, in bottles, and 200 most deadly serpents (some form of firing tube) 'for the destruction of the Christians'. The ship was actually the Saracen *Dromunda* but when hailed again she said she was Genoese, bound for Tyre. This time however she was recognised and one English galley-man advised that a galley be sent after her, looking as if it was about to attack, and then there would be no doubt about her identity. The great ship replied to this encounter with a shower of darts and Greek fire. Clearly, she was an enemy and quite capable of raising the siege of Acre if she were allowed to reach the harbour.

It was a fine day, with a smooth sea, and there was plenty of daylight left, but Richard's galleys, understandably, rowed cautiously round this formidable opponent. Their 'ardour relaxed', as the chronicler said. But Richard was as forceful a leader at sea as he was on land. 'Will you allow this ship to get away untouched and

34

uninjured?' the chroniclers reported him as saying. 'Shame upon you! Are you grown cowards from sloth, after so many triumphs? The whole world knows that you engaged in the service of the Cross, and you will have to undergo the severest punishment if you permit an enemy to escape while he lives, and is thrown in your way.'

At this urging, some of Richard's men dived over the side and swam to the Saracen's rudder, tying ropes round it, to prevent it being used. Others climbed ropes to the Turkish deck where the Turks met them 'manfully, cut them to pieces as they came on board, and lopping off the head of this one and the hands of that, and the arms of another, cast their bodies into the sea.'

The Crusaders drove the Turks up into the bows, but more Turks rushed up from below, so that the Christians were forced back until they had to retire to their galleys. They then surrounded the great ship and repeatedly rammed her with their 'spurs' until she sank. King Richard saved 35 Turks, namely, the 7 admirals 'and men who were skilled in making machines, but the rest perished, the arms were abandoned, and the serpents sunk and scattered about by the waves of the sea'.

Fire-ships were a regular part of naval armouries for centuries. It was, after all, an obvious and simple expedient to fill an expendable ship or ships with combustible materials, set fire to them, and let them drift in the hope that they would fetch up against an enemy. But in the Middle Ages and for centuries afterwards, many more fire-ship attacks failed than were successful, almost always due to miscalculations of wind, tide or timing. In August 1304, for example, a major naval battle was fought between the French and the Flemish off Zeiriksee, in Holland. The Flemish filled two vessels with pitch, oil, grease and the usual combustible materials and towed them to windward of 4 French ships which had gone aground. Unhappily the wind shifted after the vessels had been fired and they eventually did more damage to the Flemish than to the French.

In Chinese naval warfare, traditionally full of ruses, decoys and devices, fire was a favourite weapon, as much for display and to hearten one's own side as to intimidate or actually damage the enemy. Many Chinese war-junks belched fire and smoke from their dragon-shaped mouths set in their bows, to frighten and impress an opponent. Two or more fire-ships were often chained together and allowed to drift down-river so that they hung round the bows of an enemy, where they were very difficult to disentangle.

In the late sixteenth century, a Korean admiral called Yi used a novel, fire-belching warship to defeat the Japanese, who had invaded Korea, brushed aside the Korean army, and settled down to live off the Korean countryside while they assembled greater forces from

35

Japan for an expeditionary advance into China itself. With absolute command of the sea, and complete control over a mostly terrorised and demoralised population on land, the Japanese position seemed unassailable.

Admiral Yi built a new warship, large for her time, at 1000 tons, and over 120 feet long. Her decks were completely covered over with an arch of iron plates, giving her a great curved back, studded with spikes, from which she got her name, the *Kwi Sun* or 'Tortoise Ship'. She had a rudder at each end and could move either way, being propelled by eight or nine long oars on either side, worked by rowers who sat under the shelter of the turtle-back. Some accounts said that she also had a paddle-wheel mounted in the centre, worked by hand. Her chief weapon was her ram, but she had six ports cut in her back, through which archers shot flights of fire-arrows. Up forward, she had an enormous dragon figure-head, which belched forth flames and smoke. She probably had a small mast, not for sailing but for signalling.

In this extremely effective flagship Admiral Yi put to sea in June 1592 with a small Korean fleet in company. At first, Japanese ships in the Bay of Fusan ignored their approach, quite confident that any ships at sea must be Japanese. Yi fell upon them and destroyed them all. Soon afterwards, Yi's scouting vessels reported that a vast new Japanese armada had put to sea. Yi pretended to flee, and when the Japanese pursued, turned and attacked them. The *Kwi Sun* was reported to have sunk some 120 ships by fire and ram that day, in the Battle of Okpo. The Japanese were utterly defeated. Deprived of their seaborne support, their armies disintegrated and broke up or surrendered in small groups, much as they did in 1945, although the process took a long time: the war dragged on until 1598. The hull of the *Kwi Sun* was reported to be still lying in the village of Ko-Sung in Korea as late as 1884, and the villagers held an annual festival to celebrate Admiral Yi and his Tortoise Ship's victory.

Paddle-wheels were, in fact, known to the Chinese from quite early times. In the twelfth century the Emperor Kao Tsung sent an army and a fleet under Yo Fei to crush a rebellion led by Yang Yao which had broken out up country near the T'ai Hu Lake. At first, according to the imperial chronicler, Yang's vessels 'went along as if they were flying; they carried poles over the sides to strike and break up any vessels they might run against'. Yo Fei defeated Yang by scattering rotten straw, wood and other debris on the water's surface, which obstructed the paddle-wheels and rendered Yang's vessels helpless. Yang himself leaped over the side and was drowned.

But perhaps the most favoured Chinese fire-weapon of all, used against ships of the Royal Navy until well into the nineteenth

36

century, was the 'stink-pot'. This was an earthenware jar, filled half with black powder, sulphur, small nails and other metal fragments, and half with miscellaneous materials for producing smells. Clusters of stink-pots, each placed in a calico bag tied at the neck with string, were hoisted in baskets up to the junk's masthead. A man climbed up with a lighted fuse or joss stick and ignited the pots. The hope was that the 'stink-pots' would fall upon an enemy's deck and burst there, confusing him with their explosions, flying shrapnel, smoke and foul odours.

The search for missiles and weapons at sea sometimes took unexpected directions. One small merchant ship in the Mediterranean, with a crew of only some 40 or 50 men, happened to have amongst its cargo some earthenware beehives. Pursued by a Turkish galley with 500 seamen and soldiers on board, the crew flung the beehives down on their opponents' decks. Protecting themselves with masks and gloves, they then captured the galley. King John, in 1213, sent quicklime to his fleet, to fling in the faces of their enemies, and soft soap, to make their decks slippery (the great Dutch seaman De Ruyter, becalmed in the Mediterranean, smeared his bulwarks with butter to deter Algerine pirates).

Quicklime was actually used in action in 1217, shortly after King John's death. The naval defences of the country had by 1216 sunk so low that Prince Louis of France was able to cross the Channel with an invasion fleet of 600 ships and 80 cogs under the command of the notorious sea-rover Eustace the Monk, who had made himself more hated and feared by the English than any other Frenchman in previous history. Although Louis' ships were dispersed by bad weather he himself landed unmolested at Sandwich.

When Louis was defeated in a battle in the streets of Lincoln in May the next year, his kinsman Roger de Courtenay gathered another fleet, of 80 ships, with some galleys and some small craft, once again under Eustace. They were opposed by Sir Hubert de Burgh, Governor of Dover Castle, who had 16 large and well-equipped ships from the Cinque Ports, and about 20 smaller vessels.

When the English ships put to sea from Dover on 24 August 1217, Eustace's fleet was already in mid-Channel, some miles out of Calais, heading almost north on a brisk south-south-easterly wind, steering to round the North Foreland and enter the Thames. At first, Sir Hubert did not head directly for his enemy but across the Channel, so that Eustace believed he meant to attack Calais. This did not worry Eustace. He knew Calais was well defended.

In fact, Sir Hubert had no intentions of sailing to Calais. He was gaining the weather-gauge – one of the earliest examples of this primary tactic in the days of fighting sail. Having once got his enemy in his lee, Sir Hubert altered course to the south and his ships bore down on the French rearguard. The English sailors flung unslaked lime downwind into the eyes of the French, and followed it with grapnels, to prevent them getting away. While English archers poured a stream of flaming arrows into the French ships, the English men-at-arms boarded and cut the French rigging and halyards with axes, before engaging the blinded and bewildered defenders in hand-to-hand combats which were mostly short and ended in immense slaughter amongst the French. The English ships were fitted with iron beaks, which also did tremendous execution, sinking several Frenchmen.

Most of the French ships were captured or sunk. Only 15 escaped; 25 French knights and more than 1000 soldiers were taken prisoner. Eustace the Monk was found shivering and cowering in the hold of his ship. He was taken ashore, where his head was lopped off and exhibited throughout England. He had made the elementary mistake in naval tactics of attempting an operation without first ensuring that a hostile fleet, no matter how inferior on paper, was first eliminated, and had paid the penalty. The battle, off the South Foreland, was decisive and ended the war.

When the King's Ships were next in action, in Edward III's great victory over the French at Sluys in 1340, there is evidence that guns may have been used by the Royal Navy for the first time. Certainly, in a sea-fight in 1362 between ships from Denmark and from Lübeck, a Danish prince was killed by a ball shot from one of six 'Donnerbuschen' ('Thunderboxes') on board one of the Lübeckers. But there can be no certain, definite date for the first introduction of guns at sea. They co-existed on board with catapults and throwing machines from the ancient world, and with longbows and crossbows, for very many years (Henry VII's *Regent*, built in 1488, had 225 guns, but she also had 200 bows of yew-wood on board).

Venetian galleys were armed with cumbersome bombards, discharging huge stones, by 1400. Lighter guns were added later, but always in the bows, so as not to interfere with the rowers. Very probably, guns were first used regularly by merchantmen, which had neither the money nor the space for large numbers of fighting men on board. Guns were more economical of manpower than archers, and though the guns themselves may have been inefficient, and even dangerous to their users, the noise, the smoke of their discharge and the almost supernatural awe they evoked, would go a long way to deter attackers and pirates.

The gunner himself was a man of mystery, a man conversant with the black arts, learned in arithmetic and astronomy and able to discourse about 'disparts' and 'windage', a man very probably in league with the Devil himself (*Lights to the Art of Gunnery*, a textbook published as late as 1689, related the fate of a certain profane and godless gunner, Cornelius Slime, who was carried off by the Devil before the astonished eyes of onlookers).

The gunner was popularly supposed to gather his saltpetre, or 'burning salt', from vaults, inside tombs and other appropriate places. Burning salt, according to medieval writers, grew like a flower out of the walls of cellars, or in the ground which is found loose inside vaults, tombs or desolate caves, or in abandoned dung-hills. One writer of the seventeenth century found it in places that 'men use to piss in', or where many dead bodies have been laid and earth thrown over them. Likewise, a gunner was supposed to make his touchwood from toadstools gathered in a graveyard and dried over a slow fire. He himself was protected meanwhile from the frightful violence of his charges by St Barbara, patron saint of artillerymen.

But while the development of the gun progressed, some navies, especially the Dutch in the wars of the seventeenth century, refined the science of the fire-ship for use in a tactical setting or to meet a specific tactical problem. Dutch fire-ships burned the *Triumph* at Scheveningen in 1653. During the Four Days' Battle in 1666, the *Royal Prince* ran aground on the Galloper Bank and was there attacked and burned by two Dutch fire-ships. At Terschelling later the same year, English fire-ships joined in the burning of some 170 Dutch ships. The Dutch used fire-ships in the Medway in 1667, and set the *Royal James* on fire at the battle of Solebay in 1672. The Royal Navy at the time of the Revolution of 1688 had 26 fire-ships, in service or commissioning. English fire-ships assisted in the burning of 6 of the 12 large French warships trapped and destroyed at the head of La Hogue bay in 1692.

But by the time of that defeat at La Hogue, the French themselves had evolved an important change in naval tactics – the use of the bomb-ketch. Bombs, as they were known, were used for the first time by the French admiral Abraham Du Quesne in July 1682, when he bombarded the pirate stronghold of Algiers with several *galiotes à bombes*. Designed first by a young Basque engineer, bombs were usually three-masted vessels of about 200 tons, with the foremast removed to make room for the mortars, which were short, fat, tubby-barrelled guns firing bombs of some 2 hundredweight each in a high, howitzer-like trajectory. The mortars rested on specially prepared decks, reinforced with old rope cables, specially cut and packed close together, to provide a resilient mounting.

With their lop-sided rig and peculiar appearance, bomb-ketches were not elegant. But they certainly were effective in their place. With practice, a bomb-ketch crew could drop their shells with extreme accuracy into a fortified town or harbour which could not have been damaged in any other way. At Algiers, the forts were badly damaged and the town itself partly set on fire, with about 700 people killed. According to one account, the bombs 'struck the whole piratical fraternity with immediate awe'. So enraged were the pirates, however, that when they had recovered from their awe they lopped off the heads of the French ambassadorial staff and fired them back as missiles.

From Algiers Du Quesne moved on to Genoa which he also bombarded in the same way and with even greater effect. 'An incessant shower of bombs, which continued, till the whole number, amounting to 14,000, with which the fleet was furnished, had been expended, laid the greater part of the city, and the whole of the many superb buildings which it contained, completely in ashes.' This was certainly a new and very effective weapon which helped the French to gain temporary maritime control over the Mediterranean.

Fire-ships and bomb-ketches served in most of the Royal Navy's fleets of the eighteenth century, from Byng to Keppel, to Howe, Rodney and Jervis. They eventually achieved a kind of respectability, with a Master and Commander in command. They had appropriate names, to mark their associations with the Devil or with violent explosion and eruption, such as *Infernal*, *Blast*, *Thunder*, *Carcass*, *Salamander*, *Firedrake*, *Grenado* and *Basilisk*. Vernon bombarded Cartagena with bombs for many hours, though not to much effect, and Rodney bombarded Le Havre in 1759. Generally, bomb-ketches were a useful weapon, without being a lasting strategic menace. They could assist, but not finally solve, the problem of breaching a defended enemy position.

It was the explosive shells which the bomb-ketches lobbed over on to their targets which caused one of the very few tremors of conscience ever to trouble the gunnery world. When the French used them in the Revolutionary wars, they were regarded by the British as cowardly, ungentlemanly, and underhand. To fire such devices as these at men in wooden ships was inhumane; they were really only suitable for bomb-ketches against shore targets. Some captains even frowned upon the throwing of hand-grenades from out of fighting tops.

But it was actually an Englishman, Sir Samuel Bentham, who first fitted some Russian long-boats with bronze, recoil-less cannon to fire shells at Turkish warships in the mouth of the Liman river, in the Sea of Azov, in 1788. The Russian shells blew great holes in the Turkish ships but left the Admiralty's conservatism intact. They showed no interest in the shells, nor in the experiments of a

Lieutenant Shrapnel which were being carried out at the same time.

The Admiralty's indifference was excusable. It was not in their interest to sponsor any great improvement in naval ordnance, which might depreciate Great Britain's enormous advantage in ships and guns. In other words, as always, such experiments lay with the weaker power, in this case France, which took up research into explosive shells with enthusiasm. Lieutenant General Count Andreossy, a French artillery officer, carried out an impressive series of trials on explosive shells at various ranges. Despite the disadvantages of 'hollow' shells, which could not be cast as accurately as solid, and could not withstand the force of as heavy a charge, thus falling short in range, the explosive shells clearly had the potential of a very deadly weapon indeed.

But they also had one other serious disadvantage. They were extremely dangerous to store and handle. There were many accidents, and French explosive shells killed as many Frenchmen as Englishmen. The one terrible example of an internal explosion was *L'Orient*, which blew up during the Battle of the Nile. The admiral and the captain had already been killed and discipline on board had disintegrated; fires started during a prolonged gun action were permitted to spread and eventually reached the main magazine. The lesson of *L'Orient* was underlined almost a year later, on 14 May 1799, during the siege of Acre, when there was a shell explosion on board *Theseus*, which killed 40 men and injured another 47.

Curiously, although the French used shells themselves, they objected to them being fired back. In October 1798, British gunboats were having some success while bombarding the castle at Aboukir, so much that a party of French officers came out under flag of truce to object formally to the use of such unfair devices as exploding shells. When the gunner was sent for, to produce some of the shells complained of, he explained that these had been found on board the French *Spartiate* captured after the battle of the Nile.

After the Napoleonic wars, another French artillery officer, Henri-Joseph Paixhans, carried on the work of Andreossy. Paixhans, a man well in advance of his time, advocated what was in fact a naval revolution: all sailing ships to be replaced by smaller steam-ships, manned by smaller crews, and armed by fewer but more destructive guns of one calibre throughout, firing explosive shells. After trials in 1824, in which the old wooden 84-gun *Pacificateur* was blown to pieces by shell-fire, Paixhans guns were eventually accepted into the French fleet, in 1837.

The deadly efficiency of shells was demonstrated again, in earnest, at the so-called 'Massacre of Sinope', one of the preludes to the Crimean War in 1853, when a squadron of Turkish frigates was blown out of the water by shells from Russian ships, with tremendous loss of life. Even so, the Admiralty were slow to adopt shells, just as they were slow to adopt one of its antidotes, armour plating. In that, as in shells, the French were to show the way, with the commissioning of the world's first ironclad warship, *La Gloire*, in 1859.

After the Crimean war, and for some years in the latter half of the nineteenth century, the navies of the world were diverted by rams. In 1861 the citizens of New Orleans subscribed to a fund to convert the small tug *Manassus* (387 tons, 128 feet long) into a ramming vessel. She looked like a floating metal cigar, with two funnels mounted abreast of each other, and a 32-pounder carronade up forward, firing through a shuttered port. But her chief weapon was her ram, which was made of 20 feet of solid timber. Her hull was protected by 12 inches of oak, with an outer skin of $1\frac{1}{2}$-inch iron plate.

This sinister little warship threw a long shadow. She was credited with driving away a whole blockading squadron from the mouth of the Mississippi. Federal reports said she 'was the most troublesome vessel of them all', although she was herself badly knocked about by fort gunfire in October 1861.

The most famous Confederate ram was the *Merrimac* (actually renamed *Virginia* but for some reason holding on to her original name for posterity). The hull of a steam frigate was cut down to within 3 feet of the water-line, strengthened with armour plating and covered with a bomb-proof, sloping-roofed house made of 20 inches of oak and pine, and sheeted with iron $4\frac{1}{2}$ inches thick, to cover the screw and rudder. Bow and stern were sheathed in steel plate. She was armed with 11-inch guns, and a ram. She had no mast, but a smoke stack, pilot-house and ensign staff broke the smooth expanse of her upperdeck. Under way, she looked like a 'huge half-submerged crocodile'. The Federals scoffed at her, calling her 'that Southern Bugaboo' and that 'old Secesh curiosity'.

She may have looked a curiosity but in Hampton Roads on 9 March 1862 she engaged and defeated three orthodox Federal warships, ramming and sinking the frigate *Cumberland*, setting the *Congress* on fire, and badly damaging the *Minnesota*.

Next day, *Merrimac* faced another ironclad as peculiar-looking as herself – the *Monitor*, designed by John Ericcson. She was a floating metal platform, with a very low freeboard, surmounted by a pilot-house, a funnel, and a huge steam-trained gun turret, mounting two heavy Dahlgren guns and protected by 5 inches of armour.

These two grotesques circled round each other at close range, exchanging shots which bounced futilely off each other's plate.

Merrimac attempted to ram *Monitor*, without damaging her, and the somewhat inconclusive battle was broken off, perhaps marginally in *Monitor's* favour. However, it seemed to everybody that ironclads and rams were now the coming thing.

The point seemed to be underlined beyond all argument by the Battle of Lissa, in the Adriatic, on 20 July 1866. An Italian fleet containing some modern warships but commanded by a peculiarly inept admiral, Count Carlo di Persano, spent two days bombarding the forts on the island of Lissa and attempting to land troops ashore. On the third day they were brought to action by a smaller Austrian fleet under Rear Admiral Wilhelm von Tegetthoff. The action itself took place in scenes of utter confusion, with most of the ship movements shrouded in thick smoke, and the ships themselves crossing and criss-crossing each other's bows and wakes, attempting to ram or to avoid being rammed, whilst firing guns at very close quarters.

At about 11 o'clock the Austrian ship of the line *Kaiser* actually did succeed in ramming the Italian ironclad *Re di Portogallo* abeam just abreast of her machinery space, while going at full speed. The ironclad turned to port just before impact and so lessened the blow, or she would probably have been sunk. As it was, she lost two anchors, several boats, one gun knocked overboard, and more than 60 feet of her side-armour was displaced.

Ironically, *Kaiser's* self-inflicted injuries were much worse. Her bowsprit and her entire stem were torn out. The foremast toppled over and took the funnel with it. However, she took another ironclad *Maria Pia* under fire but during the engagement, a serious fire was started, steam-pipes were shot through and the steering gear damaged. *Kaiser* then had to retire.

Tegetthoff's flagship *Erzherzog Ferdinand Max* had rammed two Italian ironclads but at too sharp an angle to damage them although she did remove the ensign of one of them (afterwards found to be *Palestro*). *Palestro* also received such severe damage from gunfire that, later in the day, she blew up and sank.

At the height of the battle Tegetthoff sighted an Italian ironclad, apparently stopped and surrounded by four Austrian ships. She was no longer obeying her helm and could only move straight ahead or astern. Conning his ship from half-way up the mizzen shrouds, from where he could see through the smoky gloom, *Erzherzog Ferdinand Max's* Captain, Freiherr von Sterneck, manoeuvred his ship to ram the ironclad, which was actually *Re d'Italia*.

Re d'Italia's engines were going full astern, but she had not yet made any sternway and was still stationary in the water when the Austrian ram hit her just over her engine-room with the force of

5000 tons going at a speed of $11\frac{1}{4}$ knots. Armour, plates, frames, beams and planking all collapsed before that titanic hammer blow, punching a hole about 300 feet square, half of it below the water-line.

Obeying previous instructions for ramming *Erzherzog Ferdinand Max*'s chief engineer immediately reversed engines after the impact, withdrawing the ram which had penetrated to a depth of $6\frac{1}{2}$ feet.

Re d'Italia heeled slowly over about 25° to starboard, swung back rather suddenly to port, driving that ghastly gash in her side well under water, and then sank almost at once. *Erzherzog Ferdinand Max* had some plates bent, a few rivet-heads sheared off, and a slight leak, but was otherwise undamaged.

The Italians were clearly defeated, although di Persano claimed a victory when he returned to Ancona (exactly as the Peloponnesian admirals did on their return to Mytilene after the Athenian victory off the Argusinae islands in 406 BC) and it was some time before the truth emerged.

When the truth did emerge, the ram was acclaimed as the paramount weapon at sea. 'The Power of the new weapon was conclusively proved,' wrote Admiral Colomb in *Lessons from Lissa* in 1867, 'and it is henceforth impossible to doubt its practical value.' Russia, he wrote, now thought the ram the only weapon of value against a fleet, while France firmly believed that the ram, and the ram only, need be feared at sea. Sir Edward Reed, the Chief Constructor of the Royal Navy, agreed and saw the ship itself, as a 'steam projectile', as the 'most formidable weapon of attack that man's ingenuity has devised'.

The most influential advocate of the ram was Admiral Sir George Sartorius, who had been a midshipman, aged 15, in the *Tonnant* at Trafalgar. Sir George wanted the ram pure, the ram simple, with no other armament at all so that 'there should be no possible cause or temptation to distract the attention of the commander from the Ram Power'. Largely as a result of Sir George's pressure (and he was supported by many other senior naval officers) the Royal Navy commissioned one of its more extraordinary warships, the 2649-ton torpedo-ram *Polyphemus* (the model for H G Wells' *Thunder Child* in *The War of the Worlds*).

Designed by Nathaniel Barnaby, Director of Naval Construction, *Polyphemus* was laid down at Chatham in 1878, launched in June 1881 and completed in February the next year. She looked like a long cylinder with tapered ends, flattened to form a deck and protected over the flattened portion by armoured steel. She had 6 Nordenfelt quick-firing guns and 5 torpedo tubes: 2 in a broadside on each side, and the fifth mounted at the extreme forward end of her

12-foot long steel ram. The cast steel conical cap which shut off the end of the torpedo tube actually formed the tip of the ram.

Apart from her ram, *Polyphemus* had several other unusual features: a bow rudder, for added manoeuvrability, and a unique system of balance weights fitted in her keel, which could be jettisoned by hand or hydraulically, to compensate for any compartments flooded in action. She was washed down from end to end in most seas, when only her hurricane deck was habitable. She had an unpredictable and violent movement in a short beam sea. Below decks she was extremely hot, temperatures in her machinery spaces regularly reaching 140°F.

After three years of trials, she went to Bantry Bay in Ireland in July 1885, where she was to try and break the boom across the harbour, one of the tasks for which she had been designed. It was thought that the heavy steel hawser of the boom would ride up over her ram-shaped bow and sweep the upper deck clean of every fitting. But nothing of the sort happened. *Polyphemus* slowed down gradually after the impact but then her momentum cut cleanly through the boom.

But *Polyphemus'* trials led nowhere. This was not the way to attack enemy strongholds. *Polyphemus* went out to the Mediterranean, where she served for 20 years, normally based at Gibraltar. Painted dark grey, she patrolled the Straits of Gibraltar during the Boer War.

Very few rams were actually built, and they had no military value or significance. Meanwhile, as a series of ramming accidents in the 1860s and '70s showed, any warship fitted with a ram bow was a constant source of danger to friends as well as foes. The preoccupation with rams proved to be only a temporary aberration. It was soon realised (and in fact many officers had never lost sight of it) that the big gun remained the final arbiter of naval battles, as it had been for centuries and as it was to be until the advent of the strike aircraft of the 1940s. Guns stood squarely in the mainstream of naval history, from Hawkins' long guns which defeated the Armada, to the close-range 'smasher' carronades of the French wars, to the monster muzzle-loaders of the Victorian ironclads, to the superb 15-inch gun of the twentieth century. Developed from broadside, to battery, to barbette, to turret, their size increased to the giant 18-inch of the Japanese *Yamato* class. The best talents of each generation laboured to improve their range, explosive, recoil systems, director control, range-finding and rate of fire. Their battle honours − Trafalgar, Navarino, Alexandria, Tsushima, Coronel, Jutland, Cape Matapan, *Bismarck*, Salerno, Normandy, *Scharnhorst* − reverberate like a tremendous roll of drums. At the same time, gunnery officers were

45

promoted and honoured. They were men of influence and power, if no longer with the Devil, then certainly with the establishments of their navies.

But, as the big guns thundered and the gunnery officers went up to receive their rewards from kings, emperors and presidents, there was always another view of naval history, another range of naval weapons, which gunnery officers might almost have considered subversive. This school of thought believed in the unobtrusive rather than the demonstrative, in silence rather than salvoes, *under* rather than over.

Above: A French bomb-ketch. (By De Passebon)

Below: *Monitor* versus *Merrimac*, Hampton Roads, 9 March 1862. (Author's Collection)

Above: The brig *Dorothea*, blown up by Fulton's torpedo off Deal, 15 October 1805. (From *Torpedo War and Submarine Explosions* by Robert Fulton, 1810)

Below: The torpedo-ram *Polyphemus* (the *Thunder Child* of H G Wells' *The War of the Worlds*) in dock in Malta. (From *Navy & Army Illustrated*, 9 April 1898)

CHAPTER 3

'*Hic homo est machinae inventor* ... This man is the inventor of a machine ...' wrote Mr Tutor Lewis of Yale to Ezra Styles, President of the College, on 15 August 1775. '... *nunc est fabricata et fere perfecta* ... now made and almost perfected ... for the destruction of the fleet in the harbor of Boston, by the explosion of gunpowder. The machine is so constructed that it can move rapidly 20 or more feet underwater, and can carry and attach to the hull of a ship 2000 pounds of gunpowder. Either immediately, or in ten minutes, or in half an hour, according to the will of the operator ... *horologium totam massam inflamabit* ... a clockwork will ignite the whole mass.'

Thus, in the dry Latin of one scholar's letter to another, was described the advent of the first operational submarine in naval history. The time was the American War of Independence. The fleet in Boston referred to was the British, and the man was David Bushnell, a farmer's son, born at Saybrook, Connecticut, in 1742. In 1770 Bushnell inherited the family farm but left the running of it to his brother Ezra, while he took himself to Yale as a scholar in 1771. He studied divinity, but he had an enquiring, sceptical turn of mind, combined with unusual technical ingenuity. Throughout his time at Yale it was probable that war with England was on its way. Without any prompting or advice or outside financial assistance of any kind, Bushnell began to ponder the possibilities of certain original weapons, and to make experiments.

He began by proving that an explosion did not dissipate itself harmlessly underwater. On the contrary, water tamped and increased the explosive effect. Bushnell put 2 pounds of powder in a wooden bottle and fastened it under a hogshead, with a 2-inch thick plank between hogshead and powder bottle. A wooden pipe, primed with powder, led down through hogshead and plank and into the powder bottle. A match was put to the priming powder.

There was a terrific detonation. The hogshead was completely demolished. Broken staves rose into the air, with stones torn from the bottom, in a towering column of water and debris, to the utter astonishment of the 'first personages in Connecticut' who had gathered to watch the demonstration.

This device was undoubtedly a primitive form of underwater mine. Bushnell's problem was now to carry the mine towards its target. Whilst still continuing his divinity studies, Bushnell began to consider ways of delivering his weapon by perfect stealth, underwater.

The idea of a submersible vehicle was not new. Medieval illustrated manuscripts showed a wide-eyed Alexander the Great descending in a form of submarine. There was Robert Valturio's wooden submarine of fifteenth century Venice, and there were sealskin submarines in sixteenth century Greenland. An eighteenth century French traveller described an attack by forty Cossacks, breathing through reeds, rowing a cowhide submersible against Turkish ships at Constantinople. William Bourne, an Elizabethan gunner, wrote down quite feasible principles for constructing a submarine, with ballast tanks operated by jack screws, in his *Inventions and Devices* published in 1578. One Cornelius Drebbel actually built a 12-oared 'eel boat' in which he was supposed to have taken James I, that cautious and fearful monarch, on a trip beneath the surface of the Thames. A seventeenth century bishop, John Wilkins, foresaw that submarines would be useful against pirates, for setting up blockades, and for exploring the sea. But the first man really to consider seriously the submarine as a weapon of war was Leonardo da Vinci and, clearly, the more he thought about it the more uneasy he became about the uses men might make of his designs. 'This I do not publish or divulge,' he wrote in his Notebooks, 'on account of the evil nature of men who would practise assassinations at the bottom of the seas by breaking the ships in their lowest parts and sinking them together with the crews who are in them.'

'Assassinations at the bottom of the seas' were precisely what David Bushnell had in mind. His submarine took about four years to plan and build, and it was completed at Saybrook in the spring of 1775. He himself wrote of it simply as a 'submarine vessel' but it has since been called the *Turtle*, or the *American Turtle*.

Turtle was a truly marvellous technical achievement, years ahead of her time. Alone, and with no formal scientific or engineering training, Bushnell solved some formidable problems of submarine construction, control and instrumentation which have since exercised the combined talents of whole shipyards. A contemporary drawing by a Lieutenant F M Barber in 1775 and Bushnell's own account describing *Turtle* as resembling 'two upper tortoise shells of equal size joined together', made of oak timbers, bound with iron bands and sealed and made watertight with pitch.

The single operator entered through an elliptical brass hatch set in the top with ports cut in its sides for visibility when proceeding awash. *Turtle* measured 7 feet from top hatch to keel, in which were 900 pounds of lead ballast, of which 200 could be jettisoned in emergency. She had two Archimedes propellers, one mounted horizontally and cranked by the operator to make about 3 knots in ideal conditions. The other, mounted vertically, forced the submarine down. There were two air-pipes and a ventilator drew fresh air through one and expelled stale air through the other. Both tubes were fitted with devices, the world's first schnorkels, 'so that they shut themselves whenever the water rose near their tops so that no water could enter through them.' There was air for a dive of about 30 minutes.

The operator dived the submarine by pushing his foot down on a brass valve spindle which opened a kingston valve to admit water into a ballast tank fitted next to the keel, at the same time cranking the vertical propeller. Water was pumped out by two hand-operated 'force pumps', one on either side of the operator. There was a line and lead for taking soundings, a compass for steering, which was by a hand-operated rudder at the stern, and a depth-gauge, consisting of a cork float in a glass tube half-filled with water. Cork and compass needle were phosphor-coated. Illumination inside the submarine whilst underwater was provided by the glow of rotting wood, known locally as 'fox fire'. The controls were all conveniently placed so that the operator could use them without having to stretch.

The mine, or magazine, was egg-shaped and fitted closely, like a hump, on to the back of the *Turtle*. Made of curved pieces of oak, scooped out of the solid, it contained 130 pounds of gunpowder, a clock, and a gun-lock with a reliable flint. At the top of the submarine was a detachable awl, worked from inside, and connected by rope to the mine. The operator screwed the awl point into the hull timbers of the target ship, detached the awl and moved away, leaving the mine moored to its target by the rope.

Trials were carried out in the summer of 1775, with Bushnell's brother Ezra as crewman. There were problems with the 'force pumps'. Fresh parts had to be machined. There was also a curious snag with the 'fox fire'. It was extinguished by frost. As the weather grew colder in the autumn, trials had to stop until the spring of 1776.

Some Americans had misgivings about the propriety of using weapons like *Turtle*. James Fenimore Cooper, for example, in a history of the navy published after the war, did not regret the failure of these 'torpedoes', since, in his opinion, they were a species of warfare that tended 'to aggravate the evils of hostilities, without essentially conducing to bring them to a termination'.

51

George Washington had no such doubts. His armorial family motto was 'The End Justified The Means'. He could not afford to be squeamish or mealy-mouthed about any weapon. He had no navy to speak of, and the Royal Navy was present in strength off New York. Anything that could discommode or, ideally, disperse those ships was well worth trying. When Bushnell had spent most of his inheritance on his experiments, George Washington provided him with a further £100. The submarine was thus designed and saw its first operational debut in the classical manner of new weapons, as the brain-child of the weaker power.

In the summer of 1776, Sir William Howe had 10,000 troops on Staten Island, while his brother Admiral Howe had a large fleet of warships and transports in New York Bay. On 12 July, Howe's flagship the 64-gun Third Rate *Eagle* anchored off Staten Island, so provocatively close that the Americans could actually smell the British on board her. Clearly, there was *Turtle*'s target, and now was the time to attack.

Unfortunately, Ezra Bushnell now fell ill and took so long to recover that David Bushnell realised that his brother would not be able to carry out the attack. Another crewman had to be found. From three men who had previously volunteered for fire-ships and who now volunteered for *Turtle*, Bushnel chose Sergeant Ezra Lee, from Lyme, Connecticut. It was Sergeant Lee who, in New York harbour on the night of 5/6 September 1776, carried out the first operational submarine attack in history.

The night was fine, calm and dark, with the moon due to rise later on. Three whale-boats towed *Turtle* for the first part of her journey. Lee embarked, shut the top hatch and trimmed *Turtle* down until her ports were just above water level. A strong ebb tide carried *Turtle* down harbour. The tide in fact took her too far and Lee had to propel himself back up tide to his target. It took him 'the space of five glasses by the ship's bells, or $2\frac{1}{2}$ hours' to get under the stern of *Eagle*. He could hear the bells and men's voices clearly underwater.

Eagle drew 10 feet, a fairly deep dive for *Turtle*, but Lee manoeuvred her successfully under the target, and began to screw the awl into the bottom of the ship. But the awl would not bite. Thinking he had struck a patch of metal hull sheathing, Lee moved his position and tried again. Still the point would not penetrate the ship's timbers. By now it was growing light and the tide was starting to flood. Lee decided to break off the attack and try again the next night. His compass now went awry and he was forced to bring *Turtle* up so that he could see through the ports to steer. The top hatch was sighted and a boat put out from the shore to investigate. Lee jettisoned the mine and cranked away for the American shore. The mine later detonated with a tremendous roar, signifying what might have happened to *Eagle*.

On 15 September Lee made another attack in *Turtle* upon an unknown British frigate in the North River, opposite Bloomingdale. Again the attempt went awry. *Turtle* was swept away from her target by the tide. Lee had to crank furiously to prevent himself and *Turtle* being swept out to sea. Some time later, as the British army advanced, Bushnell loaded *Turtle* on board a small sloop, hoping to get her back to Connecticut. But a British frigate intercepted and sank the sloop with *Turtle* on board.

Bushnell, Lee and everybody else thought that Lee's attack had failed because of new copper sheathing on *Eagle*'s hull. In fact, Lee had been foiled by a simple law of physics: every action has an equal and opposite reaction. In a vessel free-floating in water, the harder an operator pressed against an object, the more he would push himself away from it. Unless *Turtle* had had enough positive buoyancy to float up and press herself hard against *Eagle*'s hull, or Lee's awl had had the fortune to snag itself in the wood and allow the circular movement of the thread to take effect, Lee had had no hope of penetrating the hull with an awl.

In August 1777, Bushnell launched another ingenious attack on the British frigate *Cerberus*, lying in Black Point Bay in the Connecticut River west of New London. He appears by then to have abandoned all thoughts of *Turtle* and any successors to her. Instead he built a 'machine', loaded with gunpowder, which drifted down river on a line until it fouled its target where, after a set interval, clockwork exploded the charge.

Unfortunately, the machine snagged first on a captured schooner, a British prize, lying just astern of *Cerberus*. It blew up while four sailors were examining it, destroying the schooner and killing three of the men. In December, still experimenting with floating mines, Bushnell prepared several kegs charged with gunpowder and set them adrift on the Delaware River, above Philadelphia. But the kegs were released too far from their targets and drifted ashore or were caught in ice. They did not arrive near their objective until daylight, when their arrival certainly caused consternation in Philadelphia. Guards and pickets were called out, and wild shots were fired, in a general pandemonium which later inspired an American rhymester, Francis Hopkinson, to compose a derisive ballad 'The Battle of the Kegs'. The kegs did no physical damage to any British warship, but Commodore Symons, flying his broad pennant in *Cerberus*, wrote of these events in outraged terms: 'the ingenuity of these [villains] is singular in their secret modes of mischief.'

Bushnell himself was actually captured on 7 May 1779 by a British raiding party who naturally had no idea of his importance. He was later released in an exchange of prisoners. The war ended on 3 September 1783, and Bushnell left the army in November with the rank of Captain-Lieutenant. He eventually went to live in Warrenton, Georgia, under the plain name of Dr Bush, and died there in 1824.

In the end, largely because of bad luck, illness, and a certain amount of bad planning, Bushnell's brilliantly inventive weapons achieved no tactical success whatever. But Bushnell was also hampered by the technology, or lack of it, of his time. For example, except in ideal conditions of fine weather, slack water, and short hauls, it was physically impossible for one man alone to propel *Turtle* towards her target whilst simultaneously steering a course, keeping a depth, pumping and flooding, aiming and working the awl, and releasing the mine. In bad weather, in strong tides, over a longer distance or where any violent evasive action was required, the physical task simply became too great.

As for the failure of some of his other devices, Bushnell was opposed by the best navy in the world in its time, a service by no means as innocent of mysterious devices nor as disconcerted by things that went bump in the night as the Americans loved to proclaim (as a matter of interest, Captain Henry Duncan, commanding *Eagle*, did not even mention the furore over *Turtle*'s attack in his Journal for 6 September 1776). Every officer and man in the Royal Navy had been brought up in a long tradition of cutting-out raids, expeditions by night into defended harbours, sightings of strange objects and, generally, of simply messing about in boats. The commotion at Philadelphia, for instance, so satirised in 'The Battle of the Kegs' was, after all, a very understandable reaction. It would have been a far better subject for satire if the British had ignored unidentified objects floating down river towards their warships in time of war.

George Washington had had no scruples about using submarines, or machines, or 'infernals', as they were called. The more ships they could sink, the better. But with the opening of the nineteenth century, the element of moral doubt about such weapons became ever more noticeable amongst senior naval officers and politicians. Paradoxically, the better the weapons became, the deeper the misgivings about using them. This paradox was personified in the curious, contradictory figure of Robert Fulton whose personality acted almost as a catalyst in his times.

Robert Fulton was born on 14 November 1765, one of five children of a poor Irish farming family at Conowingo Creek, Little Britain County (later named Fulton County), near Philadelphia. Not much is known of his early life but he was clearly a quick, intelligent lad, clever in hand and brain. He had some quality about him which made other men of talent recognise and assist him. When he was 17 he went to Philadelphia and gained some reputation as a painter of miniatures. In 1786 he went to London, under the patronage of Benjamin West, later President of the Royal Academy (where Fulton exhibited a portrait in 1791).

By 1793 Fulton had turned his hand to mechanical matters. At various times in his life he was concerned with, and even took out patents for, machines for spinning flax and making rope, for sawing marble into blocks, and for designing and improving canals. In 1797 he went to France where, in the turbulent intellectual atmosphere of the Revolution, Fulton saw a future for all mankind, free of oppression, free of slavery, free of the monarchy and, above all, free of the naval force of England which he saw as 'the source of all the incalculable horrors that are committed daily'. He evolved schemes for universal disarmament, for removing sea power with one deadly weapon, for making war impossible by the exertion of one over-powering, overwhelming, irresistible force.

Fulton himself was a very human mixture of idealism and mendacity. He genuinely wished to make war impossible and he actually developed what could have been a war-winning weapon on a strategic scale. But he also wanted to make money. The nearest modern parallel would be if somebody had invented a nuclear bomb and wished to pocket all the profits. Those who employed Fulton were just as ambivalent in their attitudes being both horrified and delighted by what he was doing. As they watched stout warships disintegrating into match-wood, they were exultant and yet fearful of the forces they were releasing into the world.

From about 1796, Fulton had been thinking of a 'plunging boat' which he later called *Nautilus* (to become, over the years, the most famous of all submarine names). On 13 December 1797, he wrote to the Directory of France: 'Having taken a great interest in all that would diminish the power of England, I have planned the construction of a mechanical machine in which I have the greatest confidence for the annihilation of this [ie the Royal] Navy.'

Fulton's letter went on to put forward an ingenious proposal for setting ocean warfare on a strict cash basis, with a price paid for every warship sunk, like a bounty payable for every pest killed. The government were asked to pay Fulton's Company various amounts depending on the size of the vessel sunk or captured. The government could also build *Nautilus* machines themselves, under licence, on payment of a royalty. Since the War of Independence Fulton had of course been an American citizen (having been born while America was a British colony) and he stipulated that the *Nautilus* was not to be used against America unless the Americans first used them against the French.

There was one other very significant demand. Fulton was evidently afraid of the high feelings his inventions would arouse. He seems to have had the notion that fire-ships were against what he called the 'Laws of War', and their crews would be hanged if captured. He therefore required an assurance that anybody serving in a *Nautilus* would be treated as a prisoner-of-war and that the French government would take reprisals on English prisoners-of-war if *Nautilus* crews were ill-treated.

In January 1798 the Ministry of Marine replied to this audacious document with Fulton's own mixture of caution and brutality. They were certainly interested. But they reduced the terms of the prize money and they refused to give the *Nautilus* crews commissions, saying that their method of destroying the enemy was repugnant and disgraceful. Thus, with those same double standards which everybody held towards submarines, the French government was willing to employ them, but not to make them respectable. As for the treatment of prisoners, there was no hope of fulfilling Fulton's conditions. The British had three times as many French prisoners in their hands as the French had British.

When Fulton continued to press for recognition of *Nautilus* crews as *bona fide* belligerents, the government dropped his proposals. Undismayed, Fulton carried on his one-man crusade against bureaucracy. He made a model of a *Nautilus* and with it succeeded in impressing the next Minister of Marine, Admiral Eustace Bruix, who appointed another commission. They reported in August 1798 that 'this arm is without doubt imperfect [but] it is the first conception of a man of genius'.

Fulton himself was at pains to explain that with *Nautilus* he was really only being cruel to be kind. 'If at first glance,' he wrote in October 1798, 'the means I propose seem revolting, it is only because they are extraordinary; they are anything but inhuman. It is certainly the gentlest and least bloody method that the philospher can imagine to overturn this system of brigandage and of perpetual war which has always vexed maritime nations; to give at last peace to the earth, and to restore men to their natural industries, and to a happiness until now unknown.'

Nevertheless, his proposals were turned down once again, so he went to Holland, where he had no more success. But in November 1799, Napoleon Buonaparte became First Consul. He had already shown some interest in *Nautilus*, and his Minister of Marine, Forfait, had been a member of the commission which had reported encouragingly in 1798. At last, Fulton was instructed to go ahead.

Fulton had always had the knack of making useful friends. Joel Barlow, an American poet and a rich man, had offered him lodging when he was hard up. Two more friends, Gaspard Mongé, the mathematician, and de La Place, the astronomer, assisted Fulton to build *Nautilus*.

She was laid down at the Perrier yard in Rouen and sailed on her maiden voyage on 29 July 1800. She was shaped like a blunt-nosed torpedo, with a rounded bow and stern and an observation dome forward. She was 21 feet 4 inches long, made of copper sheeting fastened over an iron framework. Like *Turtle*, she had several innovations: a folding mast with a sail, for use on the surface, and a 4-bladed (windmill type) propeller cranked by two men. She had a rudder and a pair of horizontal rudders or hydroplanes as they were called in later years, for depth-keeping. There was an internal ballast tank in the keel. Part of the keel could be detached in an emergency.

On the first day, *Nautilus* made two dives, of 8 minutes and 17 minutes. On 24 August, she dived for an hour, with a candle lit inside her, to see how long it would burn. On 27 August, she covered a distance of 500 metres submerged.

The weapon was a mine similar to *Turtle*'s, but towed on a line which was threaded through a hole in a spike. The spike was driven into the hull of a target, while *Nautilus* went on, thus drawing the mine up against the spike. The mine was then detonated, when *Nautilus* was some distance away.

In September, Fulton took his *Nautilus* down to Le Havre for trials in the open sea. On the 12th he reached La Hogue, having achieved speeds of a 'league and a half' ($4\frac{1}{2}$ miles) an hour and 'had the pleasure of seeing it ride the waves like an ordinary boat'. On one sortie, Fulton went 70 miles from Le Havre, to Growan near Isigny and twice tried to approach English brigs lying offshore. Both times they moved away before *Nautilus* could get near them.

On 6 October, Fulton wrote a jubilant letter to Napoleon. 'Let us see first what would be for France the immediate effects of the *Nautilus*. The loss of the first English ship destroyed by this extraordinary means would throw the English Government into utter embarrassment ... the whole navy could be destroyed by the same means ... it would be possible to blockade the Thames and cut off the whole commerce of London ... Deprived of Pitt's guineas, the coalition would vanish and France thus delivered from its numerous enemies would be able to work without obstacle for the strengthening of its liberty and for peace.'

Indeed it was a heady prospect and Fulton was summoned to

Paris to discuss it personally with Napoleon. He must have come away from the interview convinced that a great building programme for *Nautilus* was about to start. But days passed and still nothing happened. Fulton was incredulous. He had offered Napoleon a weapon which would bring him the dominion over the world he sought. But *still* the man hesitated. It was inexplicable. Fulton wrote another letter, complaining about '... the cold and discouraging manner with which all my exertions had been treated ... will compel me to abandon the enterprise in France if I am not received in a more friendly and liberal manner.'

It was not a tactful letter and Admiral Decres, who had replaced Forfait as Minister of Marine, had no great enthusiasm for *Nautilus*. In fact, he thought such warfare was underhand. He cancelled the whole project and told Fulton, pointedly, 'Your invention is good for Algerians and pirates, but learn that France has not yet given up the seas.'

That could well have been the end for Fulton, and for *Nautilus*. But Mongé and La Place seem to have smoothed their friend's ruffled feelings. More important, they convinced Napoleon again that he ought to continue with *Nautilus*. She was rebuilt at Brest in the summer of 1801 and on 3 July made her first dive, to a depth of 5 feet and then, by stages, to 25 feet. She had several improvements: a small window in the upper part of the hull, a copper globe filled with compressed air at 200 psi to extend the air supply. Fulton could make *Nautilus* travel 1300 feet underwater, follow a compass course just as if he were on the surface, and generally handle her like a proper weapon of war. It now only remained to demonstrate her.

The demonstration took place against a 40-foot sloop off Brest. Fulton dived *Nautilus* 600 feet from the target, ran underneath and fixed the mine. 'Taking my direction so as to pass near the Sloop I struck her with the bomb on my Passage. The explosion took place and the Sloop was torn into Atoms, in fact nothing was left by the buye and the cable, And the concussion was so Great that a Column of Water Smoak and fibres of the Sloop was cast from 80 to 100 feet in the Air.'

To the spectators, who included professional naval officers like Admiral Villaret and the Maritime Prefect of Brest, the demolition of that sloop must have appeared a truly terrible sight, a preview of a future in which their wooden warships had no place. The Prefect of Brest reported 'This type of warfare carries with it the objection that those who undertake it and those against whom it is made will all be lost. This cannot be called a *gallant* death.'

Admiral Villaret's account of the demonstration so impressed Napoleon that he asked to see and inspect the 'plunging boat' for himself. But Fulton had made yet another tactical error in public relations. He had already disposed of *Nautilus*. She was leaking a great deal, he explained, and he did not think her of any more use. He had taken her to pieces and sold her iron work, lead and 'Cylenders'.

The truth was that Fulton believed that *Nautilus* had served her purpose. He thought he had done enough. Surely he had shown, once and for all, the potential of his weapon? Surely nothing now stood in the way of a progression of bigger, better, more powerful plunging boats? Having apparently learned nothing at all from the past, Fulton wrote to Napoleon again.

Napoleon did not reply. After three years of working and designing, demonstrating, cajoling, pleading, Fulton was back where he started. Worse, he began to hear rumours that Napoleon now thought of him as a charlatan, an *escroc*, who thought of nothing but money. On 5 February 1803, the Ministry of Marine wrote to Fulton, finally dispensing with his services. The Minister himself, Admiral Pleville le Pelly, said that in any case his conscience would not permit him to encourage so terrible a machine. There was a general feeling amongst Napoleon's generals and advisers that Fulton's methods of warfare were fit only for cowards. Their thoughts and hopes, like Napoleon's own, were already turning to the east, to the conquest of Russia.

Fulton temporarily dropped all thoughts and plans of submarines and, encouraged by the American Minister to the French government, Robert R Livingston, he turned his attention to steam-boats, building and running one on the Seine. Here, too, ironically was what could have been a priceless weapon in Napoleon's hand: a means of towing his invasion barges across the English Channel whatever the wind direction.

If the French had lost interest in Fulton, the British certainly had not. Fulton had corresponded fairly regularly with another influential friend, Lord Stanhope, himself a talented naval inventor. The British secret service had also been watching and reporting on Fulton's experiments, and especially his demolition of that sloop off Brest. Lord Stanhope made a speech in the House of Lords warning of such dangers. On 19 June 1803, a month after the war broke out again, the Admiralty issued a secret circular to the flag officers commanding at Sheerness, Portsmouth, the Nore and Plymouth, warning them of Fulton's plans for destroying 'the Maritime Force of this Country' and giving a fairly accurate but somewhat alarmist account of *Nautilus'* attack at Brest.

A Mr Smith, a confidential agent of the British Government, was sent to France to offer Fulton £800 to go to England and demonstrate his ideas. After all the harsh words Fulton had uttered about the

British and their infamous Navy, after all his attempts to blow British men and ships into the air, he might have been expected to refuse such an offer out of hand. In fact, Fulton said that he must have £10,000 to leave France. He would require a committee to be formed within three weeks to examine his submarine inventions. If accepted, he would sell all his plans for submarines and bombs for £100,000. Clearly, Fulton had lost none of his financial audacity.

He went to Amsterdam to await the reply. Nothing happened for three months, so he went back to Paris. There, the discreet Mr Smith called upon him again with a reply, in code, from the Foreign Secretary Lord Hawkesbury who said that he could not grant such sums before an invention had been tested. But he assured Fulton he would be treated with 'the utmost liberality and Generosity'. Fulton decided to go, and travelling under the name of Mr Francis, arrived in London on 28 April 1804. He found Hawkesbury out of office, and Pitt in his chair.

Fulton's drawings show that his new designs were a great improvement on *Nautilus*. He had plans for a seagoing submarine, 35 feet long, and 10 feet in the beam, with a 6-man crew and provisions on board for three weeks at sea. The submarine was armed with 30 submarine bombs carried in individual deck compartments. There was a conventional sloop-rigged sail, with a 2-bladed propeller for underwater passages, which was jointed so that it could be folded out of the way when not required. There were two streamlined ventilation pipes and a conning tower with viewing ports cut in it. It was, like *Turtle*, a vessel many years ahead of its time.

Fulton's new submarine was never built, but he did collaborate in the design of explosive 'catamarans' used in a raid on Boulogne harbour in October 1804. Fulton's first meeting with Pitt was at breakfast at Pitt's house near Putney Common, then in the country outside London. Also there was Captain Sir Home Popham, a Fellow of the Royal Society, an excellent surveyor and astronomical observer, and adapter of a code of signalling used by the Navy for many years. He was also scheduled to lead one of the raids using Fulton's inventions.

According to Fulton's account, when 'Sir Home Popham went into an adjoining room, Mr Pitt remarked that this is an extraordinary invention which seemed to go to the destruction of all fleets; I replied that it was invented with that View, And as I had no design to deceive him or the government I did not hesitate to give it as my opinion that this invention would lead to the total annihilation of the existing System of Marine War.'

Whether he believed that statement or not, Pitt offered Fulton the facilities of the Royal Dockyards, £7000 for materials, £200 a month salary, and half the value of every ship his inventions could destroy. Even if Fulton produced nothing, he was at any rate no longer working for the French and that, in Pitt's view, was worth the money.

The only objection was from Earl St Vincent, who disliked Pitt (and Popham, too, for that matter). His objection was practical rather than ethical. 'The morning of my first interview with Earl St Vincent,' Fulton wrote, 'he was very communicative. I explained to him a Torpedo and the *Dorothea* experiment. He reflected for some time, and then said, Pitt was the greatest fool that ever existed, to encourage a mode of war which they who commanded the seas did not want, and which, if successful, would deprive them of it.' There, in a sentence, St Vincent expressed the Royal Navy's view of submarines for the next century.

The *Dorothea* experiment took place in Walmer Roads, near Deal, off Walmer Castle, Pitt's house by the sea, on 15 October 1805, at 5 o'clock in the afternoon. The *Dorothea* was a 'strong built Danish brig', 200 tons, drawing 12 feet. Two boats, each with a 'torpedo' in the stern, approached *Dorothea*, connected by a line. The torpedoes were thrown into the water. The tide carried them down on to *Dorothea*'s anchor cable. The line draped round the cable and brought the two torpedoes, one on each side, close into *Dorothea*'s hull. Each torpedo had an 18-minute clockwork delay on its fuse.

The distinguished spectators had gathered to watch. Some of them were sceptical. A Captain Kingston said that 'if a torpedo were placed under his cabin while he was at dinner, he should feel no concern for the consequence'. As Fulton drily remarked, 'Occular demonstration is the best proof for all men.'

The explosion seemed to lift *Dorothea* bodily 'about 6 feet: she separated at the middle and the two ends went down; in 20 seconds nothing was to be seen of her except floating fragments; the pumps and foremast were blown out of her; the fore-top sail-yard was thrown up to the cross-trees; the fore-chain plates, with their bolts, were torn from her sides ... the mizzenmast was broke off in two places; these discoveries were made by means of the pieces which were found afloat.'

As the roar of the explosion died away, and debris from the shattered brig rained down over a wide area of sea, the watchers were as horrified and thrilled as those at the earlier experiment off Brest. Here, truly, was a war-winning weapon. But, only a week later, Nelson defeated the combined French and Spanish fleets off Cape Trafalgar, and the British lost interest in Fulton and his machines.

Fulton began to write letters again, as fruitlessly as before. He

had been paid £13,000 in fees. The government had spent another
£11,000 on materials for the 'carcasses and machines' used at
Boulogne. Fulton claimed another £40,000. The case went to
arbitration. The arbitrators agreed with Fulton's case. But he got no
money. He wrote to the Prime Minister. Still he got no money.
Finally, in October 1806, Fulton went home to America where his
friend and benefactor Robert R Livingston encouraged and financed
Fulton's steam-boats, including the famous *Clermont*.

Fulton carried out yet another spectacular demonstration of his
torpedo (actually a form of mine) in New York harbour in August
1807, when he blew up another two brigs before an appreciative
audience of 2000 people. There was, of course, a defence against
Fulton's floating mines: nets strung round a ship. These defeated
Fulton in a test in 1810 but, ever resourceful, he designed a form of
cable cutter. The result was taken to be a draw. A committee judged
the experiments inconclusive.

Clermont brought Fulton the money and fame he seemed always
to have wanted. But his heart seems still to have hankered secretly
after his plunging boats and mines. In New York in 1815 he began to
build another submarine, 80 feet long by 22 in the beam, called *Mute*.
She was to have had a crew of a hundred, but Fulton died that year
and *Mute* was scrapped.

Another submarine boat, possibly of Fulton's design or
developed from it, took part in the War of 1812 between Great
Britain and the United States. In July 1813, off New London, this
submarine attacked the line-of-battleship *Ramillies*, which was flying
the broad pennant of Commodore Hardy (Nelson's Hardy). The boat
was sighted astern of *Ramillies* and the alarm was raised. The boat
was seen to dive. *Ramillies* got under way but the submarine boat
was sighted again, too close for the guns to be depressed to fire at it.
The boat dived once more and attached itself to *Ramillies* keel where
it remained for half an hour. The screw awl broke off and the
submarine's operator had to make his retreat. Hardy then advised the
American government that he was taking on board as many
American prisoners-of-war as possible, so that 'should the ship be
blown up, your citizens must share his fate'.

This form of warfare caused feelings to run high on both sides.
The Americans laid another device to destroy *Ramillies*. A schooner
with a load of flour had a bomb concealed in the cargo. It was hoped
that *Ramillies*, short of stores as always, would send a prize crew to
take the schooner and bring her alongside to discharge her cargo,
when the bomb would explode. The little ship was indeed captured,
but the bomb exploded prematurely, some distance away from its
intended destination. The historian William James commented: 'We

shall not trust ourselves to comment upon this most atrocious proceeding' and quoted another historian, Brenton, writing of the same incident: 'A quantity of arsenic among the food would have been so perfectly compatible with the rest of the contrivance, that we wonder it was not resorted to. Should actions like these receive the sanction of governments, the science of war, and the laws of nations, will degenerate into the barbarity of the Algerines; and murder and pillage will take place of kindness and humanity to our enemies.'

William James went on to indulge in sarcasm. He had heard it said, that this disgraceful attempt against the *Ramillies* originated with 'mercenary merchants' and it had been hinted that the perpetrators were 'adopted, not native, Americans, the latter being too "high-minded" to countenance such a proceeding'. Nobody who wished to 'escape a tar-and-feathering' would have dared to whisper a supposition 'that an American naval officer would lend his ear to so dishonourable a mode of freeing himself from the presence of his enemy'. In fact, according to James, Captain Charles Stewart of the American navy had *already* sanctioned a plan to blow up the *Plantagenet* (74 guns) in Chesapeake Bay by a torpedo conducted by Mr Mervine P Mix, one of the *Constellation*'s midshipmen. And, James went on, Commodore Stephen Decatur, that 'excellent man', that 'ornament to his country' had tried to blow up Sir Thomas Hardy with a torpedo in a whale-boat which had lain in a bay on Long Island for some weeks waiting a chance to attack, before Hardy got wind of the plan and captured those who were to carry it out.

Thus, in several attempts, with the expenditure of a great deal of money and some lives, no warships had yet been sunk in earnest by submarine attack. But the idea of such attacks was irrepressible. It was to reappear again and again. Fulton's plans and machines were now part of naval history. The notion of creeping unseen upon an enemy and destroying him by stealth, ungentlemanly though it might seem, had to many naval officers an irresistible appeal.

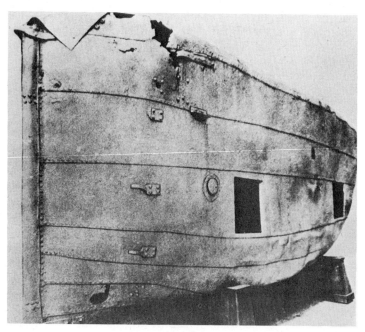

Above: The *Brandtaucher* ('Fire Diver'), the first submarine built by Wilhelm Bauer, with which he put the Danish fleet to flight in Kiel harbour, in 1850. After 36 years on the bottom it was raised and put on display at the Naval Museum, Berlin. (Author's Collection)

Below: Early photograph of Robert Whitehead with a trials torpedo, somewhat battered. (RNAD Museum, Gosport)

CHAPTER 4

Nineteenth century submarine design progressed in a curious state of inspired fantasy grappling with primitive resources. The inventors had no government support or encouragement and built their submarines almost as a cottage industry, like present day men trying to build a lunar space module in their own backyards. Their achievements were severely limited by their technical means, but nothing could put bounds to their imaginations. In 1820 an enterprising smuggler called Captain Johnson offered to spirit Napoleon away from St Helena by submarine. He actually did demonstrate a form of submersible, 100-foot long, with folding masts and sails, and did raise some money, but Napoleon unfortunately died. In 1832 a French naval officer, Captain Montgéry, planned but never built what would have been a formidable warship, *L'Invisible*: she was to have been 112 feet long, armed with 100 mines, 4 very large 'columbiads' or underwater cannon, a ram, 100 rockets and a battery of 8 carronades on the upper-deck. She was to have had paddles, driven by an 'explosion engine' in which gunpowder detonated in a cylinder. In her one can perhaps see the seeds of Jules Verne's inspiration.

Those inventions which were built took a steady toll of their inventors. In 1831 a Spaniard, Signor Cervo, built a spherical submarine in which he dived only once, and for the last time. A Dr Petit of Amiens dived several times in the river Somme before disappearing for good. An American shoemaker called Phillips successfully took his wife and two children down to the bottom of Lake Michigan, but failed to surface from a later dive.

The next submersible actually to be used in war emerged from an equally domestic, almost homely, background. In 1850 Germany and Denmark were at war over the question of the border province of Schleswig-Holstein. The Danish fleet blockaded the harbour of Kiel. A corporal Wilhelm Bauer, of the light horse artillery, who had been a woodturner at home in Dillingen, in Bavaria, offered to build a weapon to lift the blockade.

Bauer hoped that she would look like a dolphin but, as actually built by a local blacksmith, she resembled a metal sausage with flattened ends. She was 25 feet long, with a 6-foot beam and 9-foot draught, with four large square windows set in her sides, and a 4-bladed propeller hand-cranked by two men.

She was called *Brandtaucher* ('Fire-diver'), but on her first operational sortie she did not have to dive. The mere sight of her strange upper-works, this suspicious-looking object apparently propelling itself by some mysterious process, alarmed the Danish ships enough to make them retreat from the harbour entrance. Here, in fact, was a genuine weapon for breaking the blockade, if it could be developed, but *Brandtaucher*'s next dive was very nearly fatal to her inventor.

Bauer had rigged a system for adjusting the internal distribution of the submarine's weight by means of a large iron block travelling on a rail. Not realising the inherent instability of the method, Bauer planned to make the bows dip by running the weight forward, bring the bows up by running the weight aft. Unhappily, *Brandtaucher* next dived, and went on diving, coming to rest at the bottom of an unsuspected 60-foot deep hole in the harbour bed. None of the efforts of Bauer or the two men with him could bring *Brandtaucher* to the surface again. Meanwhile, well-meaning rescuers on the surface began to drag for the submarine with heavy anchors which smashed against the windows. If a window once broke, the men inside would drown at once.

In the dark and cold of a partially flooded submarine, after the shock of the accident and with the very real possibility of death, Wilhelm Bauer still kept his wits about him and worked out a means of survival (which remains the principle of one form of submarine escape to this day). The hatch could not be opened because of the pressure of water upon it. But if water were allowed to flood into the submarine until the pressure inside and outside the hatch were the same, the hatch could be opened, and the men could escape in a bubble of air.

The other two men understandably thought Bauer had gone mad, to suggest allowing *more* water in. It took Bauer some four hours, while the dragging anchors continued to scrape and smash menacingly against the hull, to convince them. But, at last, they made the attempt. The hatch opened, and all three escaped.

Afterwards Bauer embarked upon the endless peregrination round the courts and ministries of Europe, trying to find sponsors for his ideas, which seemed the usual lot of the nineteenth century submarine pioneer. In Austria, the Archduke Maximilian was intrigued and promised a grant of 100,000 francs, but the project was opposed by regular Austrian naval officers of orthodox views and eventually collapsed. Bauer went to England where he interested Prince Albert and, with Palmerston and the naval architect John Scott Russell, began on plans for an improved *Brandtaucher*. She was to have 'a hypnotic apparatus' of air-pipes leading to the surface, and a piston engine propelled by a gas of combined saltpetre, sulphur, coal and ammonia. Bauer planned for her to carry 500-pound mines, which could be fixed to the hulls of targets by the crew putting their arms in shoulder-length leather gauntlets mounted on holes cut in the hull, like modern arrangements for handling radio-active material.

Bauer fell out with his sponsors and left the country, whereupon Scott Russell and Palmerston discovered that Bauer's ideas were registered but not formally patented. Scott Russell used some of them for a submarine, in which 10 men crewed a form of diving bell, to be used in the Crimean War. But it was unsuccessful, and cost several lives.

Bauer's last submarine was built for the Russians. His patron was the Archduke Constantine, who financed *Le Diable Marin* ('Sea Devil'). She was 52 feet long, with a 12-foot beam and 11 feet from deck to keel, made of sheet iron, and propelled by a 3-bladed propeller worked by four men walking a treadmill. She also had a 500-pound mine, and gauntlet arrangements for fixing it to a target.

She was launched in 1855, and from May to October 1856 she made no less than 134 dives, some to a depth (reported) of 150 feet. On 6 September 1856, to celebrate the Coronation of Tsar Alexander II, Bauer dived *Sea Devil* to the bottom of Kronstadt harbour where a hired four-piece brass band played a selection of popular airs. But he met the same now-familiar opposition from Russian naval officers. His last trip was to France where he had the ear of Napoleon III for a time. He returned to Bavaria and died in Munich, of tuberculosis of the spine, in 1875.

In the American Civil War, both sides showed considerable technical ingenuity at sea. The war was fought with the fraternal ferocity of all civil wars. There were a few scruples to begin with, but these soon vanished under the pressure of events. The South began with no navy at all, and had to compensate with inventiveness and improvisation. One of the most inventive and certainly one of the most secret of their organisations was the Confederate Torpedo Bureau, under Gabriel James Rains.

Rains at first had to overcome opposition to his devices from some Confederate leaders who deplored the use of concealed lethal mechanisms against which there was at the time practically no defence. But as the war went on, Rains' ruthless weapons were approved by Jefferson Davies. The men who worked in Rains' department were allowed no illusions about their fate if they ever fell

67

into Federal hands. The Union had no torpedoes and did not think the use of them 'honorable warfare'. They themselves had no need of submarine defences, because the South had no ships. They announced that they would shoot or hang any man they captured who was in the 'torpedo business'.

One device the Federals found particularly offensive was a bomb disguised as a piece of coal. When added to the regular coal on board and eventually shovelled into the furnace, it exploded, wrecking the boiler and possibly even sinking the ship. One such planted bomb badly damaged the headquarters ship of General Butler, the Union army commander, when he and Admiral Porter were both on board her.

The Torpedo Division had their headquarters in a converted tug, actually called the *Torpedo*, in which they developed a variety of torpedoes (still having its old meaning of stationary underwater mines) with various containers and detonators. They experimented with hollow spherical shells of iron, filled with powder, linked by electric cable, fired by a battery, with sensitive fuses of fulminate of mercury. In December 1862, the Torpedo Division established a station on the James River 5 or 6 miles below Richmond, where they planted two giant 'tanks' each containing 1000 pounds of powder on the river bed. An attack on a Federal gunboat on her way up river narrowly failed, the detonation being slightly mistimed. The gunboat was badly shaken but survived. In a later action on the same river in May 1864, when General Butler's army, supported by the Federal navy, was advancing northwards to Richmond, another lay of torpedoes was successfully exploded, destroying the gunboat *Commodore Jones*.

The Union built several 'monitors', armoured warships armed with Dahlgren guns, after *Monitor* herself (who sank in a storm). These 'Goliaths' had their 'Davids', indeed the little ships were called 'Davids' by the Confederates. They were low-freeboard torpedo-boats, with not much more than the funnel and a slip of the hull visible above water. The South did not have the manufacturing resources of the Union, and the 'Davids' were 'backyard warships' constructed in improvised shipyards up and down the banks of southern rivers. They were between 20 and 40 feet long, driven by a steam engine stoked by bituminous coal, which gave out quantities of smoke and sparks. Later, cleaner anthracite coal, obtained at great expense, was used instead. There was normally a crew of four, including an engineer aft, who also acted as fireman.

On the dark night of 5 October 1863, a 'David' commanded by Lieutenant W T Glassell carried out an attack on the Federal ironclad *New Ironsides*, which was part of a fleet blockading the port of

Charleston. The 'David' was armed with one 'spar torpedo', also developed by the Torpedo Division, consisting of a 40-pound charge fixed to the end of an 18-foot pole. The 'David' was to run in under cover of dark, place the torpedo against the target hull, and then retire a little distance, when the torpedo would be detonated by pulling a lanyard.

The sparks and smoke from the 'David's' funnel were sighted from *New Ironsides'* upper-deck by Ensign Charles Howard who was on watch and raised the alarm. While the ironclad's ship's company ran to general quarters and manned their guns, the 'David' approached to within a few feet of *New Ironsides*, when there was a tremendous explosion. Glassell had misjudged his distance in the darkness and pulled the lanyard too soon. Flying metal from the torpedo killed Ensign Howard (the only casualty) but the ship was hardly damaged. The towering column of water from the explosion crashed down on the 'David' and washed Glassell overboard. He was picked up and became a prisoner-of-war. The rest of his crew tried to give themselves up but were ignored in the confusion. Eventually they found their 'David' still afloat and seaworthy, so made their escape unobtrusively at slow speed.

As the war went on, the South's need to break the Federal blockade of its ports became ever more urgent. In 1863, two Confederate naval officers, Hunley and McLintock, and a civilian engineer named Baxter Watson built a submersible in New Orleans, but they had to scuttle it to prevent it falling into the hands of Farragut when he took the city. The three went to Mobile, Alabama, where they constructed a second submersible, but it sank whilst being towed to attack Fort Morgan.

After these mishaps, the Confederate government's enthusiasm began to wane, but Hunley offered to build another submersible with his own money. He, McLintock, and Watson, with another engineer W A Alexander, built a third submersible in the machine shops of Park & Lyons in Mobile. Made from what had originally been a cylindrical boiler, she was 30 feet long, 4 feet in the beam, and 5 feet deep. She had a crew of one officer, to guide and direct, and eight men, sitting in a row, to work a large camshaft driving a 3-foot propeller rotating inside an iron guard. There was a raised oval hatchway, with observation ports cut in it, at each end of the boat. Cast iron ballast weights were bolted to the keel; they could be released from inside the hull. Midway between the two hatches was a 4-foot long hinged ventilation pipe. The weapon was a spar torpedo on a 20-foot pole.

The trials of this 'David', known as *Hunley* after her chief inventor, were trials indeed: a series of almost unmitigated disasters.

Below the Belt

First, she was swamped by a passing paddle-steamer; the captain, Lieutenant Payne, was the only survivor. She was raised, dried out and refitted, only to be swamped again in a storm. Again, Lieutenant Payne survived, with two of the crew. The rest were drowned. Understandably, Payne now applied for other duties. Hunley himself took his craft to sea when, again, it failed to surface after a dive. Everybody on board was drowned.

These misfortunes should have been enough to deter any further experiments but, spurred on by patriotism (and by the substantial sums of money offered by Southern businessmen for the destruction of Federal war vessels) another crew volunteered, commanded by an army officer, appropriately named Lieutenant Dixon.

So many lives had been lost since Bushnell's day. There had been so many disappointments, so many failures to damage or even to reach the target. Some day, some time, there had to be a success and it came on 17 February 1864, off Charleston, where Federal monitors and ironclads lay in harbour, protected by a boom. It was a dark night, with little wind and a calm sea, when at 8.45 pm the lookouts on board the Federal 13-gun steam corvette *Housatonic*, 1264 tons, anchored 2½ miles off Charleston bar, saw something suspicious just astern, and raised the alarm.

It was the new *Hunley*, captained by Dixon, who had just brought the craft to the surface for a last look at the range and bearing of his target. *Housatonic*'s anchor cable was slipped and the ship began to gather sternway, coming down on top of *Hunley*. Dixon therefore reached his target much more quickly than he expected and some accounts said that *Hunley* remained against *Housatonic*'s side for a full minute before the explosion. Part of *Housatonic*'s midships section was blown in by the force of the explosion and 5 men were killed. The ship went to the bottom in a few minutes, taking the wreckage of *Hunley* and the bodies of her 9-man crew with her.

In another daring attack, at Newport News on the night of 9 April 1864, the Federal flagship *Minnesota* was badly damaged by a spar-torpedo from a Confederate 'David' which succeeded in making its escape afterwards, the first 'David' to do so. In that same summer of 1864 the Confederates had considerable tactical success with their own ironclad ram *Albemarle* which, despite several Union sorties against her, for some months ruled the waterways of Albemarle Sound, at the entrance to the Roanoke river, North Carolina.

Albemarle sank the Union ship *Southfield* at Plymouth, North Carolina, in April and in May repelled attacking Union gunboats with losses. Five Union volunteers then carried two 100-pound torpedoes on floating stretchers across a swamp and swam with them almost up to *Albemarle*'s bows. But they were spotted and driven off by gunfire. Finally, in October 1864, *Albemarle* was sunk through an outstanding act of personal bravery.

Lieutenant William B Cushing, of the Union Navy, fitted out a 30-foot launch, which had a steam engine driving a propeller. There was a 12-pounder howitzer in the bows, and a short, stout derrick, with a halliard rigged for raising and lowering a 14-foot boom. On the outward end of the boom was a buoyant torpedo, which could be detached from the boom by pulling on a lanyard. The torpedo was detonated by pulling on yet another lanyard.

An attack was thus an incredibly complicated operation. Cushing steered the launch by two lines, one fastened to his wrist, the other to his ankle. He had also to give the orders for working the boom halliard, as well as manipulating the lanyard to separate the torpedo. Finally, when he judged the torpedo had drifted close enough to his target, he had also to pull the lanyard which fired the torpedo.

The attack was made on *Albemarle* where she lay behind a boom in the Roanoke river on the night of 27 October. Cushing had at first toyed with the idea of boarding the ram and capturing her, but his cutter was sighted and had to approach through a hail of fire. The boom was stoutly made of thick logs, but Cushing reasoned that they would be slippery from long immersion and, with luck, his cutter would be able to slide up and over them.

By the time they reached the boom the fire was so intense that the whole of the back of Cushing's coat and the sole of one of his shoes were torn away by buckshot. *Albemarle*'s captain hailed them, calling upon them to surrender, but Cushing's men gave derisive or nonsensical answers. At full speed the cutter hit the boom (at a place where the mouth of an 8-inch cannon gaped only 10 feet away from the crew's heads) and, just as Cushing had hoped, rode up and over. The last of her impetus carried the cutter under the overhang of *Albemarle*'s side. Cushing ordered the men on the halliard to lower away the boom. He jerked the detaching line, waited until he could see where the torpedo had come to the surface, and then pulled the firing line.

A gigantic explosion took place, just as 100 pounds of grapeshot at 10 feet range crashed into the cutter, accompanied by a column of water which swamped the boat. Telling his men not to surrender, Cushing threw off his sword, revolver, coat and shoes, and began to swim. The whole surface of the water around where the cutter was floating was soon ploughed by raking salvoes of grapeshot. Many of Cushing's men were killed in the water. But he himself swam away, found a rowing boat, paddled it until the next night when he reached the mouth of the Roanoke river and was picked up by a passing

Federal picket-boat. The crew were at first reluctant to pick him up, believing he was the 'rebel conductor of an infernal machine'. Besides, they had been told that Cushing was dead. The *Albemarle* was sunk and her captain said of Cushing's exploit that 'a more gallant thing was not done during the war'.

The Union Navy did build submarines but they saw no action. Two engineers, William W Wood and John H Lay (also inventor of the Lay torpedo) built a semi-submersible, the *Spuyten Duyvil*, which had a retractable spar torpedo fitted underwater at her bow, but she was too late to take part in the war.

In the second half of the nineteenth century submarine development began to accelerate, as it was simultaneously realised in America, in Russia and in several European countries that the submarine could be a feasible weapon of war, especially for the weaker navies. Original inspiration still came from the individual entrepreneur but, actively sponsored by governments, submarine building moved out of the backyard and into the shipyard. By 1869, when Jules Verne's *Twenty Thousand Leagues Under the Sea* (a seminal book, which both responded to and stimulated submarine design) was first published, some 25 submarines had been successfully built and had made dives.

In 1863 Simeon Bourgeois and Charles-Marie Brun built the *Plongeur* for the French Navy. She was 140 feet long, displaced 435 tons, and had compressed air in bottles for expelling air from her ballast tanks and for driving a 4-cylinder engine. She was a practical submarine, which could dive to 20 feet and, despite low speed and endurance and uncertain depth-keeping, nevertheless had the first true underwater mechanical propulsion system which did not rely on human muscle power.

Submarine designers continued to be all sorts and conditions of men. In 1872 Oliver Halstead sold his submarine the *Intelligent Whale* to the US Navy. She drowned 39 men on her trials, while he himself was shot and killed by his mistress's lover. The unlikely combination of a Swedish engineer and inventor Thorsten Nordenfelt and an English clergyman, the Reverend George William Garrett, collaborated to build a steam submarine (110 feet long, 160 tons), which was sold to the Greek Navy. Another of Nordenfelt's submarines caused a sensation at the 1887 Golden Jubilee Review of the fleet at Spithead. She was wrecked on the coast of Denmark when on her way to join the Russian Navy.

In 1888 the US Navy offered a prize of $150,000 for a submarine, which was won by an Irishman, John Philip Holland. Born in 1840 in County Clare, Holland had come to America in 1872, and worked for a time as a school-teacher in New Jersey. Like

Bushnell and Fulton before him, Holland was no lover of the English (arguably, anglophobia was by far the most potent factor in nineteenth century submarine design). In forty years, from 1859 when he first sketched out a design for a submersible in a school notebook at home in Ireland, until 1899, the year of *Holland VIII*, the forerunner of the modern submarine, Holland suffered under every kind of material and financial set-back. His submarines sank, either on launching or on tow. One was stolen by the Fenian Society, the anti-British organisation which had first sponsored it. He overcame official apathy and discouragement. He won the US Navy prize, was deprived of it on a technicality, and re-awarded it. His business partners were as unreliable as his engines. He was made bankrupt and sold his patents to Isaac Rice, of the Electric Boat Company. Yet, in *Holland VIII*, he produced the first true modern submersible. Only 74 tons, powered with a petrol engine which gave her a surface speed of 7 knots, and an electric motor giving $5\frac{1}{2}$ knots submerged, *Holland VIII* was an excellent little submarine, safe, handy, easy and simple to control. She had a single torpedo tube in the nose of her hull, from which she could fire a torpedo with enough accuracy to hit a battleship at a range of several hundred yards. In official trials with the US Navy, she was all that Holland claimed, manoeuvrable on the surface, quick to dive, although she did need sensitive handling to keep depth. Captain John Lowe, USN, who was on board the little submarine for her final official trial on 6 November 1899, wrote: 'I report my belief that the *Holland* is a successful and veritable Submarine Torpedo-boat, capable of making a veritable attack on an enemy unseen and undetectable, and that, therefore, she is an Engine of Warfare of terrible potency which the Government must necessarily adopt in its Service.'

While the development of the submersible went on, so too did the development of the torpedo, which was to prove the perfect weapon system for the submersible to use. The two weapon technologies, so to speak, advanced roughly side by side, although it was some time before the two were brought together. By then, 'torpedo' had lost its old meaning and had come to denote a mobile explosive charge with an existence and a propulsion system independent or almost independent of its launching platform.

The spar torpedo was superseded for a brief time by the Harvey torpedo, which was towed from the bows of an attacking ship, so that a target was 'swept' and caught by the charge, rather as a mine is swept up by a minesweeper's cable. But from about 1870 onwards, designs for torpedoes multiplied. The explosive charges they carried were normally about 200–300 pounds but no two designs were alike. Some were propelled by rocket (Barber, Berdan, Cunningham,

73

Ericsson), others by compressed carbon dioxide (Lay), carbonic acid (Patrick), by flywheel spun up in the parent ship before launching (Howell), by electric batteries (Nordenfelt), or were wire-powered (Brennan) or wire-controlled (Sims-Edison). Some travelled awash, others kept depth by floats suspended from the surface (Nordenfelt and Sims-Edison). Speeds went from the claimed 60 knots of Cunningham's rocket torpedo to the 12 knots of the Sims-Edison. Size ranged from the 12-inch diameter and 280-pound weight of Barber's 1873 torpedo to the giant Nordenfelt of 1888, 29 inches in diameter and weighing 5000 pounds. Range went up from about 500 to a reported 4000 yards. Torpedoes were normally fired from tubes on deck, but Ericsson designed a submerged smooth-bore underwater gun, an early torpedo tube, which fired the torpedo by compressed air.

By the end of the nineteenth century, torpedo design was dominated by the figure of one man, Robert Whitehead, the English manager of an engineering works at Fiume. Whitehead took up the original idea of Captain de Luppis, a retired Austrian naval officer, of a small, wooden, clockwork-propelled *Kustenbrander* ('coastal fire-ship'), which had a gunpowder charge detonated by a percussion pistol impact on its nose. It was not much more than an intriguing toy, with possibilities. Whitehead began first to examine it more as an intellectual exercise. But he soon went on to develop it in deadly earnest.

He began in 1866 with a primitive (for him) torpedo, powered by a compound oscillating engine driven by compressed air to give a speed of about 6 knots, carrying an 18-pound charge for about 200 yards. Whitehead's greatest advance in design, and one which put his torpedo ahead of all its contemporaries, was his 'secret', a hydrostatic balance chamber which responded to increasing or decreasing water pressure by operating elevator flaps on the torpedo's side, causing it to self-correct its running depth, and thus maintain an average depth. Similarly, a pendulum device compensated for any tilt, fore or aft, of the torpedo while running.

In June 1870, Whitehead arrived in England to demonstrate his torpedoes to the Royal Navy. He brought with him four torpedoes, two of 14-inch and two of 16-inch diameter. Both types were powered by Whitehead's own design of Vee-twin air-driven engine and both of course incorporated his depth and attitude keeping devices. Both had a speed of about 7 knots, but the larger had a range of about 1000 yards (as opposed to the smaller's 600) and an explosive charge of 67 pounds (over the smaller's 18 pounds). The iron paddle-wheel sloop *Oberon* was converted, with a torpedo discharge tube also of Whitehead's design fitted in her bows, and the trials began at Sheerness on 31 August. The torpedoes' performance and suitability as a weapon of war were to be judged by a committee of three naval officers, one of them Lieutenant (later Admiral of the Fleet Sir) Arthur Knyvet Wilson, who was to win the VC as a Captain, and become the Navy's foremost expert on torpedo warfare.

After some early stutters, both types of torpedo ran true, and the trials went very well indeed. By the final run on 7 October, all three members of the Committee were convinced of the torpedo's value as a weapon. A demonstration in which an old coal hulk, the former wooden corvette *Aigle*, was hit and sunk by a torpedo clinched the matter. Contracts were exchanged between Whitehead and the British government, awarding Whitehead £15,000 and expenses of £2000 for the licence to build Whitehead torpedoes in England, to purchase further models from Whitehead's own works at Fiume, and permission for a certain number of officers to be trained in the mysteries of Whitehead's depth-keeping devices. Whitehead's motives at all times were financial, not patriotic; and therefore it was Great Britain's good fortune that the best torpedo designer in the world was on her side and not her likely opponents', and it was purely fortuitous that some other nation had not signed a contract with Whitehead first.

The Royal Navy's first operational use of a Whitehead (and indeed the first ever) was in 1877 and, somewhat unexpectedly, off the coast of South America during a revolution in Peru. The Peruvian rebel Nicolas de Pierola had persuaded the officers of the Peruvian ironclad *Huascar* to join his cause. When Admiral de Horsey, the C-in-C, arrived at Calloa in his flagship the frigate *Shah*, he was informed by the Peruvian government that Pierola was a pirate and had, moreover, committed outrages against British persons and property.

De Horsey in *Shah*, with the corvette *Amethyst* in company, encountered *Huascar* on the morning of 29 May 1877, at anchor off the port of Ilo, and demanded her surrender for piracy on the high seas. Pierola refused to surrender, but instead of opening fire (*Huascar* was considerably more powerful than the unarmoured *Shah*) made use of the ironclad's shallow draught and steered into the shoals off the Ilo estuary, where he hoped *Shah* could not follow him. De Horsey outmanoeuvred him, and the action began at 3.06 pm that afternoon, with *Shah* steaming up and down outside the bar, peppering *Huascar* with shells, scoring more than 70 hits with her 9-inch and 7-inch guns, but without doing any damage to *Huascar*'s $4\frac{1}{2}$-inch thick armour plating.

Shortly after 5 pm, *Huascar* began to close *Shah*, apparently being about to try and ram. Captain Bedford, in *Shah*, ordered one of the Whiteheads to be fired. According to legend, *Shah*'s Gunnery Officer requested that this dire order be put in writing, because he did not feel that the Peruvians deserved the terrible fate of having a torpedo fired at them.

He need not have concerned himself. *Shah*'s log recorded: '5.14 Fired Whitehead torpedo. Not seen. Port electric broadside, 400 yards'. The torpedo disappeared and nobody was ever able to discover what had happened to it. It certainly missed *Huascar*, very probably being too slow and fired at too great a range.

The action was broken off and at 5.45, when *Huascar* had closed the town of Ilo so that the British guns were in danger of hitting the houses, Admiral de Horsey ordered the cease fire. That night an expedition was planned in *Shah*'s boats, to take a spar torpedo and another Whitehead, lashed alongside a cutter, to be launched at close range. But *Huascar* had meanwhile escaped through the shoals and in fact Pierola surrendered at Iquique the next day.

Various torpedoes – spar, Harvey, Whitehead – were used by the Russian Navy against the Turks in the Russo-Turkish War of 1877–78. Russian torpedo-launches badly damaged the Turkish ironclad *Seifez* at Braila on 25 May 1877, but further attacks with Harvey and spar torpedoes at other places later in the year were foiled by nets and booms. On 25 January 1878, the Russian torpedo-launches *Tchesma* and *Sinope* attacked shipping in Batum roads and claimed to have hit and sunk the revenue steamer *Intikbah* with two Whitehead torpedoes (although this was disputed by the Turks who hotly denied that *Intikbah* had been sunk). This, if the Russian claim was correct, was the Whitehead's first operational success.

A Lay torpedo was used in the 1879 war between Chile and Peru. The Peruvian admiral Miguel Grau embarked two Lay torpedoes and an operator who knew how to use them in his flagship *Huascar* (the same) at Iquique and sailed for Antofagusta where, on 27 August, he encountered the Chilean corvette *Abtao*. Grau closed to within a cable (200 yards) of *Abtao* before firing the torpedo, which was a massive weapon, weighing well over a ton. Grau had wanted to go even closer, but the Lay operator said that 200 yards was close enough.

He was mistaken. When the torpedo was on its way towards the target it suddenly turned through 180° and headed back for *Huascar*. The operator tried frantically to regain control but could do nothing except marginally reduce the torpedo's speed. Just when it seemed that *Huascar*'s own torpedo might succeed where *Shah*'s had failed, a very brave officer Teniente Diez Canseco jumped over the side, swam to intercept the torpedo and steered it away. Grau was so incensed by this failure that when he returned to Iquique he landed the two Lays and had them buried in a cemetery, where they were later dug up by the Chileans. No doubt it was one of these from which *Huascar* had another narrow escape on 3 January 1881, when an attempt was made to launch a Lay at her from a tug. But the tug captain either lost heart or changed his mind. He beached the tug and destroyed the torpedo.

Clearly, one of the best methods of getting a torpedo to its target was to fire it from something itself fast-moving and manoeuvrable. In the 1870s several navies commissioned Torpedo-Boats (many of them built in British yards) for this very purpose. The first of this type of vessel built for the Royal Navy was *Lightning*, launched in 1877. Numbered Torpedo-Boat *No 1*, she was 84 feet 6 inches long, weighed 27 tons, and had a speed of 19 knots. She was originally intended to be armed with a spar torpedo but was soon converted to carry two Whiteheads in upper-deck slings. The next two, *Nos 17* and *18* were built for the Russian navy but were bought from Yarrows in 1877, after the Admiralty had refused to allow them to sail during the Russo-Turkish war. There were also Second Class Torpedo-Boats, which were enlarged ship's launches, normally 60 feet long, 12 tons, with a speed of 17 to 18 knots; they were carried on board a parent battleship and hoisted out for action.

About a dozen or so torpedo-boats were built for the Royal Navy but no particular interest was shown in them until the 'Russian scare' of 1885. Alfred Yarrow, the shipbuilder, addressed the Royal United Services Institute in a lecture that year in which he pointed out that the Russian navy had by that time 115 torpedo-boats, and the French 50, whereas the British only had 19, built or ordered. A crash torpedo-boat building programme was authorised.

The Royal Navy had no opportunity to test torpedo-boats in action but the naval manoeuvres of 1890 provided a startling example of their capabilities. A flotilla of torpedo-boats dashed across the Channel from Alderney and attacked the Channel Fleet under Admiral Sir George Tryon at Plymouth just before dawn. When the exercise came to be assessed, it was seen that in the confusion and surprise of the attack, a great part of the Channel Fleet must be adjudged to have been sunk or damaged.

Meanwhile, there was more experience of torpedo warfare in South American waters, where there were several revolutions and minor naval campaigns which were practical models of applied sea power. During the Chilean revolutionary war of 1891, two Government torpedo-boats, *Almirante Lynch* and *Almirante Condell* (both built by Laird), entered Caldera Bay on the coast of Chile at 4 am on the morning of 23 April to attack the Congressionalist (or rebel) ironclad *Blanco Encalada*, 3450 tons. They were sighted from the ironclad at a range of 2000 yards and the alarm was raised. Unfortunately the bugler sounded reveille instead of action stations and in the confusion and delay the torpedo-boats closed to within 500 yards, on *Blanco Encalada*'s starboard bow. *Almirante Condell* fired one torpedo which missed and exploded ashore. *Lynch* fired two, one of which hit and sank the ironclad. A torpedo was also fired at the schooner *Biobio* which missed and ran ashore. It was recovered later and found to be a Whitehead Mark IV 'Fiume', a 14-inch torpedo, with a charge of 58 pounds of gun-cotton and a speed of 23 knots.

A very similar attack was carried out during the attempted Brazilian Revolution of 1893–94, when the rebel ironclad battleship *Aquidaban*, lying in Porto Bello Bay, was attacked on the night of 15/16 April 1894 by the Government torpedo gun-vessel *Gustavo Sampaio*, and three torpedo-boats *Silvado*, *Pedro Ivo*, and *Pedro Affonso*. *Gustavo Sampaio* hit the battleship with one 16-inch Schwartzkopf Whitehead, with a charge of 125 pounds of gun-cotton, in one of the forward compartments. The ship was abandoned but only sank until her stem rested on the sea-bed, in a depth of 24 feet. Although her two forward compartments were waterlogged *Aquidaban* was later patched up and reached Rio de Janeiro under her own steam. After repairs, she was renamed *Vinte-cinco de Mayo*.

By 1895, Great Britain had 82 torpedo-boats but was still easily outnumbered by other major navies: France had 195, Germany 158, Italy 121, Japan 124 and Russia 94. With so many navies having torpedo-boats, some defence against them had to be found. A class of warships called torpedo-catchers was evolved, the earliest of them being White's *Swift*, followed in 1886 by *Rattlesnake*, first of a new class. But the torpedo-boat-catchers proved in practice to be far too slow to catch the torpedo-boats. Finally, a new kind of warship, fast enough and heavily armed enough to destroy the torpedo-boats, began with *Havock*, launched in 1893. She was named by Admiral Fisher, torpedo-boat-*destroyer*, afterwards shortened to 'destroyer', of immortal memory. Ironically, as the torpedo-boats were relegated to the place of minor war vessels, it was the destroyers which carried torpedoes into battle.

It was the Imperial Japanese Navy, in the war against Russia of 1904–5, who demonstrated the speed and surprise effect of torpedo-boats skilfully and boldly handled. Always firm believers in Josh Billings' great strategic maxim, 'blessed are they whose cause is just, four times they who's got in *fust*', the Japanese began with a pre-emptive strike in the early hours of 9 February 1904, before the formal declaration of war (although diplomatic negotiations had been broken off on 5 February). Ten torpedo-boats of the Imperial

Japanese Navy attacked Russian ships at Port Arthur, firing a total of 18 Whitehead torpedoes, hitting the guard-ship *Pallada*, and the battleships *Retzivan* and *Tsarevitch*. Although these were the only three hits scored, they seemed to have a paralysing effect on the Russian fleet, which stayed in harbour, seemingly frozen into immobility, and made no attempt to hamper Japanese troops landings in Korea later in the year. So, Port Arthur was one case where a minor tactical success had the effect of a major strategic defeat in the mind of the enemy.

In the later stages of Tsushima, on 27 May 1905, Japanese torpedo-boats hit and sank the battleships *Sisoi Veliki* and *Navarin*, and the armoured cruisers *Admiral Nakhimoff*, *Vladimir Monomakh* and *Dmitri Donskoi*. The Japanese pressed home their torpedo attacks with tremendous panache. 'If we hit, we shall go down with the Russians,' one torpedo-lieutenant wrote to a friend, 'if we are hit, the Russians shall come down with us, for the last man alive will steer the spare torpedo into the water. What is life but a dream of summer's night?'

Meanwhile the Royal Navy watched and reported on all these events. It had flotillas of destroyers, and more than 30 years' torpedo experience. But though it had been commendably quick to seize upon the torpedo, it still remained obstinately slow to embrace the best torpedo delivery vehicle, the submarine.

Above: Launch of Royal Navy's first submarine *Holland I* at Vickers Son & Maxim Ltd, Barrow-in-Furness, 2 November 1901. (Author's Collection)

Below: Interior of an early submarine (possibly Holland's third boat, built at Delameter Iron Works, New York, 1881). 1. Captain's seat 2. Steering wheel 3. Fore-planes 4. Aft planes 5. Depth gauge 6. Air bottles. (Author's Collection)

CHAPTER 5

'Had either the Russians or the Japanese had submarines,' wrote Admiral Fisher to Admiral May, in characteristically vehement style, on 20 April 1904, 'the whole face of their war would have been changed for both sides. It really makes me laugh to read of "Admiral Togo's *eighth* attack on Port Arthur"! Why! had he possessed submarines it would have been *one* attack and *one* attack only! It would have been all over with the whole Russian Fleet, caught like rats in a trap!'

Another equally famous admiral, George Dewey, the hero of the Spanish-American War, victor of Manila Bay in May 1898, made the same point of his own campaign. 'I could not,' he wrote, 'with my squadron, fifteen ships – if the enemy had had two of those boats with determined Americans on board – have held that bay. It would have worn us out. We would have had to be under way and never known where the blow was to strike ...'

Yet, in the Royal Navy, the premier navy of Fisher's and Dewey's time, no other weapon in naval history was ever so derided, denigrated and deplored as the submarine. 'Unfair, underhand and damned un-*English*!' was Admiral Sir Arthur Wilson VC's often quoted view of submarines, when they were first mooted as possible developments for the Royal Navy. As Third Sea Lord and Controller, responsible for the procurement, design and supply of the Navy's material needs, Wilson could have been expected to voice the official opinion and to know the general feeling in the Service. But, although, he certainly did speak for a large number of senior officers, the Royal Navy's attitude towards submarines was a great deal more complex, containing many more strands of opinion, than Wilson's outburst would suggest.

In spite of Palmerston's view that 'steam has bridged the Channel', in spite of the frequent 'Invasion scares' which periodically disturbed Victorian England, there was still a basic belief in the Channel as a moat defensive. Down the years, still came the echo of St Vincent's voice: 'My lord, I do not say they cannot come. I only say they cannot come by sea.' This point was well, if obliquely, made in a short story published in *Blackwood's Edinburgh Magazine* in May 1871. Called 'The Battle of Dorking', the story was anonymous but was actually written by Colonel Sir George Tomkyns Chesney, of the Royal Engineers. It described the sudden and successful invasion of England by Germany, followed by a short, sharp campaign which ended in the defeat of England, a nation debilitated by long years of safety and sloth. The story was so well and convincingly written that it shocked the nation and caused the Prime Minister to protest in Parliament against what he called the alarmism of a clever magazine article. 'The Battle of Dorking' started a vogue for 'what could happen if' invasion stories and had a considerable influence on naval and military thinking in its time (and, in fact, its lineal successors are still on the bookstalls today).

But the story had one glaring weakness. It rather skirted the question of how the invading force crossed the Channel in the face of the Royal Navy. Chesney wrote that the fleet was scattered at the critical time, 'some ships to guard the West Indies, others to check privateering in the China seas, and a large part to try and protect our colonies on the Northern Pacific shore of America where with incredible folly, we continued to retain possessions which we could not possibly defend.'

The invasion began on a Monday, and the fleet sailed on Tuesday, 10 August, to engage the invasion forces, taking with it a submarine cable 'to lay down as it advanced so that continuous communication was kept up, and the papers were publishing special editions every few minutes with the latest news'.

The news was almost all bad. 'An ironclad has been blown up' – 'The enemy's torpedoes are doing great damage' – 'The flagship is laid aboard the enemy' – 'The flagship appears to be sinking'. It was two days before a solitary ironclad, the sole British survivor of the battle, steamed into Portsmouth. 'Then the whole story came out – how our sailors gallant as ever had tried to close with the enemy; how the latter evaded conflict at close quarters, and, sheering off, left behind them the fatal engines which sent our ships, one after the other, to the bottom.'

It was these 'fatal engines' which spoiled the story's credibility. Colonel Chesney did not elaborate any further on them. He gave no details of their construction or use, which naturally detracted from his story. Even the French did not believe in them. M Charles Yriarte, who translated the story into French, remarked on 'the affair of five lines' in which Chesney had completely disposed of the Royal Navy, 'a force without rivalry in the world'.

A submarine was designed and actually underwent trials in England in 1885, but her brief history ended in a somewhat comic episode which might very easily have turned to tragedy. Named *Nautilus*, she was designed by James Ash and Andrew Campbell, and launched at Tilbury. She was 60 feet long, weighed about 50 tons and was designed to have an underwater speed of 6 knots driven by an electric motor. She dived by admitting water into ballast tanks and by withdrawing exterior cylinders, so as to (by Archimedes principle) reduce the effective displacement of the submarine. She surfaced by the reverse of the principle, the cylinders being driven outwards by hand so as to increase the displacement.

Trials took place in West India Dock and were attended by a large number of distinguished officers and Admiralty officials. Amongst the visitors was Admiral Lord Charles Beresford, who actually volunteered to go down in *Nautilus* for a test dive. The dive was only to be for a very short time, but the minutes passed, and *Nautilus* did not reappear. Eventually, when the watchers on the dockside had become thoroughly alarmed by the delay, *Nautilus* surfaced, and some white and shaken faces appeared on her upper deck. It transpired that the submarine had dived heavily and embedded herself in mud so deeply that it was virtually impossible to force the cylinders outwards. Only by the utmost exertions of the men on board, at the last limits of their strength, had the cylinders been moved far enough to bring *Nautilus* back to the surface.

In February 1886, Thorsten Nordenfelt himself came to London to address the Royal United Service Institution on Submarine Boats, and found it necessary to begin with an *apologia* for submarines. 'I beg to be allowed to say that I cannot admit, as I have heard stated, that there is anything especially cruel or horrible in the idea of a submarine boat. War altogether is cruel and horrible, and causes an enormous amount of pain and suffering, but any invention which may tend to shorten a war, or to protect commerce and private property during war, will really diminish this suffering on the whole.'

Whether or not as a result of Charlie B's harrowing experience the year before, Nordenfelt's speech had a polite but cool reception from his audience of senior naval officers. They respected Nordenfelt's experience in the matter but were still sceptical, wanting to know, for example, 'whether in a rough sea the water does not come through the funnel?' 'There is no funnel,' Nordenfelt answered, shortly. Admiral Arthur (who had attended the Sheerness Whitehead trials) came closest to the nub of it: 'My opinion is that all torpedo-boats should be submarine boats.'

The French, meanwhile, were perennially preoccupied by the problems of crossing the Channel themselves, and of preventing the English from crossing it, and they came nearest to the solution. While the Royal Navy stayed aloof, the French navy pioneered the first submarines for war. Dupuy de Lôme, a brilliant designer and naval architect who had been largely responsible for France's lead in ironclads in the 1860s, collaborated with another gifted engineer Gustave Zede to design a submarine. de Lôme died in 1885 and for a time it seemed that the submarine design might come to nothing, but in 1886 Admiral Aube, the newly appointed Minister of Marine, commissioned two submarines: Goubet's *Gymnote*, a pioneer submarine which provided invaluable trial experience, and *Gustave Zede*, launched in 1893. The trials and experience of these two led to *Narval*, designed by M Laubeuf, who had been Engineer of the Navy.

Narval was a 'deepwater', ocean-going submarine, with an inner and outer hull (the space between being fitted for ballast tanks), a surface speed of 11 knots and a dived speed of 8. Her battery had an endurance of 5 knots for 11 hours. On the surface she could cover 500 miles at $7\frac{1}{2}$ knots. With *Narval*, the French realised that at last they had a weapon which could break a British blockade of their coasts, and also attack the British fleet in its home ports, hitherto invulnerable.

Narval was laid down in 1898, at a time when the general opinion of submarines in the Royal Navy was fairly expressed by James Wilson, a well-known writer on naval affairs in his day, in a discursive and faintly dismissive piece on 'Underwater Warfare' in the 17 September 1897 issue of *Navy and Army Illustrated*, a large format picture magazine printed on glossy paper, with superb photographs, widely read in club and mess at the time. 'It is extremely doubtful,' he wrote, 'whether any such boat will ever be of the least assistance to England ... It is impossible for such a boat to remain at sea ...'

Almost a year later, in the same magazine, the Editor in his periodical Notes and Queries for 30 July 1898 was commenting 'Submarine boats have as yet been tried very little in this country, if we except the one that nearly stuck fast in the mud at the bottom of a London dock with Lord Charles Beresford on board. And herein I think the Admiralty have shown their wisdom. Other nations have been fascinated by the manifest advantages of submarine navigation if only it could be satisfactorily managed. France, Italy, Portugal, Sweden and the United States have all been tempted to waste money and time over the pursuit of what must be called a maritime will-o-the-wisp.'

Later the same year, the French provided an ominous answer to this comment, in an exercise at Toulon, witnessed by the Minister of Marine and a party of influential officials and senior naval officers, when the *Gustave Zede* attacked three battleships and hit one, the *Magenta*, with one torpedo. The French press gave such delighted coverage to this event that, in February 1899, for the first time ever, submarines emerged into the limelight as a subject of public debate in Great Britain. Questions were asked in the House of Commons, whether the Admiralty attached any importance to these French successes and whether the Royal Navy had any intention of getting some submarines. Goschen, the First Lord, gave the cautious Admiralty answer, that it would be 'inexpedient' for him to express the opinion of the Admiralty at that stage.

The situation all over the naval world in that last year of the nineteenth century was of navies preparing (with the exception of the Royal Navy) to get submarines, or to improve the ones they had. The politicians, at the same time, were trying to get the genie they sensed had been released back into the bottle and replace the stopper, by agreement if not by force. In 1899, representatives of 26 nations attended the Peace Conference at The Hague. Admiral Fisher was the British naval delegate, and scored a tremendous personal success with his colourful personality and language. Never one to shrink from violent hyperbole, Fisher warmly recommended that captured submarine crews should be boiled in oil. After discussing the limitations of armaments for some time and in great detail, the Conference put forward motions to declare the torpedo contrary to the laws and customs of war, and to prohibit the use of submarines in war. But neither motion was adopted.

There is nothing more powerful than an idea which has achieved its time of ripeness. From 1900 onwards, the submarine was irresistible. On 7 January 1900, the United States Navy bought *Holland VIII*, their first submarine, and in June ordered five more improved Hollands, largely as a result of Admiral Dewey's persuasive evidence (in which he mentioned the dangers of submarines at Manila Bay) before a House Committee on Naval Affairs. The same year, the French budgeted for more submarines and the British naval attaché in Paris reported on 17 February that the younger generation of French naval officers were convinced that submarines were the most important for coast defence and might be the only possible weapon to take a war back across the Channel, by attacking coasts and ports and by destroying coastal trade.

But, although the dark shape of the future of a submarine war was already forming so clearly over the Channel, the Admiralty was still carefully fending off questioners in the House of Commons. In April Goschen repeated the view that submarines were weapons for maritime Powers on the defensive, and that any antidote to them 'must be looked for in other directions than in building submarine boats ourselves, for it is clear that one submarine boat cannot fight another'. In May, Goschen was again asked whether the Navy was experimenting with submarines. Again he said no, but other nations were being carefully watched.

In July 1900, the debate on the Navy Estimates fully ventilated the subject of submarines for the first time in British parliamentary history. The Admiralty was urged not to be blinded by 'lofty English scorn' for foreigners and their strange doings. Their Lordships were pointedly reminded that the French had led the way in a number of naval innovations – ironclads, breech-loading guns, explosive shells – in which we had had eventually to follow them. Arnold Forster, a Member with some experience of naval affairs, hoped that 'one of these days we may not follow a little too late.' We know all about submarines, Goschen replied, and 'it would be foolish to encourage other nations by saying how useful they might be against us.'

However, already in that year, the Admiralty were secretly changing their opinion of submarines. In October 1900, Isaac Rice of the Electric Boat Company called at the Admiralty, looking for business. In November, Goschen was writing 'it is also important to ascertain how far, apart from the question of defence against other submarine boats, these boats could be usefully employed for other important purposes in HM Navy'. Rice had made a great impression, and had seemingly provided just the stimulus which the Admiralty needed.

As usual, the French underlined the British deliberations with a dramatic publicity *coup*. In January 1901, *Gustave Zede*, dived at a depth of 4 metres, had attacked the battleship *Jauréguibery* in an exercise off Hyères and hit her with both the torpedoes she had fired. The battleship had been making 6 knots, so this was the first time ever a submerged submarine had successfully attacked a major warship under way. The French budget for that year authorised the building of 20 more submarines. In July, *Gustave Zede* pulled off another coup, hitting another battleship, *Charles Martel*, with a torpedo in an exercise off Ajaccio in Corsica.

But the tides of reaction in London still had some way to flow. Admiral Wilson, the Controller and Third Sea Lord in 1901, wrote that 'the development of submarine warfare must be detrimental to a nation depending on navigation at the surface for its supplies and necessaries of life. We cannot stop invention in this direction, but we can avoid doing anything to encourage it.' Wilson went on to suggest that when the First Lord introduced the next Naval Estimates he should state that 'as certain foreign nations had devoted considerable sums to the construction of submarine boats, and shown their intention of making use of this underhand method of attack in future wars, HM Government considers it would be to the advantage of all the Maritime nations of the world if the use of submarine boats for attack could be prohibited.' Despite the strong whiff of King Canute's courtiers about this proposal, other senior naval officers concurred. Vice Admiral Archibald Douglas commented that there were plenty of ways of making submarines harmless, by nets, and barriers of mines, and anyway it was so difficult to navigate underwater that he 'was not apprehensive of submarine boats ever proving very formidable'.

In this case, civilians proved more far-sighted than naval officers. The Secretary to the Admiralty, Sir Evan MacGregor, said that the Navy must abandon its 'policy of discouragement, to adopt one of unostentatious progress, both in the direction of using and meeting these new engines of war ...' He feared 'it would only excite ridicule if we were now to attempt to put down submarines as "underhand". I cannot see much difference between them and the torpedo from a naval standpoint except that they involve much greater risk to the user of them.' Arnold Forster, now Parliamentary and Financial Secretary to the Admiralty, also disposed of the moral objection. 'Our moral objection to any weapon will not prevent a foreign power using it against us, if it can be used to our injury.' We really must abandon the view 'that the submarine being undesirable is also negligible'.

In the event, the Royal Navy took up submarines unobtrusively, almost surreptitiously, without any public or parliamentary comment or even an announcement. Five submarines, of the Holland type, were to be built by Vickers at Barrow-in-Furness, with the assistance of the Electric Boat Company. The five were to be allocated one each to Chatham, Devonport and Portsmouth, with the remaining two to the torpedo schools to practise with destroyer flotillas methods of dealing with submarine attacks.

At first the Royal Navy's intention was genuinely experimental. As Wilson said, 'Our primary object is to test the value of the submarine boat as a weapon in the hands of our enemies.' Sir William Clowes, in his monumental history of the Royal Navy, made just one reference to submarines (in the seventh and last volume published in 1903) and then as experimental. The Navy's reasoning seemed to be that the French, albeit an excitable nation, seemed to be having some success with these machines. Certainly they were making enormous claims. It was always possible that the French might eventually do as they always seemed to be hankering to do, to cross the Channel and attack British ports. Maybe there was something in the idea after all. The best thing was to get some of them and find out. The first orders were placed, the first submarine personnel appointed. *Holland I* was launched in November 1902 and was ready for trials early in 1903.

From the very first fleet exercises submarines attended in 1904, it was clear to those who were ready to see it that here was a new weapon with a terrible potential. They seemed immune to gunfire even when awash: in a practice shoot by destroyers at a dummy conning tower at ranges of 400 to 800 yards, only two hits were scored from 271 rounds. Nor were explosives fitted on the ends of booms of any effect, nor any of Admiral Wilson's counter-measures such as nets, lassos, grapnels and hand grenades (although, to be fair, Wilson was inhibited and reluctant to press some of his designs after *A1* was rammed and sunk by SS *Berwick Castle* off Spithead).

Worse still, one Holland closed to within 80 yards and torpedoed the flagship. Fisher, in the same explosive letter to Admiral May, described the incident. 'It's astounding to me, *perfectly astounding*, how the very best amongst us absolutely fail to realize the vast impending revolution in naval warfare and naval strategy that the submarine will accomplish! Here, just to take a simple instance, is the battleship *Empress of India*, engaged in manoeuvres and knowing of the proximity of submarines, the flagship of the Second Admiral of the Home Fleet 9 miles beyond the Nab Light (out in the open sea), so self-confident of safety and so oblivious of the possibilities of modern warfare that the Admiral is smoking his cigarette, the Captain is calmly seeing defaulters down on the half-deck, no one caring an iota for what is going on, and suddenly they see a Whitehead torpedo miss their stern by a few feet! And how fired? From a submarine of the 'pre-Adamite' period, small, slow, badly fitted, *with no periscope at all* − it had been carried away by a destroyer lying over her, fishing for her! − and yet this submarine followed that battleship for a solid two hours under water, coming up gingerly about a mile off every now and then (like a beaver!) just to take a fresh compass bearing of her prey, and then down again!' 'In all seriousness I don't think it is even *faintly* realised − *The immense impending revolution which the submarines will effect as offensive weapons of war.*'

Admiral Wilson had his own ripostes for submarines. When as C-in-C Channel Fleet his flagship was torpedoed by an 'A' class submarine who signalled 'Respectfully submit have torpedoed you. Respectfully submit you are sunk. Respectfully submit you are out of the exercise' he went out on to the flag-bridge wing with a pair of semaphore flags and himself signalled back 'You be damned'.

During the first years of the twentieth century, the French, Russians, Japanese and Italians all built up submarine fleets. In countless fleet exercises, the submarines began to prove their worth. One officer, Lieutenant K Michell joined *B9* in 1909 and took part in Fleet manoeuvres for the first time that year. 'Up to this time the Navy had not had very friendly feelings towards the submarine branch and had been reluctant to accept us as of any value in the war programme which was then building up with the advance of the German Navy. We cruised to the West Coast of Ireland but the Battle Fleet, as far as I am aware, avoided us like poison.'

Other more senior officers had realised that the time had come to take submarines more seriously. Admiral May, C-in-C of the Home Fleet, wrote in May 1910: 'I think the time has now arrived when Admirals and Captains should be more conversant with submarines and their methods, and that more exercises should take place in conjunction with the Fleet.'

In the naval manoeuvres which took place off the West Coast of Scotland in May 1910, the submarine *D1*, first of a new and larger class, drove home Admiral May's point with tremendous force. *D1* was part of the Red (British) Fleet which was matched against a smaller Blue (German) Fleet, which was supposed to be trying to break the blockade of the (simulated) Heligoland Bight. *D1* went up to the exercise area alone and unescorted, and patrolled off the 'Blue' harbours. There was no submarine depot ship with the 'Red' Fleet and it was therefore a shattering surprise to the 'Blues' when *D1* 'torpedoed' two of its cruisers before returning to Portsmouth, undetected and totally unscathed.

Two years later, in the manoeuvres of 1912, *D2* took *D1*'s feats a stage further when she entered the Firth of Forth, slipped unseen past patrols and defences, penetrated upstream of the Forth Bridge and 'torpedoed' her own depot ship anchored off Rosyth Dockyard. In the German Navy's exercises of the same year, 12 U-boats distinguished themselves by keeping the sea in far rougher weather than anybody had believed possible, and achieving a higher percentage of hits than the 80 or more destroyers and torpedo-boats also taking part, for the adjudged 'loss' of only two U-boats.

Germany, having been almost the last major Navy to embark upon a submarine building programme, had now, virtually unrealised by themselves, possessed themselves of a formidable, ocean-going submarine force. 'There are a lot of idiots who lecture at the Naval War College and write in the papers that Tirpitz won't use his submarines to sink merchant ships!' Fisher wrote to the Prime Minister, Asquith in May 1914. 'The civilised world say they would execrate him!'

Although, in fact, Tirpitz had said in 1901 that Germany had no use for submarines, he meant submarines which were only able to cruise in home waters. *U1* was not completed until 1906, but the Germans were very quickly building boats capable of crossing the North Sea and had thus an offensive capability. They were also fitted with serviceable radio from quite an early stage. But the German annual building programme was small, compared with the French, and even the British, and the German Navy still intended to use submarines against warships, to redress the Royal Navy's superiority.

This point of view was put by Winston Churchill, then First Lord, in a survey of the current naval situation before the Committee of Imperial Defence on 11 July 1912: 'Now we come to the submarine. If ever there was a vessel in the world whose services to the defensive will be great, and which is a characteristic weapon for the defence, it is the submarine. But the German development of that vessel, from all the information we can obtain, shows that it is intended to turn even this weapon of defence into one of offence, that is to say, they are building not the smaller classes which will be useful for the defence of their somewhat limited coast-line, but the larger classes which would be capable of sudden operation at a great distance from their base across the sea.'

The shape of submarine warfare as it was to become seems to have been first perceived by Arthur Balfour in 1913. Certainly, Fisher was much impressed by his opinion. '*Submarines are the coming Dreadnoughts* and *aviation will* SURELY *supplant cruisers*,' he wrote to Arnold White in March 1913, 'and only such a brain as Balfour's (with whom I lunched last Friday) seems capable of this grasp of the future! *What a brave man he is!*'

Balfour wrote to Fisher in May 1913: 'You know how long, and how earnestly, I have preached the case of submarines. The question that really troubles me is not whether *our* submarines could render the enemy's position intolerable, but whether *their* submarines could not render *our* position intolerable … In other words, what is to prevent the Germans sealing up every port, military or commercial, round our whole coast – and this whatever our superiority in battleships and cruisers might happen to be?' Balfour took the proposition a stage further in a letter a fortnight later. After discussing submarines generally, he envisaged a possible state of affairs where the seas around the British Isles were safe from enemy battleships and which no enemy troops could cross, and yet, because of the infestation of enemy submarines, we ourselves had equally as little control over those waters. Finally, Balfour wrote, 'Should we not, among other things, have to reconsider our views about the capture or rather the destruction (for a submarine could not capture) of private property at sea?'

It was this concept, that a submarine could not capture her prey and would have to sink it, be it warship or (by inference) a merchantman, which so many people found impossible to grasp. It was, quite literally, unthinkable. Their minds could not be shaken free from the old proposition of the privateer capturing his prize, and bringing it triumphantly back. But to Fisher, typically, it was quite feasible. 'There is nothing else the submarine can do except sink her capture, 'Fisher wrote in a 'Memorandum on The Submarine and Commerce' in 1913, which developed Balfour's ideas, 'and it must therefore be admitted that (provided it is done, and however inhuman and barbarous it may appear) this submarine menace is a truly terrible one for British commerce and Great Britain alike, for no means can be suggested at present of meeting it except by reprisals ... It has been suggested that it should be obligatory for a submarine to fire a warning gun, but is such a proceeding practical? We must bear in mind that modern submarines are faster on the surface than the majority of merchantmen, and will not necessarily need to dive at all. Therefore, as the submarine would in most cases be sighted, and as she has no prize crew to put on board, the warning gun is useless, as the only thing the submarine could do would be to sink the enemy; also the apparently harmless merchant vessel may be armed, in which case the submarine may but have given herself away if she did not sink her ...'

'Moreover,' continued Fisher with remorseless logic, '... under numerous circumstances can a submarine allow a merchant ship to pass unmolested? Harmless trader in appearance, in reality she may be one of the numerous fleet auxiliaries, a mine-layer, or carrying troops, and so on. Can the submarine come to the surface to inquire and lose all chance of attack if the vessel should prove to be faster than she is?'

Fisher's argument was inescapable, but nevertheless the politicians and the other naval officers of his day found it impossible to believe. Churchill said he had 'read and reread ... the brilliant and most valuable paper on Submarines' but there were a few points on which he was not convinced. 'Of these the greatest is the question of the use of submarines to sink merchant vessels. I do not believe this would ever be done by a civilised Power.' After comparing such outrages with the spreading of pestilence and the assassination of individuals, Churchill considered these 'are frankly unthinkable propositions, and the excellence of your paper is, to some extent, marred by the prominence assigned to them.' Prince Louis of Battenberg, the First Sea Lord, agreed with Churchill that Lord Fisher's brilliant paper 'was marred by this suggestion'. Commodore Roger Keyes, then Commodore of Submarines, felt that this possible behaviour by submarines 'we all discarded as impossible and unthinkable'. Many years later, Churchill conceded that 'in his diagnosis of the German character Lord Fisher was right and the Admiralty was wrong'.

In the summer of 1914, there was an extended public discussion on submarines which admirably sums up the current state of thinking in the Navy on submarines. It was started by Sir Percy Scott, an energetic, inventive and somewhat peppery admiral, who, in a phrase, had taught the Royal Navy to shoot straight. He, with a handful of others, including Fisher and Jellicoe, did most to haul the Navy's gunnery out of its late nineteenth century torpor and prepare it for twentieth century war.

In 1913 Sir Percy discovered that, in his opinion, the Admiralty did not realise the potential of the submarine nor the deadliness of the torpedo, believing that the submarine was an untried weapon and the torpedo was not accurate. Scott believed that this state of affairs was 'a danger to the country'. He was going to write to the newspapers about it but was persuaded to desist lest the 'Little Navyites', who wanted to reduce the Navy Estimates, use his letter as ammunition. But when the Navy Estimates were eventually published, Scott felt confirmed in his view that the Admiralty had no idea of the dangers of submarines nor of the urgency of preparing some form of defence against them. So, on 4 June 1914, a very long letter appeared in *The Times*.

In short, Sir Percy said that the country already had enough battleships, but did not have nearly enough submarines or aircraft. We should stop building battleships and start building submarines and aircraft. These two had revolutionised naval warfare. If we went to war, we must lock up our battleships in a safe harbour. The enemy would have to do the same. No fleet could hide from aircraft. Submarines could attack in broad daylight. Battleships could not bombard enemy ports if those ports were protected by submarines. Enemy submarines could come and lie off our coasts and sink everything in sight. In other words, the whole function of the battleship, its very *raison d'etre*, had gone, like Othello's occupation.

For Admiral Sir Percy Scott, the master gunner, architect of so many gunnery innovations, the great apostle of the big gun, to write in this vein caused the veil of the ark of the tabernacle at Whale Island to be rent from top to bottom. After a moment's pause for stupefaction, Scott's readers reacted with a torrent of violently hostile criticism. Admiral Sir Edmund Fremantle said it was 'a mischievous scare'. Lord Sydenham said it was 'a fantastic dream'. The *Pall Mall Gazette* said Scott's ideas 'approached the boundaries of mid-summer madness'. 'As a romance, or even a prophecy,' wrote the *Manchester Courier*, 'the forecast is fantastic, but as practical tactics it is so premature as to be almost certainly fatal.' 'The imaginative, fancy-picture-making spirit of the thing is out of place over Sir Percy Scott's name,' said the *Manchester Guardian*. The *Spectator* called the letter 'a most approved example of the mare's-nest'. Mr Hannon, Secretary of the Navy League, said in the *Globe* that Sir Percy's letter contained statements that were 'premature, ill-advised and calculated to do serious harm to the cause of the maintenance of British supremacy at sea.' Occasionally, there were some who thought Sir Percy might have a point. 'Is Sir Percy Scott a dreamer of dreams like Admiral Aube? Or is he a precursor of practical achievements?' said the *Daily Graphic*. 'Let us not forget that the dreams of today are often the realities of tomorrow.'

Some of the arguments rehearsed in the letters had an antique ring. 'We have yet to hear of a case in which a submarine has made a hit from an underwater shot in any colourable reproduction of war conditions', wrote one correspondent under the initials 'RN' on 11 June. 'The submarine is a craft which can operate by daylight only. It must come to the surface often, and when it does is visible for some miles. The torpedo, its only weapon of defence, has no flexibility of aim.'

In July, Sir Percy replied to his critics and in so doing, repeated the argument first suggested by Balfour and put forward so vehemently by Fisher. 'All war is, of course, barbarous, but in war the purpose of the enemy is to crush his foe; to arrive at this he will attack where his foe is most vulnerable. Our most vulnerable point is our food and oil supply. The submarine has introduced a new method of attacking these supplies. Will feelings of humanity restrain our enemy from using it?'

Sir Percy and all his detractors were to have their answer very soon. On 5 September 1914, the small light cruiser *Pathfinder*, 2940 tons, leader of the 8th Destroyer Flotilla, was patrolling the line St Abb's Head–May Island–Bass Rock off the entrance to the Firth of Forth when she was sighted by Lieutenant Otto Hersing in *U21*. Hersing could not at first get close enough to attack, but when, at about 3.45 pm *Pathfinder* returned on her patrol beat, Hersing fired one 19.69-inch Type G (Whitehead) torpedo which hit *Pathfinder* just abaft her bridge. The explosion counter-mined the ammunition in *Pathfinder*'s forward magazine and the ship virtually disintegrated. The fo'c'sle forward of the bridge was blown off, the foremast and the forward funnel were blasted over the side, and the ship was soon awash up to her upper deck, lying under a vast black pall of black smoke. A survivor later wrote that: 'It must have been about 5 minutes after we were hit that the bulkheads down below carried away – some of them. The ship gave a heavy lurch forward, and took an angle of about 40° down by the bow. Water came swirling up to the searchlight platform, and the Captain said "Jump, you devils, jump!".' Some men were picked up but 259 of her crew were lost. This was the first warship ever sunk by a submarine.

On 13 September, 6 miles south of Heligoland, Lieut Cdr Max Horton in *E9* torpedoed and sank the old German cruiser *Hela*. On 20 September, Lieutenant Otto Weddigen in *U9* sighted a squadron of three very elderly British cruisers, actually known as the 'live-bait' squadron, who patrolled the Dogger Bank and the nearby Dutch coast in support of the Harwich-based destroyers. Bad weather had forced the destroyers to return to base and the three ancients, *Aboukir*, *Cressy* and *Hogue*, were quite alone, when Weddigen attacked them.

The first torpedo hit *Aboukir* at 6.20 am. She listed heavily to starboard and some 25 minutes later, turned right over, floated bottom upwards, and then sank. The others thought their sister had struck a mine and *Hogue* was stopped, picking up *Aboukir*'s survivors when she was struck by two torpedoes and sank within 10 minutes. *Cressy* had lowered her boats for *Aboukir*'s people and made no attempt to abandon them now. Weddigen had one of *U9*'s bow tubes reloaded and hit *Cressy* with two more torpedoes shortly after 7 am. A quarter of an hour later, *Cressy* too rolled over and sank. Nearly 1400 officers and men, many of them reservists who had just joined up, were lost.

On 20 October, 14 miles off the Norwegian coast, Lieut Cdr Feldkirchner in *U17* sighted the small steamer *Glitra*, sailing from Grangemouth to Stavanger, with a cargo of coal, coke, iron plates and oil. Having no prize crew, Feldkirchner ordered her crew to abandon ship and then scuttled *Glitra* by opening her sea-cocks. *U17* then towed *Glitra*'s boats towards the coast for some miles. She was the first merchantman to be lost to a U-boat in the Great War.

Feldkirchner had acted correctly, but on 26 October in the Channel, Lieut Cdr Schneider in *U24* torpedoed the French steamer *Amiral Ganteaume*, which had some 2500 Belgian refugees on board, of whom about 30 were drowned. Schneider claimed that he thought the vessel was a troopship.

From then on, discussion about the propriety of submarines became academic. There were those, like Admiral Campbell the Q-ship hero, who as late as the 1930s were agitating for the total abolition of submarines, but for all practical purposes the great debate was over. So, too, was the last age of naval innocence.

Above: Popular pre-1914 idea of the fate of submarines in the next war: *Hermione* running down *B3*. (From *Trafalgar Refought* (1905) by Sir W Laird Clowes and Alan Burgoyne)

Below: The reality of submarine attack: HMS *Aboukir* sinking after torpedo attack by *U9*, 22 September 1914. (Picture by Charles Dixon)

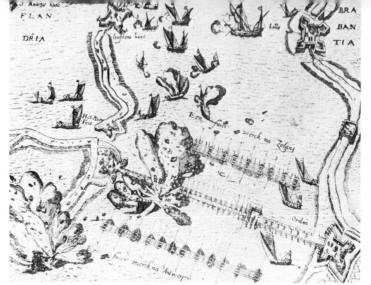

Above: Machine vessels at Antwerp, 1585. (Willem Baudart)

Below: Lieutenant R D Sandford RN winning the VC by driving the old submarine *C3*, loaded with explosives, against the Mole at Zeebrugge. He and his crew can be seen escaping in their dinghy before the submarine blew up. (Author's Collection)

CHAPTER 6

'Many times in history has a need arisen to strike at enemy warship squadrons or merchant ships ensconced within strongly defended harbours; and one frequently used method had been to force the harbours, and then send in fire-ships to wreak havoc among the enemy vessels. The midget submarine, or X-craft ... can reasonably be regarded as the descendant of the Elizabethan fire-ship.' Thus, Captain Roskill the official historian of British naval operations from 1939 to 1945 succinctly expressed the ancestry of one particular naval tradition: the penetration of an enemy stronghold. It has always been the kind of operation which required ingenuity as well as bravery and which has occasionally aroused anger as well as retaliation from the enemy so attacked.

For a successful fire-ship attack, certain conditions had to be fulfilled. The enemy had to be, in the word, 'ensconced' and stationary within a confined harbour or anchorage. The enemy had also to be down wind, tide and current of the fire-ship's launching place. The enemy should also have been inspired beforehand with a proper terror of fire-ships. The most famous example, which led to an historic strategic victory, was the English fire-ship attack on the Spanish Armada as it lay off Calais in the early hours of 29 July 1588 (8 August in the Spanish accounts using the new Gregorian Calendar of 1582).

The psychological ground-work had been well laid 3 years earlier during the siege of Antwerp in 1585. In April 1585, Antwerp had been besieged for 10 months by Spanish troops under Alexander Farnese, Prince of Parma. To link his forces north and south of the Scheldte, and to prevent relief reaching the city from the sea, Parma had built a tremendous bridge at Kalloo, 4 miles below Antwerp, where the Scheldte was some 2400 feet wide and 60 deep. By pile-driving, two great piers were built, reducing the river to almost half its original width, at some 1300 feet. Two defensive positions, Fort St Mary at the Flemish and Fort St Philip at the Brabant end, were also built, and were connected by a floating bridge of boats, carrying a roadway 12 feet wide. The bridge was also protected by floating rafts, up and down stream.

The people of Antwerp had commented upon this improbable structure with some derision at first, until they realised that it would cut them off completely from help from the sea. Luckily, an engineer from Mantua, Federigo Gianibelli, who had settled in Antwerp and who had a wish for revenge against Spain, produced a plan for destroying the bridge, by means of what were variously called 'those terrible ships', 'Hellburners', or *maquinas de minas* (mine-machines).

These were, in effect, floating bombs. Two ships, the *Fortune* (80 tons) and the *Hope* (70 tons) were filled with about 3 tons of explosive, tightly packed in special chambers prepared for them. A seventeenth century description says that 'upon a flooring of thick planks was built a masonry chamber composed of marble slabs to a thickness of 5 feet. The internal dimensions of this chamber were 40 feet in length, with a width and breadth each of $3\frac{1}{2}$ feet, and contained, in one case 6000, and in the other 7000 pounds of gunpowder. The chamber was covered over with big blue stones on edge giving a thickness of 6 feet, as a protection against chance cannon shot, but leaving several holes to be fitted with slow matches'. To make these machines look like ordinary fire-ships, wood was piled over the top of the explosive chamber. Thirty-two ordinary fire-ships were also fitted out, to be sent down the tide in groups of eight, to draw the enemy's fire before the 'hellburners' were dispatched.

The ordinary fire-ships were floated down on the evening of 4 April 1585 but, through the incompetence of Admiral Jacob Jacobzoon, the operation was bungled. The fire-ships were bunched together, and the two 'hellburners' went with them. Each boat had a light skiff, for the man in charge to make his escape. *Fortune* grounded before reaching the bridge and her slow-burning fuse fizzled out. An Englishman serving under Parma cut the fuses out and the vessel was towed harmlessly away.

But *Hope* floated straight down on the bridge and struck it at the Kalloo end, near Fort St Mary, where Parma himself and several of his staff happened to be standing. Her clockwork fuse worked perfectly and she exploded with such force that she blew a gap in the bridge 200 feet wide. About 800 men were reported to have been killed and many more wounded. Parma himself was supposed to have been knocked unconscious by a falling baulk of timber.

But Gianibelli's efforts miscarried in the end. A long-boat was supposed to row up to the bridge and fire rockets if it were breached. But the crew panicked when they were fired at, turned round and reported that the bridge was still intact. Parma recovered, set to work to repair the bridge and the siege finally ended with the capture of Antwerp on 17 August.

Flaming wreckage from the 'hellburner' had fallen in a wide circle on the city of Antwerp. But much wider were the ripples of horror which the news of the 'hellburners' aroused in the men of the Armada. Philip II warned the Duke of Medina Sidonia that the English had many diabolical inventions and fiendish fireworks. Sir Edward Stafford, the English Ambassador in Paris, played his part in the psychological warfare, whispering rumours of devilish weapons and devices in the ears of Mendoza, Philip's Ambassador.

When the Armada sailed, Medina Sidonia knew, and thought he was alone in knowing, that Gianibelli was in England, working for Queen Elizabeth. Actually, it was common knowledge in the Armada. Ironically, Gianibelli was in England, and he was working for the Government, but on an inoffensive and eventually futile scheme to build a boom across the Thames at Gravesend. But, when the time came, the mere mention of his name was enough.

Thus, by Sunday 28 July 1588, every officer and man in the Armada was unusually sensitive to any rumours about fire-ships, hellburners, *maquinas de minas*, or indeed any event or ship that appeared strange or untoward. By that day, the Armada was lying off Calais, having fought three brisk but inconclusive naval actions on their passage up the Channel, off Plymouth and the Isle of Wight. The ships were short of ammunition, with stores and water much reduced, but they were still in a tight fighting formation, having lost only 3 galleons.

Medina Sidonia now looked to Parma to embark his troops and launch the planned invasion. Parma had heard of the Armada's arrival. He was very glad they had arrived, and promised that embarkation of troops would be complete in 6 days. But Don Rodrigo Tello, who brought Parma's message, said that he had visited Dunkirk where the invasion fleet was gathering and in his opinion Parma's force was nothing like ready, even in 6 days. With the weather as it was, and Dutch flyboats blockading the coast, the incomplete state of the invasion barges, it was more likely to be a fortnight. Medina Sidonia still believed it perfectly feasible to cross the Channel. But wiser heads, such as Juan Martinez de Recalde and Alonso de Leiva, better versed in naval affairs than the Duke, knew that it was impossible while Howard's fleet was still undefeated.

That Sunday, Howard's ships were actually anchored only a culverin's shot up-wind and up-tide of where the Armada lay in its tightly packed anchorage. The English could see and hear this floating army of the great Spanish empire. There were the massive shapes of the ships, with the clear lanterns burning in their ornamented sterns, with the striking of the bells on the hours, and the hails of the guard-boats as they rowed around the fringes of the fleet. Anybody who saw the Armada, counted its ships and its guns, could not doubt that victory would surely go to Spain. The only niggling uncertainty, more than a little worrying, was the sight of some eight or nine strange unidentified ships joining Howard's fleet towards the evening.

Actually, the newcomers were harmless supply ships, but the question of fire-ships was already being discussed. Walsingham had sent to Dover earlier in the week for fishing smacks and supplies of faggots and pitch. But when the English commanders conferred on Sunday morning they decided they could not wait for fire-ships from England. Drake provided one of his own ships, the *Thomas* of 200 tons, Hawkins the *Bark Bond* of 150 tons. Six other ships, from 200 to 900 tons, were also selected. The fire-ships were led by Captain John Young in his own ship *Bear Yonge* and Captain Prowse. Any guns left in the fire-ships were loaded. There was no time to remove them and in any case the detonations might well add to the fire-ships' effect and cause greater alarm amongst the enemy. This decision, perhaps accidental, perhaps intentional, did more to destroy Spanish morale than anything else.

The tide was flowing at nearly 3 knots towards the Armada, with an extra $\frac{1}{4}$ knot of North Sea current backing it up. The wind was a brisk south-westerly. The distance the fire-ships had to cover was about a mile and a half. So, from the moment the first flames were sighted, the Armada had about 30 minutes to act.

Medina Sidonia did his best. He sent pinnaces out to windward to intercept the fire-ships and tow them clear. Working in pairs, the pinnaces were to close the fire-ships so that their crews could fling grapnels in their sides. In spite of the wind, tide and current, bearing the flames down upon the Armada at a furious rate, the pinnaces did tow two of the fire-ships away. But, just then, the flames reached the guns in one of the other ships and there was a series of shattering detonations. Here, at last, were the terrible sounds the Spaniards had half-expected, half-dreaded, to hear. Those ships which had joined the previous evening must have been Gianibelli's handiwork after all. These then, were the diabolical hellburners of Antwerp, the *maquinas de minas* designed and fashioned as though by the Devil himself.

Something close to panic broke out in the Spanish ships. As Hakluyt's account says, 'which fire in the dead of the night put the Spaniards into such a perplexity and horrour (for they feared lest they were like unto those terrible ships, which Frederic Jenebelli three yeeres before, at the siege of Antwerpe, had furnished with gun-powder, stones, and dreadfull engines ...) that cutting their cables whereon their ankers were fastened, and hoising up their sailes, they betooke themselves very confusedly unto the maine sea.'

Medina Sidonia later said that he gave the order for his flagship to weigh, and also for the rest of the Armada to do the same, intending, when the fire-ships had passed, to return and recover the same position. That may or may not have been his intention but it was impossible in practice to carry it out. Most of the ships simply cut their cables and fled, slipping rapidly away down to leeward. They were to regret the loss of those anchors and cables in the weeks to come.

But worst of all, the Armada's tight formation was broken by the fire-ships, as all the mid-Channel manoeuvres of Howard and Drake had not succeeded in doing, and once broken it was never properly reformed. Medina Sidonia did anchor, and fired a gun to signal to the others to do the same. Few heard it and only three or four ships obeyed or were able to obey. The great galleass *San Lorenzo* ran aground under the guns of the fortress of Calais, where she was plundered by Howard's men the next day. But the rest were gone for good.

Of the 123 ships in Medina Sidonia's fleet that night, only the *San Lorenzo* was lost. The fire-ships went aground and burned themselves out, with the occasional desultory explosion as the flames reached the last guns. They were not 'hellburners', not *maquinas de minas* at all, but they had done their work and, at an estimated total cost of £5111.10s (which was the compensation paid to the owners of those eight ships), they were among the most cost-effective weapons in all naval history. Off Gravelines on Monday the English ships closed to within the killing range of their long guns and inflicted the final and irreversible defeat on the Armada.

Events in the seventeenth century showed both the limitations of fire-ships and their possibilities for the future. Fire-ships were used, without much success, by Mansell at the pirate stronghold of Algiers in 1621, and by the Earl of Denbigh at La Rochelle in 1628. Sudden showers of rain or equally sudden enemy sorties were blamed, but the real reason was that the fire-ships were released too far from their targets or in the wrong place. However, in 1627, there was a flavour of things to come. The Duke of Buckingham, commanding the naval expedition for the relief of La Rochelle, issued a warrant for the delivery of '50 water-mynes, 290 water-petards and two boates to conduct them underwater'.

Prince Rupert, commander of the Royalist fleet during the Civil War, always showed great interest in technical devices and inventions (he spent the later years of his life in scientific researches and was a leading member of the Royal Society). In 1650 Rupert's ships were lying in the Tagus, actually within sight of the Commonwealth fleet under Blake. Because of the political situation, neither side could take action against the other but both indulged in a war of nerves and propaganda. Both wrote to King John of Portugal, protesting that the other was a pirate and an enemy of the human race. Parliamentary officers persuaded Rupert's men to desert, and then spread rumours that Rupert's ships were undermanned. Rupert hanged ten recovered deserters, *pour encourager les autres*. Rupert's officers attacked Blake's boats when they landed for water. There were frequent scuffles, each side claiming to have been provoked by the other.

Rupert was persuaded that Blake was plotting to assassinate him and his brother. He retaliated with an actual plot to blow up Vice Admiral Robert Moulton's flagship, *Leopard*. He sent a fruit boat, with two negroes and a sailor dressed as a Portuguese peasant, alongside *Leopard* with what looked like an ordinary barrel of oil amidships. It was, in fact, a primitive form of torpedo: 'a bomb ball in a double-headed barrel with a lock in the bowels to give fire to a quick match'. It had a pistol attachment, with a trigger pulled by a string passing through the bung.

When the boat came alongside *Leopard*, Rupert's sailor found the lower deck ports all shut. Understandably frustrated, he 'uttered an exclamation', a native English expletive, which betrayed his nationality. He was captured, the boat and barrel were investigated, and the bomb was disarmed before it exploded. In his diary for 14 March 1662, Samuel Pepys made an oblique reference possibly to this device and other incidents, when he mentioned a proposal by one Kuffler for an engine to blow up ships. 'In the afternoon came a German Doctor Kuffler to discourse with us about his intention to blow up ships. We doubted, in the matter of fact, it being tried in Cromwell's time, the safety of carrying them in ships, but he do tell us that when he goes to tell the King his secret (for none but kings successively and their heirs must know it) it would appear to be of no danger at all.' Dr Kuffler was a son-in-law of Cornelius van Drebbel, so perhaps there was something in his ideas. Pepys went on, 'We concluded nothing, but shall converse with the Duke of York about it.' But nothing seems to have come of it, in the end.

Late in the seventeenth century, Gianibelli's hellburners were given a new lease of life. After the defeat of their fleet at La Hogue in 1692, the French turned to privateering as a policy of the state. Licensed pirates like Jean Bart and Rene Duguay Trouin conducted a superbly successful *guerre de course* against English and Dutch commerce (in the years 1688–97, one ship alone, the *Capers*, was reputed to have taken back to St Malo as prizes the staggering number of 3384 English and Dutch merchantmen, and 62 convoying ships).

By the summer of 1693, the continuing success of the French *guerre de course*, capped by the commercial disaster of the French Admiral de Tourville's brilliant action against the Smyrna convoy, which caused a near-panic in the City of London, made some sort of punitive expedition against French coastal ports imperative. On 24 October Captain (later Admiral) John Benbow sailed from Cowes with a fleet of 23 sail, including five bomb-vessels and the fire-ships *Strombolo, Flame* and *Vesuvius*, bound for St Malo which he reached (after spending a fortnight at Guernsey) on 17 November.

While the bomb-vessels got to work, shelling the town, *Vesuvius* was filled with 100 barrels (10,000 pounds) of gunpowder and 230 carcasses (shells). At about 7.30 on the evening of 19 November, she was floated up to St Malo walls, where she grounded within her own length of the nearest fortifications. A pinnace was waiting to take off her crew but she blew up prematurely, killing her pilot, one Michael Thomas, and mortally wounding four other men. Her commander, Captain Guy, came back later with another eight men who had been given up for dead.

The explosion did enormous damage. 'This concussion,' wrote one eye-witness, 'was so appalling that the earth shook with it, and the reverberation of the air such that chimney stones fell two leagues from St Malo.' The whole town was covered with the debris of the ship; her bell, her galley boiler, her yards and chains were hurled on to the roofs and streets, and her capstan crashed through the Crescent Inn from top to bottom. Benbow reported that part of the town wall was blown down, and houses set on fire in three or four places. Some people were injured, but the only fatal casualty was a cat killed in a gutter.

Vesuvius and other 'machines' of the time were designed by a Dutch artillery officer called Willem Meesters, a somewhat mysterious character who, as Pepys' account suggested, often confided his secrets to, and was commissioned by, only the King himself, with few orders or payments recorded on paper. Meester brought seven of his vessels from Holland in 1693, but by the spring of 1694 they were in bad repair and in fact were always leaking and in a poor state of efficiency throughout their careers.

The Royal Navy commissioned thirty of these machines or 'infernals' as they were called between 1694 and 1695. The first, called the *Nicholas*, was commissioned under Captain Robert Dunbar on 30 April 1694 and took part in the action against the town of Dieppe in the fleet under Lord Berkeley in July 1694. After the bombs had fired some 1100 shells into the town, reducing much of it to ashes, *Nicholas* went into action on the night of 12 July. In spite of

Dunbar's brave efforts (he returned on board to relight the fuse after it had fizzled out) *Nicholas* ran against a pier and exploded but did no serious damage.

Benbow had bombs and machines under his command when he bombarded Le Havre on 16 July and again on the 18th, when the dangers of service in bombs was demonstrated by the fate of *Granado*, which blew up into fragments after a direct hit from a shore battery. One of Meester's larger 'machines' called *Abrahams Offering* with 90 barrels of powder took part in the attack against Dunkirk on 12 September but was carried by the tide past the mole and blew up harmlessly.

Eight of Meester's machines, with seven 'smoke-ships' took part in an equally unsuccessful attack on Dunkirk on 1 August 1695. The French came out with pinnaces to attack the 'smoke-ships' which were ignited prematurely and abandoned by their crews. Meesters blamed the commander-in-chief, Lord Berkeley, who in turn accused Meesters of not doing his part properly. Leaking, unhandy, and unpopular with everybody in the fleet except Meesters, the machines were not used again and the last of them, *Mayflower*, was paid off on 17 September 1695. They had had a short vogue and now seemed, like their inventor, thoroughly discredited. As so often happened with this weapon, it was tried and discarded and forgotten, only to be revived with fresh enthusiasm by another generation.

The next revival was during the Napoleonic wars when the English fleet were once again faced by the problem of an enemy safely ensconced behind a defended position. In this case, the target was the French invasion flotilla, which had to be either destroyed where it lay, or lured out from behind the protection of their batteries.

The device was a form of torpedo known as a 'catamaran' and Robert Fulton was one of those concerned in their design. It was a lead-lined chest, about 21 feet long, by 3 feet 3 inches wide, with a flat top and bottom and wedged-shaped ends. It contained about forty barrels of gunpowder and assorted inflammable materials, a clockwork machine for the fuse, and ballast, to bring the top of the catamaran down to the level of the sea surface, to make it less conspicuous. The whole contrivance was caulked and sheeted in well-tarred canvas to make it waterproof, and all together weighed about 2 tons.

The method of attack was to tow the catamaran towards its target, and as it had to be towed astern it was very unwieldy. A buoyed grappling iron enabled the catamaran to be hooked on to its target's anchor cable. When a peg was withdrawn, the clockwork ran for between 6 and 10 minutes, enabling the crew to escape, before a pistol was actuated and the charge exploded.

They were first used in action by Lord Keith in a combined fire-ship and catamaran attack on some 150 French invasion craft moored outside Boulogne Pier, on 2 October 1804. The French under Rear Admiral Lacrosse were fully alert, rowing guards around the harbour, with shore batteries manned and ready. Four fire-ships were released, with a strong tide and a fresh breeze in their favour. The four blew up almost innocuously, only wounding a few men. Of the four or five catamarans also used, none achieved anything directly, although one blew up by accident and killed 14 men in a French pinnace who had run foul of it at the time. Thus 4 fire-ships and 5 catamarans were expended for the loss of 14 men killed, about 7 wounded, and one pinnace destroyed. It hardly seemed worth the trouble.

Nevertheless, the catamarans aroused a good deal of adverse comment, much more than their actual tactical value deserved. The implications of this kind of attack were realised by both sides. From England as well as France, there was something of a clamour that Great Britain had returned to barbarism by using such methods. There was a good deal of hypocrisy in both sets of complaints, for the catamarans seemed no more barbarous than any other similar weapon. Much more serious, tactically, was the premature disclosure of a weapon before it had been properly tried out and improved. The French at once strengthened their booms, redoubled their patrols, and the catamarans, like the earlier machines, had a short and unsuccessful operational life. They were not used again in this form.

The same tactical situation, on a much larger scale, reoccurred in March 1809, when a French fleet under Admiral Willaumez (relieved on 17 April by Admiral Allemand flying his flag in *Ocean*, 120 guns) lay behind a stout boom and overlooked by gun batteries in Aix Roads, off the mouth of the River Charente. The British naval commander this time was Admiral Lord Gambier, the C-in-C Channel Fleet, who was not the most daring of seamen nor the most inspiring of leaders. A cautious, religious man, Gambier had his opponent safely bottled up, but then seemed quite at a loss to know what to do next. He had already discounted the use of fire-ships as being too dangerous. In any case, fire-ships were in Gambier's opinion 'a horrible and anti-Christian mode of warfare'.

At home, the Admiralty was determined that some form of attack on the French must be attempted. The First Lord, Lord Mulgrave, sent for Captain Lord Thomas Cochrane, to discuss possibilities. Cochrane said it was feasible to attack the French with fire-ships, but when Lord Mulgrave urged him to carry out the operation himself, Cochrane was reluctant. He knew very well that any such enterprise would have difficulties which were nothing to do

105

with the French. Events proved him right. But Mulgrave was insistent. 'My Lord,' he wrote to Cochrane, 'you must go. The Board cannot listen to further refusal.'

Lord Cochrane, heir to the Earl of Dundonald, was one of the most brilliant and perhaps one of the least tactful officers ever to serve in the Navy. Six foot two in height, red-haired, dashing and impetuous, yet at the same time calculating and technically inventive, Cochrane had already made a name for himself in command of the *Speedy* sloop and the *Pallas* frigate. When he arrived in the *Imperieuse* frigate on 3 April to join Gambier's fleet, Cochrane found an emotional atmosphere of Dostoyevskian complexity. Rear Admiral Eliab Harvey, the second-in-command, was using the most disrespectful language of his C-in-C to anybody who would listen. Cochrane himself was the most junior of the Captains present, and the others naturally resented him as an interloper, sent out from England to do what Their Lordships evidently felt they were incompetent or unwilling to do.

Nothing more had been done to attack the French or even to prepare for an attack by taking soundings of the approaches to their anchorages. The French indeed were so confident of their immunity that they goaded their blockaders, derisively flying the English ensign under the quarter gallery (where the latrines discharged) of the *Calcutta* which had been captured from the English.

Cochrane prepared his own design of explosion vessel for the attack. 'The floor of the vessel,' he wrote, 'was rendered as firm as possible, by means of logs placed in close contact, into every crevice of which other substances were firmly wedged, so as to afford the greatest amount of resistance to the explosion. On this foundation were placed a large number of spirit and water casks, into which 1500 barrels of powder were emptied. These casks were set on end, and the whole bound with hempen cables, so as to resemble a gigantic mortar, thus causing the explosion to take an upward course. In addition to the powder casks were placed several hundred shells, and over these again nearly three thousand hand grenades; the whole, by means of wedges and sand, being compressed as nearly as possible into a solid mass.' His description has a familiar ring to it and although Cochrane claimed that his plan, to make the French believe that all the fire-ships were explosion vessels, 'was new to naval warfare', it was in fact exactly the ruse of using Gianibelli's 'hellburners' against the Armada, and his explosion vessels were very similar, in explosive content and the manner in which it was stacked and laid, to those of Meester.

The fire-ships and explosion vessels arrived in the Basque Roads, where the British force lay, by 10 April 1809. Willaumez, a careful and competent admiral, noted their arrival and guessed at their purpose. He gave cautionary instructions to his guard-boats to be ready to tow away fire-ships as they approached. He ordered his largest ships to strike their top-masts and send down top-gallant masts, to reduce inflammable top hamper. He told his frigates to be ready to sail at an instant's notice.

On the afternoon of 11 April Cochrane anchored *Imperieuse* closer inshore, about a 1¼ miles from the nearest French frigate inside the boom. There were 20 fireships, 3 frigates anchored outside *Imperieuse*, ready to receive their crews when they returned, the *Aetna* bomb-vessel, placed opposite the Aix batteries, with the *Whiting* schooner and 2 hired cutters, *King George* and *Nimrod*, both fitted with the new Congreve rockets, having their first taste of action. (William Congreve himself was present to see how his invention performed.) Cochrane himself embarked in the larger of his two explosion vessels, the *Marie Anne*.

Cochrane led the way in, on board *Marie Anne*. With a 2-knot tide behind the fire-ships, and a strong wind and a choppy sea, the crews had to struggle to row away from the fire-ships after they had abandoned them. *Marie Anne*'s fuse detonated too early, when she was still some way from the boom, but she successfully blew a breach through which Cochrane saw the 32-gun *Mediator* and two fire-ships pass. The second explosion vessel was set adrift without any attempt to blow her up and she was wasted.

But *Marie Anne*, according to Cochrane, 'did her work well, the effect constituting one of the grandest artificial spectacles imaginable. For a moment, the sky was red with the lurid glare arising from the simultaneous ignition of 1500 barrels of powder. On this gigantic flash subsiding, the air seemed alive with shells, grenades, rockets and masses of timber, the wreck of the shattered vessel ...' The fire-ships, on the other hand, were a failure. They had been released too far away, only four reached anywhere near the enemy, and none did any damage. One fire-ship in fact only narrowly missed *Imperieuse* herself (and had been the reason why the second explosion vessel had been so hurriedly cast adrift).

However, the effect was just as Cochrane had hoped and believed. In great confusion and believing they were about to be blown apart by explosion vessels, the French ships slipped their cables and ran, just as the Armada had. But they had no room to flee, and when dawn came, all but two of the French fleet were hard aground.

Now was the time for Gambier to close with his ships and destroy the French where they lay helpless. But despite repeated and ever more frantic signals from Cochrane, Gambier declined to take any action, explaining afterwards that he could see no need: the French fleet had already been destroyed, thus the object of the attack had been achieved. To Cochrane's fury, the majority of the French ships were refloated and eventually escaped. The resulting accusations at home, which took place in the lurid glare of publicity, led to a court-martial at which Gambier was exonerated by the court, and led to the effective end of Cochrane's career in the Royal Navy. He was, though it could not have been of any satisfaction to him, vindicated by Napoleon himself, at St Helena, who remarked that the French admiral 'was an *imbecile*, but yours was just as bad. I assure you, that if Cochrane had been supported, he would have taken every one of the ships.'

But before he left the Navy, Cochrane sent the Prince of Wales what he called 'a new and most formidable method of attacking and destroying an enemy's fleet and of performing other warlike operations on a large scale.' The Prince appointed a Secret Committee in 1812, which included Sir William Congreve, the rocket inventor, to consider the proposals. According to Lord Keith, the mode of attack was 'irresistible' and the effect of the power and means proposed, 'infallible'.

Cochrane proposed a series of combined operations, to seize islands lying off French-held territory, such as Ushant, Ile Groix, Hiérès and Elba, to alarm their inhabitants, cut off coastal trade, intercept blockade runners; to break the chain of French semaphore telegraph stations, linking the coastal towns with each other and with Paris, by destroying every other station; and by attacking French garrisons in Spanish coastal towns.

But these were subsidiary operations to annoy and preoccupy the enemy. Cochrane's main intentions were against the French fleet, which he proposed to attack with 'temporary mortars'. This meant converting old hulks into nothing less than giant floating mortars by reinforcing their bottoms with old cannon barrels and pigs of cast iron, embedded in a layer of clay, with a stout frame of timbers bolted over them. The sides of the vessel were to be constructed at an angle, so that the whole ship was like an elongated cannon's mouth, yawning upwards. The sides were also strongly reinforced, with baulks of timber, backed by stones and clay, bound together by cables and hawsers. The hold would be filled with thousands of pounds of gunpowder, topped by shells, grenades and carcasses.

These mortar vessels were to be towed in pairs towards the enemy position, manned by skeleton crews, who would trim the sails, steer the vessels, then light the fuses and make their escapes in time. Cochrane calculated that the ships' contents, when ignited, would fly 'in the line of least resistance, an angle of between 40° and the Zenith'. The fuses had, of course, to be regulated according to the distance required.

So far, Cochrane's invention was a further development of Gianibelli's. But his other idea was quite new: sulphur ships, moored up-wind of an enemy, to allow toxic gas to waft down upon his position. The ships were to have layers of sulphur and charcoal, lying on another layer of clay. Ventilation arrangements were organised so that the sulphur burned evenly and slowly. 'Volumes of noxious effluvia,' according to Cochrane, 'evolved from Masses of Charcoal and Sulphur, burning close to the Lines, and driven by the wind into the interior of the place, would have destroyed every animal function ...'

The Committee confessed that Cochrane's ideas were completely new to them. Cochrane had originally put forward his proposals for using explosion vessels and sulphur ships against Toulon. But when Lord Melville suggested that Cochrane use a part of his plan against Toulon 'on a small scale', Cochrane thought the suggestion pre-posterous. It would only show an enemy, on a small scale, how to put Cochrane's plan into operation against Great Britain on a large scale. The Committee, whilst admitting its novelty, also had the usual objec-tions to the plan of any major power to any new device which might aid a weaker. They believed it might imperil Great Britain's colonies.

Cochrane himself thought his plans were infallible. In his autobiography he remarked that 'if the same plan had been known to the rebels in the late Indian Mutiny, not a European in India would have escaped'. In later years, during his South American adventures, Cochrane claimed that he was more than once confronted with a fortress which would have certainly succumbed (to his own great financial advantage) had he used even a part of his plan. But this would have released his secrets for possible later use against Britain and Cochrane said 'no amount of neglect or persecution could induce me to betray my country'.

In 1847, when Cochrane had for some years been reinstated in the Navy, another committee considered his plans. Cochrane had now added smoke screens as a preliminary to the sulphur vessel attack. The first Committee had rejected Cochrane's ideas because they, quite frankly, thought they would not and could not succeed. The new Committee thought that they probably would succeed and rejected the ship mortars, because they could not be used exclusively by this country once they had been revealed and the sulphur vessels, because they 'did not accord with the feelings and principles of civilised warfare'.

Cochrane's reply to charges that his devices were inhuman had a familiar ring. 'No conduct that brought to a speedy termination a war which might otherwise last for years, and be attended by terrible bloodshed in numerous battles, could be called inhuman, and that the most powerful means of averting all future wars would be the introduction of a method of fighting which, rendering all vigorous defence impossible, would frighten every nation from running the risk of warfare at all.'

When the Crimean War broke out Cochrane was in his seventies but once again he brushed the dust off his plans and once again presented them, this time for an attack on Kronstadt. Once again, they were rejected. The Committee thought they were too hazardous. They would probably fail and discredit the service, as well as giving the enemy a chance to boast. They doubted whether the smoke screen would be thick enough to cover the sulphur vessels' approach. The men in the sulphur vessels ran the risk of being gassed themselves. Even if the sulphur did work, nobody would be able to occupy the forts because of it.

The most damning criticisms came from Robert Faraday who was called in to advise the Committee. He said the gas cloud, though potentially lethal enough, would be too much dispersed by the time it reached its target, and the water over which it passed would 'absorb some of the noxious vapour and weaken it'. Lastly, he said that 'if the project were known or anticipated it would not be difficult for the attacked party to provide Respirators which would enable the men in a very great degree, or even altogether, to resist a temporary invasion of any atmosphere such as that described.'

The Committee told Cochrane that his plan was 'inexpedient' but because they did not also include Faraday's advice, Cochrane went on indefatigably and a year later in 1855, was preparing yet another plan for Sebastopol, which included drenching the water surface with naphtha and then igniting it with balls of potassium. Palmerston, the Prime Minister, was inclined to favour this plan, especially if Cochrane himself led the attack. As he said, somewhat cynically, to Lord Panmure the Secretary of State for War, if it succeeded it would save English and French lives, and if it did not, Cochrane would take most of the blame. But Sebastopol fell before anything could be done, and Cochrane never put his plans into effect.

However, they were resurrected in 1914, when the inventor's grandson, the twelfth Earl of Dundonald, took the plans first to the War Office and then, when rebuffed by Kitchener, to the Admiralty, where Winston Churchill was interested in the possibility of the smoke screen. As for the sulphur, he said 'we could not employ it ourselves unless and until the enemy himself began', because the use of noxious or poisonous fumes was implicitly prohibited by International Law. In March 1915 a technical Committee was formed, with Dundonald as president, to investigate possible development and uses of smoke, within the accepted framework of the Laws of War. But it was the Germans, at Ypres on 22 April 1915, who first used gas in war.

The Chinese had done their best, with an equally offensive explosion vessel in November 1856, during the war which had begun the previous month with the seizure of the British 'lorcha' *Arrow*. By 13 November a British fleet lay in the river off the city of Canton. The Chinese could not reach the ships from above or below river of the city but that day launched two junks prepared with explosives – and a new ingredient. Their decks were covered with excrement, so that when the junks came alongside the 13-gun screw vessel *Niger* (commanded by another Cochrane, Captain Hon Arthur) and there exploded, the warship's decks were covered with these disgusting missiles.

To *Niger*'s injury was soon added the fleet's insult. The wretched ship got precious little sympathy but was at once dubbed with a nickname to match the offending debris. (And when, towards the end of the nineteenth century, another *Niger* was commissioned in the fleet, her officers and men discovered that the nickname had stuck.)

The tactic of using a whole vessel as a missile, to be blown up when she reached her target, always suggested itself when there were special circumstances to be met. Towards the end of the First World War a very daring attempt was made to block the exit of the canal at Zeebrugge on the coast of Flanders, and so cut off the submarines based at Bruges from the sea. The plan was for troops to be landed from the converted cruiser *Vindictive* and two ex-Mersey ferries, *Iris II* and *Daffodil* to attack a battery of guns at the end of Zeebrugge Mole and to cause a diversion whilst the block-ships *Iphigenia*, *Intrepid* and *Thetis* were scuttled in the canal entrance. Success would depend upon accurate navigation, exact timing, the cover of smoke, and surprise.

It would also depend in part upon the Germans being unable to bring up reinforcements along the Mole from the shore. Zeebrugge Mole was 1½ miles long, built of solid masonry, except for one 300-yard length which was made of steel girders, through which the North Sea tides and currents raced, to scour out the canal entrance and the approaches to it. If this more vulnerable part of the Mole could be blown up on the night, the seaward end of the Mole would be cut off from the shore.

Two old submarines, *C1* and *C3*, were prepared as explosion vessels, each having 5 tons of Amatol explosive packed in her fore-ends, with 12-minute fuses. Each had a crew of 2 officers, 1 petty officer, and 4 ratings. All were bachelors, and volunteers. Their job was to take the submarines in, and ram the steel girders.

The hawser towing *C1* to Zeebrugge broke on passage and she was unable to take part. But *C3*, commanded by Lieutenant Richard Sandford RN, duly arrived off the Mole shortly after midnight on 23 April 1918. She had been provided with special gyroscopically stabilised steering gear, so that she could be set on her course for the Mole and then abandoned by her crew before the last stretch to the target was reached. But Sandford chose to stay on board and conned the submarine into the target himself. He ordered his crew up on deck, so that nobody could be trapped on board.

Sandford made his last alteration of course when the Mole was only about a hundred yards off. At about 12.15 am, *C3* ran in under the viaduct at about 10 knots and hit it with such an impact that her conning tower was wedged in the steel girders, and her bows projected out on the other side. Sandford ordered the crew to lower the motor skiff which had been provided on special davits and meanwhile himself set the fuse going.

So far *C3* had been unmolested, but the Germans on the top of the roadway at last sighted the submarine underneath their feet and began to fire down at her. Sandford, the coxswain and a stoker were all hit by bullets. The skiff's engine failed to start so they got out the paddles and began to paddle, literally for dear life. (*C3* had also been provided with a scaling ladder so that if necessary the crew could mount the girders and join the main party from *Vindictive*, but Sandford and his crew were determined to get away by sea.) Sandford was hit by another bullet, and both the paddlers were also wounded. Two others took over.

They had only managed to get about 300 yards away from *C3* when the 5 tons of Amatol blew up with a tremendous detonation which wrecked the steel girders of the Mole and caused a roar of sound which many men near *Vindictive* at the end of the Mole could hear even above the noise of their own adventures. A hundred feet of the viaduct were blown out and no reinforcements were brought up that night. Sandford and his crew were picked up by a picket boat which, by a coincidence, happened to be commanded by Sandford's brother Francis.

Although Sandford modestly said afterwards that 'we only got there because every bally thing went wrong', he won one of the nine VCs awarded for that night's work. The blockships were not precisely in position and in fact the canal was not completely obstructed. Nevertheless, they had, in Commodore Keyes' words, given the dragon's tail a damned good twist. Sadly, having survived the dangers of Zeebrugge, Sandford died of typhoid fever shortly after Armistice Day.

There was a very similar exploit in the Second World War, early in 1942, when Allied intelligence reported that the new German battleship *Tirpitz* was completing her trials. If she broke out into the Atlantic and then, like *Bismarck*, headed for France, there was only one dock on the western seaboard of Europe which could take her: the Normandie graving dock at St Nazaire, on the mouth of the river Loire. On 3 March 1942, the Chiefs of Staff Committee approved a very bold plan to crash those dock gates and blow them up.

The explosive was to have been delivered in a motor gunboat but this was thought too vulnerable to enemy fire and might be sunk before reaching the dock. Then the explosive was to be transported in a destroyer and carried out and placed on the dock after impact. Finally it was decided to make the destroyer herself the explosion vessel. The destroyer chosen was HMS *Campbeltown*, one of the 50 old ex-US Navy 'four-stackers' transferred to the Royal Navy earlier in the war.

To reduce her draught, her torpedo-tubes and main armament of three 4-inch guns were removed. The depth-charges, throwers and all ammunition were landed. Instead, eight 20-mm Oerlikon guns were fitted. Four rows of bullet-proof plating were fitted on deck, to protect soldiers lying behind them during the run in. The bridge was also covered with specially hardened steel plates, with visibility slits cut in them. The two after funnels were removed and the two remaining funnels cut on a slope at the top, to make the ship look like one of the German torpedo-boats which operated from the Biscay ports at that time.

The explosive consisted of 24 Mark VII depth-charges, as used against submarines, each weighing 400 pounds so that the total charge was $4\frac{1}{2}$ tons. They were placed behind the steel column which had supported the foremost gun; this was the most forward strong point, to resist the crumpling of the ship's bows after ramming. The charges were placed in a special steel tank on top of the fuel compartments, the steel plates being supported by wood blocks and concrete filling. The charges were laced together with 'cord-text' instantaneous water-proof fuse, with two time-set fuses: one to go off after $2\frac{1}{2}$ hours, and another, as a precaution, of an 8-hour delay pencil inserted in every third depth-charge. The fuses would be set going before impact. The ship was to be scuttled after impact.

Besides *Campbeltown*, commanded by Lieutenant Commander S H Beattie, the force consisted of *MGB314*, carrying Commander R E D Ryder, the naval force commander, and his staff, 16 MLs in two columns carrying Commandos under Lieutenant Colonel A C Newman, *MTB74*, with delayed action torpedoes for use on the dock gates if *Campbeltown* should fail, and two escorting destroyers.

The force left Falmouth on 26 March 1942 and headed out into the Atlantic, to allay any suspicions about their destination. They sighted and attacked *U593*, who later reported the force heading west. With this misleading report, brilliant navigation by Beattie, and the greatest good fortune, the force arrived off the Loire estuary intact at 12.30 am on 28 March. Though *Campbeltown* had been lightened (she carried fuel only for a one-way passage) she touched ground briefly crossing the estuary banks. However, she came off promptly and, led by *MGB314*, headed up the river, wearing a German ensign.

By means of these ruses, and by behaving as boldly as though they belonged in the Loire, Ryder's ships were not challenged until 1.20 am, when they were only just over a mile from their objective. Even then, a bold reply to the challenge, an almost-correct Very light recognition signal, a long, meandering and unintelligible morse message flashed to shore in German by Leading Signalman Pyke in *MGB314*, and above all, the sheer unlikelihood of an attack on St Nazaire in this fashion, all caused the Germans to hold their fire for another full 8 minutes. Then, the search-lights stabbed out from all round the river banks, *Campbeltown* struck the Swastika and hoisted the White Ensign, and the batteries opened up an intense fire from both sides of the river.

Guns and search-lights concentrated upon *Campbeltown*, the largest ship. She was hit many times. Her forward 12-pounder gun was blown away, her hull was penetrated in several places to the decks below where almost half her company were killed or wounded. On the bridge, though half-blinded by the search-lights, Beattie had picked out his aiming point, a lighthouse to port on the end of the Old Mole, passed it at 20 knots, and gave the order 'Stand by to ram'.

Two hundred yards from the Normandie dock, *MGB314* swung aside, leaving the way clear for *Campbeltown*. With all her remaining guns firing, *Campbeltown* headed towards the outer dock gate; her bows sliced through an anti-torpedo net and crashed into the dock. Over 30 feet of her bows was crumpled back by the impact, but the tip of her fo'c'sle hung over the inner face of the dock gate. She was well and truly wedged in the correct position. The time was 1.34 am – only 4 minutes late on schedule.

Whilst Beattie and the survivors of his ship's company prepared to scuttle their ship, Newman's Commandos landed from *Campbeltown* and from two of the MLs and fanned out into the dock area to their assigned objectives in the U-boat pens, harbour installations, and, above all, the operating gear for the great dock. The main dock pumphouse was stormed and blown up, and the gate winding house was wrecked. The Germans replied with machine-gun fire from rooftops and from positions beside the dock. In the darkness and confusion, fierce street battles took place all over the dock complex.

Most of the Commandos in the Motor Launches never got ashore at all. German resistance at the Old Entrance to the dock was so intense that only two MLs of the starboard column got alongside, and one of those was shelled and abandoned. A third withdrew, very badly damaged by shell-fire, and three more were blown up and sank. Of the port column of MLs, attacking the Old Mole, four were forced to withdraw without coming alongside, and three more were disabled or sunk. Only *ML177* got her Commandos ashore at the Old Entrance, and came off with survivors later from *Campbeltown*.

By 2.40 am, *Campbeltown* had been successfully scuttled, the force had been under heavy fire for over an hour, the main object had been fulfilled, so Ryder ordered the withdrawal. Ryder and *MGB314* returned to England, but the ML carrying Beattie was sunk going down river and her survivors picked up by a German trawler. *MTB74* had fired her torpedoes into the Old Entrance but was hit and sunk on her run down the Loire.

Campbeltown's charges did not blow up until about noon the next day, when Beattie was being interrogated by a German staff officer who was just remarking on the futility of trying to destroy a dock the size of the Normandie merely by ramming it with a destroyer. *MTB74's* torpedoes also blew up later, causing added confusion. *Campbeltown* took with her a party of German officers who, with incredible stupidity, were inspecting her at the time of the explosion. German troops opened fire and killed a number of their own men, with some French labourers, and their final casualties were much greater than those of the raiding force, who lost 169 killed, of a total of 630 taking part. Five VCs were awarded for the exploit, three of them to Ryder, Beattie and Newman.

Below the Belt

Above: HMS *Campbeltown* in the lock gates at St Nazaire. (Imperial War Museum)

Below: 55-foot Coastal Motor-Boat of the type which attacked Kronstadt harbour in 1919. (Imperial War Museum)

116

CHAPTER 7

'The dark night for our expedition arrived at last. The spot for embarkation was only separated by a spur of land covered by thick scrub and bush, but the darkness of the night enabled our guide to take us to the water. At half past twelve the punt left the rough slips and was immediately lost to sight, nor was there the slightest sound.'

So wrote Captain Hon Henry Keppel RN, commanding the 101-gun screw line-of-battle ship *St Jean d'Acre*, in his diary for 16 July 1855, in the last months of the Crimean war, describing the start of one of the most daring single-handed exploits in the Navy's history.

The Allies had complete command of the sea throughout the Crimean war. Early on, the Russians had withdrawn their major warships into Sebastopol harbour, sunk blockships in the channel, and built a boom across it. There, their ships stayed. But if the Russians would not come out, then some means had to be found of getting in to them.

One of the most ingenious and dangerous schemes was suggested by the captain of the 50-gun frigate *Diamond*, Captain William Peel, who had been serving ashore with the Naval Brigade in the trenches before Sebastopol since the early days of the campaign. In February 1855, Allied soldiers in the trenches were complaining of shells from two Russian men-of-war moored in the outer harbour, some 300 yards offshore; their guns had been dismantled and reslung with their barrels at angles of 45° to the deck, as improvised howitzers.

Peel proposed to lower six boats under cover of darkness down the cliffs of Inkerman, almost opposite where the Russian ships lay. The boats would be rowed across, the Russians boarded, their crews killed or captured, and the ships towed back in triumph. Lord Raglan, the army commander, approved, but Admiral Lord Lyons, the C-in-C, vetoed the scheme. (Even Peel's aide-de-camp, 18-year-old Midshipman Evelyn Wood, who was to be recommended for a Victoria Cross, and actually won one in the Indian Mutiny, thought this proposal rather rash.)

In April 1855, Peel was appointed in command of another 50-

gun frigate, *Leander*, which he proposed to use in another operation, to crash the Sebastopol boom by frontal assault. He would lash two fully-laden steam colliers, one on either side of *Leander*, and with everybody else below and only himself on deck to steer, hit the boom with all three ships together at full speed. But this, too, was not approved.

However, these schemes of Peel's eventually became general knowledge through the fleet and inspired an unexpected sequel. On 23 June, Keppel entered in his diary: 'Preparation by Quartermaster John Shepherd to destroy alone a Russian three-decker.' Next day, Keppel took Shepherd to see Admiral Lyons who 'was amused and approved, leaving the time for the experiment to me [Keppel]'.

Boatswain's Mate John Sheppard (his name was variously spelled) had been mulling over plans to force Sebastopol by stealth, not from the sea, but from the inland side, from a place on the inner shore of Sebastopol Bay which was held by the Allies.

In the Royal Navy of the 1850s it was most unusual for any seaman, even a senior rating like Sheppard, to show such initiative. But Sheppard was an unusual man who was not only a skilled professional seaman but an expert carver and whittler in bone and wood. He could sew and mend clothes 'invisibly' and could play exquisitely on a home-made wooden flute. He had joined the Navy as a young man in 1840, and after 10 years in the Coastguard Service, he had been conscripted for *St Jean d'Acre* on commissioning in 1853. He was now nearing 40 and might have been thought a little old for messing about in secret boats at dead of night. But, in fact, he had designed and built a kind of canoe, or 'duck-punt' which seemed to Keppel to have a real chance of success.

Keppel described the plan in his diary: 'to prepare a light iron case a foot long by eighteen inches, with a loop at each end. The case to be fitted with a Bickford fuse, which burns underwater. A sort of canvas duck-punt was to be fitted to exactly hold the case amidships. The after part was to hold one sitter, who could easily steer with a canoe paddle without noise.'

First, Sheppard had to convince sceptics in the fleet. The 90-gun sailing line-of-battleship *London* was chosen for a trial. Sheppard assured her Captain and officers that he could come by night in his canoe and chalk up their name on her ship's side without being detected. Sheppard painted his canoe white and dressed himself all in a suit of white canvas, while *London* took up the challenge. The sentries were doubled. Volunteers amongst the officers kept special watch all night. Nothing was seen by anybody, and all in *London* were utterly convinced nobody could possibly have come near their ship. Yet, when the sun rose, there were the letters L O N D O N, chalked just above the water line, just as Sheppard had promised.

Garbled stories of Sheppard's feat circulated in the fleet and rumours reached the army. General Sir George Higginson, in his autobiography *71 Years of a Guardsman's Life* wrote that Sheppard had a 'dummy bag, big enough to hold a hundredweight of explosive', which he 'screwed to the forefront of the British flagship'. Many could not believe he had used a surface craft, but must have had some form of submarine. Reports appeared in the press at home. The *Illustrated Times* of 11 August 1855 called it 'an atmospheric boat, capable of being guided when sunk beneath the surface and supplied with a reserve of air enough to last a given time for the support of its adventurous owner.' He (Sheppard) 'is in possession of a secret method by which he can move along beneath the surface of the water.'

The newspaper report was a serious breach of security because, by the time it was published, Sheppard had already made one attempt and was about to make another. The night, specially chosen for the dark of the moon, was 15/16 July 1855. The launching place was on the northern shore of the Sebastopol peninsula, in the inner reaches of the Bay. Keppel, his coxswain and an army colonel went with Sheppard down to the water's edge, helped him launch his canoe and saw him on his way.

Sheppard had just over 2 miles to cover to the mouth of Dockyard Creek, where most of the Russian battle fleet lay. After paddling for 1½ miles, he could see the masts of ships and the great towering sides of his main target, the giant 120-gun Russian flagship *Twelve Apostles*. He had passed undetected between two lines of Russian steamers which he ignored because they were minor targets and was within 400 yards of the nearest Russian battleship when he heard the sound of many oars approaching him. It was a large Russian cutter, crammed with soldiers, which passed so close he could have tossed a coin into it. He started to paddle forward again, but again had to back-water, for another Russian boat. And after that, there was a third.

The line of boats seemed unending. In fact, Sheppard had chanced upon the main Russian reinforcement route, by which hundreds of troops were ferried across to Sebastopol by night. Sheppard had not expected to find this route so far up the harbour. It later transpired that Allied gunfire had forced the Russians to re-route their ferries.

It was now 2 hours since Sheppard had started. The summer nights were short and to the east behind the Allied lines the dawn sky was already lightening. Sheppard decided to abandon his attempt. If he could return without compromising his canoe, he could make another attempt. He could not now get back to where Keppel and his party were still waiting before dawn came, so he turned aside into Careening Bay and landed at a point he knew was held by the French.

When Sheppard had not returned after 3 hours, Keppel began to fear the worst. 'I was distressed at having helped to lose poor John Shepherd – as, if caught, he would be shot as a spy'. However, an hour after coming back to camp, Keppel was delighted to hear of Shepherd's safe return.

Sheppard made another attempt at the next dark period of the moon, on the night of 15/16 August. By then, a great many people including the press knew of his doings and a feeling had grown amongst some army officers that all this sneaking about in the dark, stealthily paddling up on an unsuspecting enemy with lethal explosive charges, was not above board, not cricket. However, the French did not play cricket and Sheppard's second sortie was made from the French side of Careening Bay. He was briefed to penetrate the Russian fleet anchorage and place his explosive if he could. If not, he was to remain concealed in the harbour for the whole of the following day, returning after dark. During daylight he was to keep watch, observe the comings and goings in the harbour, and make notes.

Once again, Sheppard's passage down harbour was hampered by a bridge of boats. But he lay concealed for 24 hours and eventually returned safely to Careening Bay. After the French had taken charge of his notes and debriefed him, Sheppard went back to the Naval Brigade lines, a French soldier being detailed to carry his canoe for him.

Keppel, to his own great joy, was appointed in command of the Naval Brigade on 19 July and did not mention Sheppard again in his diary. But he and Lord Lyons both included Sheppard's name and exploit in their dispatches. Sheppard was in the list of the first Victoria Cross winners (as was Captain Peel, for three separate acts of sublime bravery during the campaign) published in the *London Gazette* of 24 February 1857. He was not present in Hyde Park to receive his Cross from Queen Victoria herself at the first VC Investiture on 26 June 1857, as he was then serving in *Highflyer* on the China Station. He retired from the Navy as a Boatswain, First Class, in 1870, and died in December 1884.

Sheppard's sortie into Sebastopol Bay might have been a model for more clandestine operations of the same kind, but his initiative was never followed up. The times were against it. Queen Victoria's Navy was in a constant turmoil of technological invention, so that a squadron of six battleships might well consist of six entirely different ironclad designs. But this energy and effort were devoted to surface ships, and especially capital ships. 'Canoes', 'duck-punts' and such-like, these were the toys of weaker naval powers. Nevertheless, John Sheppard was the direct ancestor of all the 'sneak craft' crews, midget submarines, special boat services and 'cockleshell heroes' of the First and Second World Wars.

Sheppard had plenty of kindred spirits in America during the Civil War, but at home, his idea slept for nearly 60 years, until the beginning of the twentieth century, when in 1909, Lieutenant Godfrey Herbert RN, a submarine officer serving a watch-keeping appointment in the cruiser *Monmouth* on the China Station, began to while away the long hours on deck by thinking of schemes for what he called his 'Devastator'.

'Devastator' was a manned torpedo, to be carried on board a battleship or heavy cruiser and hoisted out when the enemy fleet was sighted at a (suggested) range of 20,000 yards. It had a crew of one, who steered his weapon towards the target by compass and by periscope observation. But it was not a suicide weapon. When the operator was certain his 'Devastator' was properly on course for the target, he would detach the buoyancy chamber in which he was sitting (it was lined with air cushions to make it more comfortable). He and the buoyancy chamber would be picked up by a destroyer later.

The idea was submitted to the Admiralty who replied, a few months before the outbreak of the First World War, that 'their Lordships do not propose to proceed further in the matter at present'. By the time war broke out, Herbert was once more in the submarine service, commanding *D5*. (On 21 August 1914, in the North Sea, *D5* fired two torpedoes at a sitting duck, the German cruiser *Rostock*. To Herbert's amazement and fury, both missed. The warheads were appreciably heavier than the dummy heads of peacetime and the torpedoes ran deep. Otherwise Herbert would have been the first man to sink a warship by torpedo attack from a dived submarine.) Herbert's 'Devastator' was taken up by Commodore Keyes, who persuaded the Admiralty to consider it again. But the reply was, once again, that it was a dangerous device to develop and in any case would be the weapon of a weaker power. It was Lord St Vincent's argument, coming down through the years.

In 1915 Robert Davies of the firm of Siebe Gorman (later Sir Robert and chairman of the company) patented types of one-man and two-man submarines. The one-man crew wore a self-contained diving suit, with a shield to protect his head from the force of the water as the submarine went along. The two-man submarine had a diver in an air-lock and a coxswain, sitting in a water-tight compartment, with a glass dome over his head. Both submarines had oxygen bottles and electric storage batteries.

None of these, or indeed any midget submarines, were used operationally during the war. But the Royal Italian Navy brilliantly carried on the tradition of daring penetrations of enemy harbours with a variety of weapons. It was in the Adriatic that a combination of contrasting national temperaments and coastal geography provided ample chances for some of the bravest exploits of all time.

On one side were the Italians, an explosive, experimental, daring and flamboyant race, faced by a long Austrian coast-line, studded with superb natural harbours and bristling with possible targets. On the other were the Austrians, with a stolid, cautious siege mentality, putting their faith in booms and harbour defences, faced by an Italian coastline which had no natural harbours between Venice in the north and Brindisi in the south, and very few artificial shelters for shipping in between them. Venice was only 60 miles across the sea from the Austrian stronghold of Trieste. The other Austrian base at Cattaro was 300 miles to the south. Thus, in one of the rare instances in naval history, the side with the most aggressive approach were given the most opportunities. (Goaded by Italian successes, the Austrians did eventually make one sortie against the Italian MAS base at Ancona, 90 miles from Pola, but the 60 participants in the venture were in the hands of the Italian constabulary within a short time of landing.)

The initials MAS stood for *motobarca armata* SVAN (SVAN: Societa Venziana Automobile Nautiche, who built the earliest Italian motor-boats before the war). They were handy, 42-foot, 12-ton motor-boats, very small but sea-worthy, being completely decked over. They were armed with three machine-guns and two 18-inch torpedoes, one slung on each side, and could make about 24 knots. Some of the later boats had electric motors, driven by battery, for silent running within earshot of the enemy. The boats had a crew of 3 or 4 *masista*, normally commanded by a lieutenant or sub-lieutenant, or even sometimes by a senior artificer or yeoman, and the officers were nearly all Reserve or volunteers. MAS also stood for *Memento Audere Semper*, the unit motto given them by Gabriele d'Annunzio, together with the slogan 'One against a hundred – attack!'

The MAS *masista* certainly did their best to carry out the urging, so much so that the Austrians came to believe the MAS had more phenomenal speed and capabilities than they actually had. In the end, the *masista* had a destructive moral effect on their enemy out of all proportion to their actual achievements, although these were real enough.

On 5 June 1916, two MAS commanded by Lieutenants Berardinelli and Pagano were towed from Brindisi by destroyers 70 miles across the Adriatic and slipped off the harbour entrance of

Durazzo. Both MAS penetrated the harbour nets, found a transport and sank her with one torpedo. Surprise was complete. Both MAS escaped unharmed.

Ten days later the same two boats raided San Giovanni di Medua, 40 miles to the north, where they found nothing to attack but were themselves attacked by the shore batteries. The MAS and the towing destroyers retired under a smoke screen. Obviously, the enemy was now on the alert. The MAS were given longer-ranged torpedoes, and smoke floats for their own use. Two boats attacked Durazzo again on 24 June, sank 2 steamers out of 3 in the harbour, and returned untouched.

This was the last success of the year for the MAS flotilla at Brindisi. Bad weather, engine breakdowns, or the heightened alertness of the enemy, aborted further attacks. In November 1916, two boats under Pagano returned again to Durazzo. Their target steamer they found anchored behind a boom, so Pagano rode the bows of his boat up on the boom, taking the risk of being unable to get back if the whole boat had slipped over, and fired both his torpedoes, but both missed. The MAS escaped under enemy fire, but Pagano's boat collided with the towing destroyer and sank with the loss of one of the crew.

Another MAS flotilla operated from Venice against Austrian bases in the north. Its first raid was on the night of 1/2 November 1916 against ships lying in the Fasana Channel, between the Brioni Islands and the mainland just north of Pola. It was a roadstead used as an outer anchorage by the Austrian fleet at Pola. The expedition was led by Commander Ciano in the destroyer *Zeffiro*, with Lieutenant Commander Cavagnari in a torpedo-boat, and one MAS captained by Lieutenant Goiran. They reached the entrance to the Channel undetected at about midnight. While the *Zeffiro* stayed in the entrance, Cavagnari towed Goiran's MAS in as far as the boom, where Cavagnari made a way through with a specially contrived contraption of chains and weights, to force the boom underwater. Goiran went in, looking for the battleship *Ferdinand Max* but failed to find her, so fired both torpedoes at the aged battleship *Mars* which happened to be the only ship in the anchorage. The torpedoes missed, or were entangled in *Mars'* nets.

Now thoroughly alarmed and wary, the Austrians began to blockade their harbours with even bigger and better booms. In the new year of 1917, the MAS turned to mine-laying, using their electric motors for the last quiet mile of approach, or for landing agents, or raiding parties to destroy lighthouses or coastguard stations, also picking up prisoners for interrogation.

The MAS next took part in an attack on 16 November 1917, at

Cortellazzo, on the mouth of the Piave river, 20 miles east of Venice. On land, the Austrians were advancing against Venice, and at sea, two old battleships *Wien* and *Budapest*, with an old light cruiser and some destroyers in support, were bombarding the Italian batteries at Cortellazzo. A combined force of Italian aircraft, destroyers, submarines and three MAS carried out a counter-attack. But the MAS were the only members to have any success. The aircrafts' bombs dropped wide. The submarines were forced down by Austrian aircraft. The destroyers were driven off by Austrian guns. But two MAS under Ciano (the third had broken down) closed to within a mile of the Austrians, with the sun behind them and the enemy's own cordite smoke acting as a screen. They pressed on to within 1000 yards, under heavy fire from the battleships and the destroyers, and fired all four torpedoes. The MAS escaped, after a prolonged chase by the destroyers. Their torpedoes missed, but the Austrians broke off their naval attacks on Cortellazzo.

On 9 December 1917, *Wien* and *Budapest* were attacked again in Muggia Bay, near Trieste, by two MAS, *No9* under Lieutenant Luigi Rizzo, and *No13* (Yeoman of Signals Ferrarini). Rizzo, one of the best and boldest of all the *masista*, and also one of the most successful, had prepared throughout the previous autumn for this attack, by exploring and charting channels, marking down the booms, landing on jetties and moles to examine the construction and securing arrangements of booms. The MAS were slipped off the entrance to the bay at midnight, closed the boom on electric motors, and Rizzo got out on to one of the moles to reconnoitre. There was nobody about, so the *masista* set out to cut the boom hawers with specially provided hydraulic chisels, a task that took more than 2 hours.

When the boom broke open, both MAS entered the bay and found the battleships anchored about 600 yards apart. Each took deliberate aim and fired torpedoes from close range. Ferrarini missed *Budapest* with both torpedoes, but Rizzo scored twice on *Wien* which sank soon afterwards. In the confusion and bad visibility of the night, both MAS then escaped unscathed. This feat, coming as it did only a few weeks after the great defeat at Caporetto, and at a time when large stretches of Italy were in Austrian and German possession, came as a tremendous morale booster for the entire Italian nation. Once again, the moral effect of the *masista*'s exploits was out of all proportion to the actual physical damage inflicted upon the enemy.

On another sortie, on 10 February 1918, the *masista* were accompanied by Gabriele d'Annunzio himself, serving as a volunteer. Ciano was in charge of the expedition, with Rizzo in command of three MAS, for a raid into the Quarnaro, a narrow gulf east of the

Istrian peninsula, leading up to Fiume. The targets were shipping lying in Buccari roadstead, at the head of the gulf. The MAS went up the gulf on electric motors, changing to petrol when it widened, and arrived off Buccari, where there were four steamers at anchor, at about 1 am on the morning of the 11th. All six torpedoes missed, the alarm was given and the MAS raced back down the gulf to the waiting torpedo-boats. D'Annunzio, however, left sealed bottles behind in Buccari Bay, each containing taunting, derisive messages for the Austrians.

In June 1918, Admiral Horthy became C-in-C of the Austrian fleet and on the 9th led a force of 2 battleships, *Svent-Istvan* and *Tegetthoff*, with a screen of 10 destroyers, southwards to attack the anti-submarine barrage the Allies had laid across the Otranto Straits. At about 3 am on 10 June, Luigi Rizzo, who happened to be patrolling in the area, sighted heavy dark smoke to the north. Rizzo should already have returned to base but he had been delayed by an engine break-down. Rizzo assumed the smoke was from destroyers sent out to catch him and when he had his engines going again he made up his mind to attack.

The night was very dark and Rizzo was able to approach close enough to see that he was opposed by battleships as well as destroyers. His torpedoes were set to run at shallow depth and if he fired from long range there was always the chance that they would hit an intervening destroyer before they could reach a battleship. So, with extraordinary coolness, Rizzo decided to penetrate the destroyer screen. He slowed to 9 knots and quietly ghosted unseen between the destroyers, until he sighted his target, actually *Svent-Istvan*, at a range of 300 yards. He fired and hit the battleship with both torpedoes. Rizzo turned away at full speed, pursued by the nearest destroyer whom he distracted by dropping a depth-charge in his MAS wake, and eventually made his escape. He and his accompanying MAS, who had missed *Tegetthoff* (Rizzo's colleagues had little luck) came safely back to Ancona.

At first, it seemed possible *Svent-Istvan* might creep back to harbour. But the flooding and the list increased, there was a long delay before *Tegetthoff* took her stricken sister ship in tow, and eventually, about 3 hours after Rizzo's attack, the crew abandoned ship, the great battleship lifted her stern, rolled over, and sank. Two officers and 120 men were lost in her.

Rizzo's tremendous *coup* had a shattering effect upon the morale of the Austrian Navy. It virtually ensured that the fleet never put to sea again. The memory of that loss added an extra psychological burden to the land-locked Austrian sailors, contributed to the unrest in the fleet later in the year, and reinforced the defensive mentality of their service.

As the Austrians improved and strengthened their booms, doubling and redoubling their numbers and width, so the Italians devised ever more ingenious methods of surmounting them, and by the summer of 1918 had developed an astonishing species of 'jumping' or 'creeping' boats. On either side of the keels of these curious craft ran two endless sprocket chains, led over gear-wheels mounted on deck at bow and stern. The chains were studded with three rows of 7-inch long steel teeth and driven by a 30 hp motor. When the boat reached a boom or other obstruction, its overhanging bow projected over it. The chains revolved. The teeth bit. The whole boat was thus hoisted up and over the obstruction. The propeller, sheathed in a protective tunnel to prevent damage as the boat crossed the boom, was driven by another, 15 hp motor to give a speed of about 5 knots and a range of some 20 miles. Armed with two 18-inch torpedoes, the jumping boats were towed like the MAS to the scene of their attacks.

Four of these craft were built early in 1918 and trials carried out. Two boats were lost, having to be destroyed to prevent them falling into Austrian hands. On 14 May 1918, 5 destroyers, 2 torpedo-boats and 2 MAS, all under the command of Ciano, convoyed a jumping boat called *Grillo* ('Cricket') commanded by Lieutenant Antonio Pellegrini for an attack on Pola. Pellegrini reached the outer boom unseen, in spite of bright Austrian search-lights sweeping the entrance, but he was spotted by a guard-boat as he was engaging his chain drive to cross the boom. Pellegrini hoped to be able to go on and fire his torpedoes nevertheless, but a search-light caught him as he was crossing the boom (which had five rows of timber baulks and wire hawsers 6 feet apart). Sentries on the jetty saw the craft perched on the boom and fired warning Very lights. A second guard-boat came up, *Grillo* was hit by a shell and sank. Pellegrini and his 3-man crew were taken prisoner. Ciano, waiting outside, heard two explosions and saw the Very lights which happened to mean in the Italian code 'Have torpedoed a battleship and scuttled *Grillo*'. Ciano withdrew, well satisfied, and it was some time before Pellegrini's fate was known.

Pellegrini had failed, but another officer, Major Raffael Rossetti, of the Constructor Corps, had developed an equally ingenious craft for an attack on Pola harbour. He took the body-shell of an old German torpedo which had been fired against an Italian ship and failed to explode, and fitted twin propellers and an air engine driven by air at 2000 psi from a bottle. At the front he fitted two mines, each of 440 pounds of explosive, with a delay timing fuse. The craft was called *Mignatta* ('Leech') and had a crew of two, Rossetti himself, and

Below the Belt

Surgeon Lieutenant Raffaele Paolucci, a man who had great experience of long-range swimming. He had swum up to 10 kilometres in training, towing a mine behind him, his idea being to swim into an enemy harbour with the mine and fix it to a target ship.

The two men began serious training in July 1918, swimming for long distances and learning to handle *Mignatta* under all conditions. For the actual attack, they wore special rubber suits and steel helmets shaped, so the story goes, to look like the necks of wine flasks or carbuoys. They set out from Venice on 31 October, with two torpedo-boats under Ciano towing two MAS, *Mignatta* being carried on board one of the MAS.

The tows were slipped some miles short of Pola, and *Mignatta* was hoisted out and towed onwards by one of the MAS. At about 10.45 pm that night, *Mignatta* was slipped, with just a ¼ mile to go to the boom. The first obstacle they crossed by simply pushing it down and riding over it. But the next was far too big and they had to work inshore towards the breakwater, hoping to cross where the boom was secured. There was a sentry standing above, looking down, and they were sure they had been spotted. But Rossetti waggled his helmet, to imitate a floating flask, and a lucky rain shower drove the sentry indoors.

The obstacle was a 180-foot long boom bristling with 3-foot long steel spikes. By now, the sortie had taken much longer than they had expected, and the tide was beginning to ebb strongly, against them. *Mignatta* slipped free of their grasp, and Paolucci had to plunge in after it and swim some distance to retrieve it. They were confronted by three rows of steel mesh nets. They hauled *Mignatta* over them and met three more rows of nets. Paolucci could not believe there was a second row and insisted that somehow in the confusion they had turned right round and were now climbing back out to the open sea. But Rossetti was confident they were on course. The tide was now running even more strongly, and once again they had to swim hard to pull *Mignatta* back. 'Rossetti made signs that he wanted to speak to me,' said Paolucci. 'I got near, and he told me that of the 205 atmospheres of initial pressure, more than one half had already been consumed: so what was left was hardly enough for the return, even if we should give up the enterprise now. Immediately we resolved to give up the intention to return. As we still had three hours before dawn, we decided to carry on ...'

By the light of the Austrian search-lights, sweeping to and fro across the harbour, Rossetti and Paolucci could make out the silhouettes of several battleships. There were in fact, 3 pre-dreadnoughts, and 3 super-dreadnoughts, *Prinz Eugen*, *Tegetthoff* and *Viribus Unitis*. At 4.15 am *Mignatta* was alongside *Viribus Unitis*.

127

The two could hear cheering and laughing on board, as though someone was having a party, but they paid no attention. It took them over an hour to fix the mine. They started the fuse going on the other mine and set *Mignatta* on her way across the harbour, where she eventually struck the hull of the auxiliary ex-liner *Wien*, and sank.

As dawn was breaking, a search-light picked out Rossetti and Paolucci swimming in the harbour. They were taken on board *Viribus Unitis*. It was 5 minutes to 6 and the mine was set to explode at 6.30 am. They were puzzled to see that the sailors around them had Jugoslav cap ribbons. It was the cause of the revelry. The Austrian Navy was no longer at Pola. Sailors had taken over the ship which was now Jugoslavian. Rossetti told the captain Voukovitch about the mine, whereupon there was a frantic evacuation.

Rossetti and Paolucci swam away with the rest, but were picked up by a boat full of angry seamen who insisted they return on board *Viribus Unitis*. On the quarterdeck the two were surrounded by a menacing crowd, demanding to know where the mine was placed, or accusing the Italians of telling lies so that they could escape. 'I looked at the stern clock,' said Paolucci. 'It was 27 minutes past 6, and at $\frac{1}{2}$ past 6 the torpedo was to explode. I heard a sailor shouting, 'Let us take them to the hold: if it is true that the ship will blow up.'

The mob was pressing the Italians closely, trying to cut away Rossetti's rubber suit to search him, when the mine finally detonated, nearly 15 minutes late by Paolucci's reckoning. 'A dull noise, a deep roaring, not loud or terrible but rather light. A high column of water followed. Under my feet I felt the deck vibrate, shake, tremble. I turned round, and nobody was there any longer. Everyone had thought of saving himself.'

The mine did its work. *Viribus Unitis* settled in the water, sinking slowly as though still fighting for her existence. The water lapped over her decks, and she began to list, ever more quickly, until she rolled over and disappeared. The two Italians were taken to a hospital ship where a furious Austrian sailor assaulted Paolucci, but both men survived and, 5 days later, rejoined their own people when the Italian Navy entered the harbour. The second mine exploded under *Wien* and sank her.

In 1919, several months after the Armistice, Great Britain was still at war, with the revolutionary Bolshevik regime in Russia. A naval squadron operated in the Baltic, blockading the fortress of Kronstadt, from a base at Bjork Sound, some 30 miles east of Kronstadt, on the Finnish shore. But there was another secret base at Terrioli, north of Kronstadt, from where Lieutenant A W S Agar, on special service for the Foreign Office, ran a high speed 'courier' service for secret agents and information, in and out of Kronstadt, in his shallow draught, 35-knot coastal motor-boat, *CMB4*.

When an anti-Bolshevik insurrection broke out in Kronstadt in June 1919 and Russian warships were bombarding the forts and harbour, Agar for once dropped his clandestine role and hoisted the White Ensign. He and his crew of two, Sub Lieutenant J Hampsheir RNR, and his faithful mechanic Beeley, wore uniform on the night of 16/17 June, when *CMB4* made a daring solo run into Kronstadt Bay.

Agar had penetrated a destroyer screen and was closing a larger vessel inshore, actually the cruiser *Oleg*, when *CMB4* broke down. Her hull had been damaged by gunfire and Agar was obliged to take her alongside a breakwater to make repairs. When *CMB4* got under way again and Agar was preparing to fire, he ordered Hampsheir to remove the safety pin from the cartridge in the firing chamber. In doing so, Hampsheir unfortunately fired the torpedo. The stops were still down and held the missile in position. Hampsheir and Beeley fitted another cartridge, while *CMB4* rocked about in the choppy water. 'I, of course, dared not leave the wheel and controls,' said Agar. 'I could see the black hulls of the destroyers and waited for their gun flashes. We were a "dead sitter" but, luckily for us, remained unseen.'

CMB4 had one 18-inch torpedo, so there was only one chance of a shot. 'Finally, the job was done though the waiting seemed endless and nerve-racking. Again I put on more speed and we were soon through the screen and in position. After removing the stops I fired our torpedo at the target, the *Oleg*, as if it were an ordinary practice run. I aimed at the centre of her three funnels. Once clear of the torpedo, I increased to full speed, turned round and made towards the Estonian coast hoping to mislead the enemy destroyers and forts as to where we had come from. Within a minute there was a thick column of black smoke from the *Oleg*. I waved to both Beeley and Hampsheir in lieu of the old naval custom of cheering when one hits the enemy, as the din inside our boat was terrific with the engine all out and the boat enveloped in spray.

'Flashes came from all directions; the forts, the destroyers, the ship itself, followed by splashes as the shells threw up columns of water soaking us to the skin as we went through them.' *CMB4* got safely away, while *Oleg* sank. Agar was awarded the Victoria Cross.

The Bolsheviks put a price of £5000 on Agar's head but that did not deter him from playing a part in another raid on Kronstadt in August. Eight more CMBs had been towed across the North Sea. One sank on passage but the remaining seven left Bjorko on 18 August 1919 and reached Kronstadt in the early hours of the morning.

Led by Commander C C Dobson, in *CMB31*, the motor-boats slipped past a line of forts and at 4.25 am roared into the inner harbour, where many of the guns could not fire at them because they were afraid of hitting each other or could not be depressed far enough. Conned by Lieutenant McBean, *CMB31* pressed on into the furthest part of the harbour and torpedoed the battleship *Andrei Pervozvanni*, lying alongside an inner jetty. *CMB31* stayed for some time in the harbour, under very heavy machine-gun fire, whilst Dobson directed the other surviving CMBs (some had been sunk on the way in) to their targets, before retreating under the shelter of the harbour walls to the open bay.

During the run into the harbour the captain of *CMB88*, Lieutenant Dayrell-Reed, was shot in the head and mortally injured. His unconscious body slumped over the steering wheel so that the boat began to career out of control. His second-in-command, Lieutenant Gordon Steele, man-handled his dead captain's body out of the way and took charge himself, steadying the boat on her course once more for her target, which was also *Andrei Pervozvanni*. Steele fired one torpedo at 100 yards range, and then had to manoeuvre the boat in a very confined space to get a clear shot at another battleship, *Petropavlosk*, which was obscured by the hull of *Andrei Pervozvanni* and shrouded in the smoke already billowing from her.

Steele had only just room to turn but headed for the entrance, firing at the guns along the wall with his own Lewis gun as he went, until he too gained the safety of the bay outside, where Agar, in *CMB7*, was waiting and acting as guide and traffic marshal. They were joined there by Lieutenant Bremner in *CMB24* who had sunk the submarine depot ship *Pamyat Azova*. Back in the harbour, both battleships were sinking, as the remaining CMBs formed up on Agar and roared away across the water and back to Bjorko.

This brilliant *coup de main* severely embarrassed the British Cabinet, who were at that very time conducting the most delicate negotiations with the Bolsheviks for the withdrawal of large British land forces then in Archangel. The raid had another unexpected and unfortunate result. The Russian Baltic Fleet, and especially the Kronstadt garrison, had until then been scornfully critical of the Bolsheviks. The sheer audacious cheek of the raid caused them temporarily to turn over to the Bolshevik side. Happily, Victoria Crosses are not awarded by politicians and Dobson and Steele were duly gazetted for theirs in 11 November 1919, the first anniversary of Armistice Day.

In 1924 a notable wartime submariner, Max Horton, who was Captain (S) at Fort Blockhouse, the submarine base at Gosport, produced designs for three small submarines. The first, Type A, was 30–40 tons, with a detachable conning tower and, like Herbert's 'Devastator' (from which it was developed) was intended to be carried to the scene of operations by another larger vessel. Horton's Type B was a further advance, a two-man submarine of 40 tons with a double hull, the top containing the crew and the bottom the warhead and the engines. Type C was a true miniature submarine, with its own propelling power, carrying a torpedo slung beneath the hull. But this too had to be transported to its target. This disadvantage prevented its adoption, although St Vincent's argument was still running strongly. The Royal Navy of the 1920s and 1930s was as indifferent to Horton's ideas as the Victorian Navy had been to Sheppard's.

The Japanese Navy, however, took the greatest interest in such weapons. In 1933 there were press reports in Britain that the Japanese had invented a 'torpedo with room for a pilot inside'. The Japanese Ministry of War were supposed to have called for 400 volunteers from amongst young naval reserve officers, and no less than 5000 responded. In 1934 two very small submarines were built at Kure Naval Yard. They were intended as auxiliary weapons, to take part in 'decisive fleet actions', being transported in the hangars of *Chitose* class seaplane tenders.

They were called *A Hyoteki* ('A Targets') to conceal their real purpose. In fact, they were torpedo-shaped, with no conning towers, just under 80 feet long, weighing 46 tons, driven by electric motors which gave them 24 knots for about 50 minutes, and they carried two 18-inch torpedoes. Conning towers were added after trials. In 1936, two more were built, called *Ko Hyoteki*, and launching trials were carried out from *Chitose* the following year. From then onwards, Japan began to build numbers of these weapons for the war which she could plainly see coming.

When the war did come, it began with an exploit worthy of Cochrane, Rizzo or Fulton. The Royal Navy had been uneasy about the vulnerability of the fleet base at Scapa Flow to submarine attack during the First World War and they were not to be much reassured at the start of the Second. The plan, devised by Admiral Karl Doenitz, commanding the German U-boat service, was to penetrate Scapa Flow by U-boat and sink major units of the Home Fleet at anchor there.

The U-boat chosen was *U47*, a Type VIIB submarine, of 750 tons, with four torpedo-tubes forward and one aft, commanded very ably by Leutnant Otto Prien. *U47* sailed from Kiel on 10 October 1939 and by the 13th was dived off Scapa Flow. After a day's rest, the crew had 'breakfast' at 5 pm that evening and prepared for the attack. Two torpedoes were placed in what Prien called 'rapid loading position' before tubes 1 and 2. Explosives were broken out, in case *U47* had to be scuttled. The crew's morale, according to Prien, was 'splendid'.

U47 surfaced at 7.15 pm and headed for Scapa, intending to pass through Holm Sound at the eastern end. At 11.07 pm Prien had to dive for a merchant ship, noting that he could not make her out clearly through either of his periscopes, even though it was a clear night, with bright lights all around. *U47* surfaced again at 11.31 pm, and entered Holm Sound, with the flooding tide behind her. The whole passage was made on the surface.

Prien could see quite clearly a sunken blockship in Skerry Sound and for a time thought he was already in Kirk Sound. After a moment's alarm when he had to go hard to starboard, Prien took *U47* smoothly towards Kirk Sound, the main fleet anchorage. 'It is a very eerie sight,' Prien wrote. 'On land everything is dark, high in the sky are the flickering Northern Lights, so that the bay, surrounded by highish mountains, is directly lit up from above. The blockships lie in the sound, ghostly as the wings of a theatre.'

Prien intended to pass the blockships on their northern side, that is, leaving them on his port hand. He passed a two-masted schooner with only metres to spare and then the current suddenly caught *U47* and swung her to starboard. Prien picked out the anchor cable of the northernmost blockship, about 45° on his port bow. With port engine stopped, starboard engine slow ahead to counter the swing to starboard, *U47* touched bottom and her stern grazed the anchor cable, before she slid free and, after some more rapid manoeuvring, entered Scapa Flow. 'It is disgustingly light. The whole bay is lit up.'

To port, Prien saw the Hoxa Sound coastguard to which, as *U47* turned to starboard he must present the whole of the submarine's port side, as a perfect target. If she was sighted 'all would be lost'. There was no shipping to the south, so Prien steered north, where at, 5 minutes to 1, he sighted 'two battleships' (actually one battleship *Royal Oak*, and a seaplane tender *Pegasus*), lying an estimated 3000 metres apart.

Prien closed to about 4000 yards range and at 1.16 am (although this time was queried in pencil in *U47*'s log and 12.58 suggested) fired three torpedoes. The fourth forward tube misfired.

One torpedo from this salvo hit *Royal Oak* right forward, possibly even on her anchor cable. On board, the impact was felt only as a shudder and a dull thud. Some flooding of forward compartments was discovered. Admiral Blagrove and the Captain agreed that some internal explosion had taken place. Some forward bulkheads were shut and the paint store, which was right forward in the peak, was flooded as a precaution. Then the ship's company fell out from emergency stations. The alarm died down. The emergency, if indeed it had been an emergency, was seemingly over.

Prien had seen one torpedo explode but disappointingly the ships stayed afloat. He turned *U47* and fired the stern tube torpedo. Two torpedoes were reloaded in the forward tubes and at 1.21 he fired a salvo of three, all of which hit. 'After 3 tense minutes come the detonation on the nearer ship. There is a loud roar, an explosion, and rumbling. Then come columns of water, followed by columns of fire, and splinters fly through the air.'

At about 1.30 am *Royal Oak* rolled over and sank to starboard, with the loss of 24 officers and 809 men. The drifter *Daisy II*, lying alongside the battleship when she was hit, saved men who scrambled across on to her, and she also rescued men from the water. Some of the wounded, badly burned, she took across to *Pegasus*. Meanwhile, 'the harbour springs to life,' Prien noted. 'Destroyers are lit up, signalling starts on every side, and on land, 200 metres away from me, cars roar along the roads.'

It was now high time for *U47* to go. Prien withdrew at full speed. At one point where the channel was very narrow he seemed to be making no progress against the tide. At full speed he shaved the southernmost blockship with nothing to spare. At 2.15 Prien set course south-east for base. At 6.30, dived, Prien could see the glow of Scapa in the sky. 'Apparently they are still dropping depth-charges.'

Ironically, the one blockship which would have prevented Prien entering arrived at Scapa the day after the attack. Between the wars, one senior naval officer after another had reported again and again on the insecurity of Scapa Flow as a fleet base. The nets and defences of the First World War had been removed in peace-time, and the shore batteries had been dismantled. There could, and should, have been a major political scandal over Scapa's defences, but the First Lord, Winston Churchill, had only just assumed office and could not be blamed. The Home Fleet moved to Loch Ewe, where it led an uneasy, jumpy existence, ever afraid of submarine attack, until Scapa Flow had been strengthened.

When Prien returned to Kiel he was at once flown to Berlin to receive the Iron Cross and the congratulations of the Führer. He went on to become one of the leading U-boat 'aces' until 8 March 1941, when *U47* was sunk with all hands in the North Atlantic by the destroyer *Wolverine*.

Prien's exploit stood alone for a long time. There was an *impromptu* raid at Dakar, during the actions against the French fleet after the collapse of France in July 1940. On the 8th, a motor-boat from the aircraft carrier *Hermes*, lying offshore, went into Dakar harbour and dropped four depth-charges under the stern of the French battleship *Richelieu*. The idea was bold enough, but the depth-charges failed to explode because the water was too shallow to activate the hydrostatic pressure priming device.

Below the Belt

It was not until the early hours of 19 December 1941, in Alexandria harbour, when Italian swimmers laid mines which badly damaged the battleships *Valiant* and *Queen Elizabeth*, that the Allies were suddenly and rudely reminded of the possibilities of this kind of warfare.

Above: Cdr Antonio Pellegrini's *Grillo* ('Cricket'), the curious boom-climbing 'tank' used in an attack on Pola harbour, 13 May 1918. (Author's Collection)
Below: An Italian MAS boat with two torpedoes loaded. (Imperial War Museum)

Above: Cdr Luigi Rizzo attacking the Austrian dreadnought *Svent Istvan* on the night of 9/10 June 1918. (Author's Collection)

Below: One of the 'Sleeping Beauties' tried out by the Cockleshell Heroes: Quentin Reeves' Motorised Submersible Canoe, seen here sinking slowly to make the last stage of its stealthy approach to the target. (Author's Collection)

CHAPTER 8

The events of that December night in Alexandria were no fluke. The Italian Navy fully deserved their success. They had prepared long, worked hard, suffered many failures, but had still preserved the same spirit, a kind of romantic technical flair coupled with personal dedication, which had inspired Rizzo, Pellegrini, Rossetti and Paolucci, nearly a quarter of a century before. The Italians had realised during the Abyssinian crisis of 1935 that they needed some special weapon to counter-balance the overwhelming warship strength of the Royal Navy. They required something new and unforeseen, which could be rapidly produced and instantly employed. It had to be secret yet capable of being deployed on a massive scale and against a number of different objectives simultaneously. Variety was also required. Once known, a weapon would have far less chance of success and be more risky to use. It was a cardinal principle of such 'sneak' and 'nuisance' warfare, to develop a number of different weapons, so that as the enemy discovered one, others could still undertake operations.

Two young naval engineer officers, Sub Lieutenants Teseo Tesei and Elios Toschi, together designed a manned torpedo with a detachable warhead, electrical propulsion, steering and hydroplane controls, and a crew of two who sat astride, their feet in stirrups, protected from the oncoming water by a curved screen. The crew manoeuvred their craft to the target, being free to climb off to cut nets, remove obstacles and place their charge against the target. As developed, the SLC human torpedo, the 'pig' as it was nicknamed, was 6.7 metres long, diameter 53 cm, had a speed of $2\frac{1}{2}$ knots and an operational range of about 10 miles, a designed diving depth of 30 metres, and a warhead of 300 kg. It had two ballast tanks for diving and surfacing, and carried tools for net-cutting and clamps for fixing the charge to an enemy keel.

In spite of inevitable suspicion of conservative elements in the Navy, the idea was approved, two prototypes were built and crew training began at a camp at the mouth of the river Serchio. At about this time, the Duke of Aosta had designed a type of very small but very fast motor-boat, containing explosives. Scores of them were to be carried slung between the floats of seaplanes and launched in swarms in front of enemy naval bases immediately after the outbreak of war. Their attacks were to be carried out whilst the shore defences were distracted by diversionary air raids. They were made of stretched canvas over a light wooden hull, with the explosive, set to detonate on impact, in the bows. The one man crew had to ensure that his boat was on course for the target before throwing himself into the water. Two of these prototypes were built and tested.

These devices were a promising start, but when the campaign in Abyssinia ended the Italian Navy lost interest and it was two years, in late 1938, before an officer was appointed to command the First Light Flotilla, as it was called, crews joined for training again, and a staff created for the study of special weapons. In 1939 an order for 12 'pigs' was placed and a full scale exercise was carried out in the gulf of La Spezia early in 1940. Three craft were carried by the submarine *Ametista* and although two broke down, the third successfully fixed its dummy charge to the keel of the target which, in a real operation, would certainly have been sunk.

From the first, the Italian crews had an almost mystical belief in their mission. While they were certainly not suicide missions, personal survival had a low priority. Tesei himself, who took part in that exercise, said that 'the success of the mission is not very important, nor even the outcome of the war. What really counts is that there are men ready to die in the attempt and really dying in it: for our sacrifice will inspire and fortify future generations to conquer.'

For all their training and dedication, the first World War Two operation of the Tenth Light Flotilla, as they were later called, was a failure and indeed was the first of a sequence of failures. In August 1940, four 'pigs' were transported on board the torpedo-boat *Calipso* to the Gulf of Bomba, on the coast of Cyrenaica, where they were to be transferred to the submarine *Iride*. Leaving Bomba on the 22nd, *Iride* was to arrive off Alexandria on the night of the 25th and launch the 'pigs' to attack British shipping in the harbour. But the enterprise was first betrayed by Allied code-breaking and then confirmed by air reconnaissance, which spotted the ships lying in the bay. Three Swordfish torpedo-bombers from 824 Squadron Fleet Air Arm, embarked in *Eagle*, flew ashore to Sidi Barrani, where they arrived on the 22nd. At 12.30 pm the flight took off, made a wide board of some 50 miles out to sea to avoid Italian fighters, and then approached the bay from seaward.

Calipso was refuelling alongside the depot ship *Monte Gargano*. *Iride* was just putting to sea, with the human torpedoes on her casing, to carry out test dives. *Iride* was hit forward by one torpedo and sank with most of her ship's company, only 14 men coming to the surface. *Monte Gargano* was also hit and sank later. Seven men survived in *Iride*'s after torpedo compartment and escaped 24 hours later, using the method Bauer used: flooding up the compartment until internal and external pressures were equal and the hatch could be opened. They were as reluctant to use this method as Bauer's companions had been, and had to be threatened that the rescuers would go away and abandon them to their fates unless they obeyed instructions.

Two sorties in September were also unsuccessful. The submarines *Gondar* and *Scire* were fitted out as 'assault craft transports' with three steel shells, strong enough to withstand the full submarine's diving pressure, placed on the casing, one forward and two aft of the conning tower (*Iride*, with the unprotected 'pigs' on her casing, had been limited to their diving depth of 30 metres). *Gondar* sailed from La Spezia on 21 September, and embarked the 'pig' crews at Villa San Giovanni, in the straits of Messina (to shorten their period on board). They were to attack Alexandria on the night of 29/30th but shortly before the launching time *Gondar* received a message that the British fleet had sailed and the operation was cancelled. *Gondar* was detected and sunk by the Australian destroyer *Stuart*, with assistance from aircraft of 230 Squadron RAF, off Alexandria on 30 September. *Scire* had left La Spezia on 24 September for a similar attack at Gibraltar on the same night of the 29th, but she too was recalled.

The flotilla was not at all downhearted by these reverses. One of its officers, Commander Valerio Borghese, has described its philosophy. 'The Tenth lived a retired life of its own, resistant to every kind of interference from outside. Politics, the illusory idea of a short war, sudden fits of exaltation consequent upon a success or of depression following a reverse, did not enter into our calculations and did not distract us from our work. A single thought, a single spur, a single activity inspired us: it was to keep our men and weapons up to the mark and sharpen our wits to discover ways of striking at the enemy as hard as possible: nothing else interested us.'

Training went on, the swimmers from the Serchio travelling up to La Spezia for night exercises twice a week, using as targets the old cruiser *San Marco* anchored in Varignano Bay, or any of the battle units which happened to visit La Spezia. On 21 October, *Scire* sailed for another attack on Gibraltar. After two attempts on two successive nights to go through the Straits, *Scire* reached Algeciras bay on the

29th and launched three 'pigs' at the top end, in the mouth of the Guadarranque river, in the early hours of the 30th.

One 'pig', crewed by De La Penne and Bianchi, was detected by a patrolling motor-boat and illuminated by search-lights. They were forced deep, depth-charged, and had to abandon their 'pig' on the bottom at a depth of about 40 metres. They surfaced, took off their breathing sets and rubber suits, and swam ashore 2 hours later, where they were picked up by agents. The second 'pig', with Tesei and Pendretti, had the same fate.

The third, with Birindelli and Paccagnini, actually got inside Gibraltar harbour and laid the mine a few hundred yards from the battleship *Barham*. But they too had difficulties with their 'pig' and their breathing sets, swam ashore and were captured. The mine blew up but did not damage *Barham*. Birindelli wrote from his prison camp, 'Tell my brother that he ought to have another try for his degree. If at first you don't succeed, try, try again.'

The expedition had been valuable experience and spread uneasiness in Gibraltar. The harbour was vulnerable to such attacks, and these 'pigs' although they still required development, clearly had the potential to do a great deal of damage.

With the 'pigs' the Italians also developed the Duke of Aosta's idea into an ingenious little craft, with many novel features, called the Modified Touring Motor-boat (MTM), otherwise known as the 'explosive' or 'E-boat'. It was flat-bottomed, 5.2 metres long, driven by an Alfa Romeo 2500 engine which gave it a speed of 32 knots, with an endurance of 5 hours. Propeller and rudder were in one combined assembly, easily lifted out of the water, so that the boat could cross a boom without damaging it. The forepart held 300 kg of explosive, detonated on impact, or hydrostatically, at a set depth. The boat was piloted by one man who aimed it at the target, locked the rudder, and then threw himself into the sea. As soon as he could he climbed on to a wooden life-raft, which had been the cockpit back-rest, and which he had detached before jumping, so that he was not actually in the water at the moment of the explosion. When the E-boat hit its target, the impact caused a ring of small charges to blow the craft in two; both halves sank and the portion containing the explosive exploded when the set pressure was reached.

Two destroyers, *Crispi* and *Sella*, were converted to carry six E-boats each, with special electric davits for hoisting and lowering them. The E-boats made their successful operational debut on 25 March 1941, when the destroyers took them to within 10 miles of the harbour of Suda, in Crete, where air reconnaissance had reported British destroyers, 5 large transports, 7 smaller transports, and a heavy cruiser at anchor. Suda Bay was an *impromptu* fleet base, not properly fitted with booms and defences, and the E-boats stood an excellent chance of breaking into it.

The six E-boats under Lieutenant Luigi Faggioni set off at about 11.30 pm, on a dark but starry night, with fine weather and a calm sea. They negotiated the first two nets with very little difficulty and passed round the end of a third, in a gap between it and the shore. Inside, they paused, to look round their possible targets. The cruiser, actually HMS *York*, was only 200 yards away from the nearest E-boat. She was hit by two of the E-boats, listed heavily and began to go down by the bow. Another E-boat attacked and damaged a tanker. All six E-boat crews were captured, but *York* later became a total loss and was abandoned where she lay. The Luftwaffe subsequently claimed her, but there is no doubt she was sunk by Faggioni's E-boats.

In May 1941 *Scire* and three 'pigs' made yet another sortie to Gibraltar. Elaborate arrangements were made to shorten the time 'pig' crews had to spend on board. This time, the crews were flown to Spain, with false papers to placate the Spanish authorities, and taken to Cadiz, to the Italian tanker *Fulgor* which had been interned since the beginning of the war and was now being used as an advanced base by the Italians. *Scire* entered Cadiz with the implicit connivance of the Spanish harbour anthorities and the Spanish navy, and secured alongside *Fulgor* by night. Borghese met the 'pig' crews, took on stores to refresh his own ship's company, and received the latest intelligence of Allied shipping in Gibraltar. *Scire* then slipped and made her way out to sea, with the 'pig' crews embarked, and early in the morning of 26 May, launched the three 'pigs' in Algeciras Bay.

Once again, the mission was a failure. Once again, the crews had difficulties with their craft, and in any case the harbour was empty of shipping. One 'pig' was badly damaged on launching, and the other two were lost in the Bay. The six crewmen successfully reached the shore and, as before, the protection of Italian agents.

Each mission added to the operational experience of the Flotilla and resulted in improvements in gear and armament. Morale remained high, and even survived an operation in July 1941, in which E-boats and 'pigs' together took part, which, if not a suicide mission, was for some of the participants not far removed from it.

Ever since Italy had been at war, Malta had lain like a thorn in her side. It was a serious strategic error on the Italian's side that no invasion of Malta was ever carried out. But in April 1941, E-boats were taken down to Augusta in Sicily from where they would carry out a sortie to crash the defences of Malta. It was an operation very similar in spirit to those of the First World War. After two attempts in May and June 1941, both called off for bad weather, leaking boats, or both (the June attack after the E-boats had actually come close to success), another attack was scheduled for the new moon in July.

It was planned on an ambitious scale and in quite considerable force. The dispatch vessel *Diana*, once Mussolini's personal yacht, had nine E-boats on board and towed a special motor-boat which carried two 'pigs'. Two motor-boats, Nos *451* and *452*, towed in turn a torpedo-motor-boat in which Lieutenant Commander Giobbe was to guide the E-boats to the harbour entrance, and remain to pick up survivors.

It had been decided not to try and force the main entrance to Grand Harbour which was assumed to be guarded with booms, nets, listening posts, obstructions and all manner of protective devices, but to go instead for the narrow channel just beside the main entrance, under a bridge which crossed from the mainland to the Sant Elmo mole. The bridge was steel, supported by three pillars which stood high enough to allow small boats to pass under. A steel anti-torpedo net hung from the bridge to the sea bottom.

The plan was for *Diana* to approach Malta with the E-boats on board and towing the special motor-boat with the 'pigs'. One 'pig' would blow up the nets under the Sant Elmo bridge, the other the boom across the neighbouring harbour entrance of Marsa Muscetto where the submarine base lay. Once the way in was clear, the E-boats would enter and discharge their explosives against warships in Grand Harbour and submarines in Marsa Muscetto.

The attack took place on 25 July and was an almost total failure. Tesei, whose task it was to blow up the Sant Elmo net, was late in his approach, but blew up the net at 4.30 am, although he knew there was no time for him and his crewman to get clear. They were both killed, and from Tesei's letters and statements beforehand, and his poor state of health, it seems that he was bent on suicide.

His sacrifice was all in vain. Of 8 E-boats launched, 2 got as far as the bridge and 1 exploded but, somewhat predictably, brought down the bridge structure, blocking up the gap so desperately blown open by Tesei. The other 6 boats were caught by search-lights and sunk by gun-fire. The island's radar had picked up the intruders at some distance out and the defences were thoroughly warned and ready. Most of the E-boats crews were killed by shore fire or strafing aircraft. The rest were picked up in the morning and made prisoner. The two motor-boats were caught by aircraft at daylight. One was blown up, the other captured. The second 'pig' bound for Marsa

Muscetto ran aground, failed to get past the boom, and its crew were captured.

In all, 15 men were killed and 28 captured. One motor-boat was sunk and the other captured; 8 E-boats, the special towing craft and the 2 'pigs' were all lost. Only 11 men survived to rejoin *Diana* and come safe home.

In spite of this, the Tenth Flotilla was still undismayed and in September 1941 *Scire* was making yet another sortie to Gibraltar. The *modus operandi* was the same: crews flown to Spain, rendezvous with *Fulgor*, passage to Algeciras Bay, the clandestine launching of the 'pigs'. One tried to attack a battleship of the *Nelson* class, but could not force the harbour entrance and instead laid charges against the hull of the 2444-ton tanker *Fiona Shell*, which later sank. A second 'pig' was harassed by patrol boats, abandoned the attempt to get inside the harbour and sank the British motor-ship *Durham*, of 10,900 tons. The third 'pig' penetrated the harbour, set its mine against the large 15,000 ton tanker *Denby Dale*, which blew up and sank at about 8.40 am the next morning. The six crewmen all got ashore safely and were recovered by Italian agents.

With this exploit, it could be said that the human torpedoes finally came of age. Some 30,000 tons of shipping had been sunk, for the trivial loss of 3 'pigs'. *Denby Dale* had actually been destroyed whilst inside a defended harbour, so this was the first successful penetration by members of this arm. The Italians had taken a risk by continuing with the same weapon, long after it had been first used and suspected by the enemy. But it had finally paid a dividend.

It was shortly to pay a much larger dividend. Until then, all the flotillas' efforts had no more than pin-prick nuisance value. Ships had been sunk or damaged but the only lives lost were Italian. The debacle at Malta seemed to show that these sorties by midgets had no more effect on the progress of the general war at sea than one Lilliputian's attack would have on Gulliver. But suddenly, literally overnight, the situation changed completely. It was shown that human torpedoes could indeed have a far-reaching strategic effect upon a whole theatre of the war.

At dusk on 3 December 1941, *Scire* sailed from La Spezia, ostensibly on an ordinary submarine patrol. But, outside the harbour, a lighter came alongside, with three 'pigs' on board and clothing and breathing sets for the crews. After checking their own torpedoes and gear, the crews left that night, while *Scire* sailed on Operation EA 3, as it was called; yet another human torpedo attack on British shipping in Alexandria harbour.

Scire reached the Greek island of Leros on 9 December, where she was joined three days later by 10 operators – 6 operational crews and 4 reserves. The submarine sailed on the 14th. Her mission was to make a submerged approach through a minefield and surface a few thousand yards off the harbour entrance. Accurate navigation was vital. The success of the 'pigs' would depend upon a reliable datum starting point. Alexandria harbour was protected by a minefield which extended 20 miles to the north-west, a line of 'lobster pot' mines moored at a depth of 30 fathoms in a radius of 6 miles from the entrance, detector cables laid on the sea bottom closer in, net barriers and groups of 'lobster pot' mines in specially chosen positions. There was also continuous surveillance from shore and from patrolling vessels.

After one day's delay because of bad weather, *Scire* surfaced off Alexandria on the evening of 18 December. Conditions were perfect: a very dark night, calm sea, clear sky. Two of the reserve crews went up on deck first, to open the doors of the cylinders housing the 'pigs' to save the operational crews extra labour. They were followed by the 6 men of the operational crews, all dressed in dark rubber suits. The three 'pigs' (actually Nos *221*, *222* and *223*) were launched, manned, and disappeared in the blackness. *Scire* then submerged and headed for home (after surfacing a short time later, to retrieve one of the reserve crew who had been left on deck and very nearly drowned).

Meanwhile the three human torpedoes approached the entrance boom which, providentially, was drawn aside just as they arrived, to allow a force of cruisers and destroyers under Rear Admiral Vian to enter harbour. Blessing their luck, the 'pigs' followed. Inside the harbour, Lieutenant Luigi Durand De La Penne and Petty Officer Diver Emilio Bianchi approached the battleship *Valiant*, reached the side of her massive hull, where the 'pig' suddenly dived to the bottom. De La Penne got under the hull and looked round, to find there was no sign of Bianchi. He surfaced to look for him. Everything was still very quiet, no sight nor sound of Bianchi.

When De La Penne tried to restart the 'pig's' motor, it refused to turn. He discovered a wire round the propeller. There was nothing for it but to man-handle the 'pig' by himself across the muddy bottom underneath *Valiant*. De La Penne had to exert all his strength to drag the 'pig' inches at a time. The sweat streamed down inside his face-mask and his rubber suit, and he was blinded by the mud stirred up by his movements. He could hear the steady thumping of a reciprocating pump somewhere inside the hull (almost certainly a steam-driven furnace fuel oil pump, supplying the harbour services boiler) and used that as a sound guide.

Now in the last stages of exhaustion, De La Penne positioned his 'pig' directly under the battleship and set the time fuses running. The 'pigs' also carried a number of incendiary bombs intended to be released and ignite the surface oil on the water after the main explosion, in the hope of causing a major fire in the harbour and putting the whole naval base out of action. But De La Penne did not release his, for fear they would reveal his position. He left the 'pig' where it was on the sea bed and swam up to the surface.

De La Penne began to swim slowly away from the ship's side but he heard a hail. A search-light beam shone out and there was a burst of gunfire. It seemed foolhardy to go on, so he swam back and climbed on to the mooring buoy at *Valiant*'s bows. There to his amazement he found Bianchi. He had apparently lost consciousness during the sudden dive and risen to the surface, where he came to his senses. He had hidden on the buoy and stayed quiet so as not to jeopardise De La Penne's attack.

The two were picked up by a motor-boat and taken on board *Valiant* and then ashore for interrogation. Later in the night they were taken back to *Valiant* and put in a compartment forward, deep in the ship and, they guessed, close to where the explosion would occur. About 10 minutes before the set time, De La Penne asked to see the Captain. 'I told him that in a few minutes his ship would blow up, that there was nothing he could do about it, and that, if he wished, he could still get his crew into a place of safety. He again asked me where I had placed the charge and as I did not reply had me escorted back to the hold. As we went along I heard the loudspeakers giving orders to abandon ship, as the vessel had been attacked by Italians, and saw people running aft ... A few minutes passed (they were infernal ones for me: would the explosion take place?) and then it came. The vessel reared, with extreme violence. All the lights went out and the hold became filled with smoke. I was surrounded by shackles which had been hanging from the ceiling and had now fallen.'

'The ship had now listed through 4–5° and come to a standstill. I saw from a clock that it was ¼ past 6. I went further aft, where a number of officers were standing, and began to watch the battleship *Queen Elizabeth*, which lay about 500 metres astern of us ... A few seconds passed and then the *Queen Elizabeth*, too, blew up.'

Queen Elizabeth had been attacked by the second 'pig', crewed by Engineer Captain Antonio Marceglia and Petty Officer Diver Spartaco Schergat, who had also found the boom open and, though disconcerted by charges dropped round the entrance (precisely to deter intruders such as themselves) as they slipped inside, and though they were very nearly run down by three destroyers, eventually found themselves 'face to face with the whole massive bulk of the target', as Marceglia said. They crossed a torpedo net, and submerged beneath the hull, level with the forward funnel.

Their attack went like a copy-book exercise. They attached a loop-line from one keel plate to another and fixed the warhead to the middle of the line, so that it hung neatly about $1\frac{1}{2}$ metres beneath the centre of the hull. 'I tried to analyse my sensations at that moment. I found that I did not feel particularly thrilled, but only rather tired and starting to get cold.' They surfaced and were nearly sighted. A torch shone down on them. They could see a man walking up and down the fo'c'sle, with a cigarette glowing.

'We got out of the obstructed zone and at last took off our masks; it was very cold; I couldn't prevent my teeth chattering. We stopped again and began distributing our incendiaries after setting the fuses.' They set the fuse going to destroy their 'pig' and sank her. They swam ashore, took off their masks and breathing sets, and their rubber suits, cut them in pieces and buried them under the rocks. They waded ashore having been in the water for more than 8 hours.

The third 'pig', crewed by Gunner Captain Vincenzo Martellotta and Petty Officer Diver Mario Marino, also entered unobserved, although buffeted by the same depth-charges. They could not find the aircraft carrier which was their target (in fact there was no aircraft carrier in the Mediterranean Fleet at that time) but sighted another large warship. They were actually underneath her when Martellotta decided she was only a cruiser and broke off the attack. Finally they set their warhead under a large tanker (*Sagona*) distributed their incendiaries and made their escape. They too sank their craft, destroyed their suits and got ashore.

The submarine *Zaffiro* waited off Rosetta on the Nile delta two nights after the attack, to pick up any crews who escaped. Marceglia and Schergat actually got to Rosetta and stayed at a small inn. Next day, when they were trying to get down to the seashore, they were stopped by police and recognised as Italians. (In one story, the manageress of the small inn was offended by these two guests appearing at every meal in dirty overalls; after they had seemingly ignored her protests, she complained to the police.) Martellotta and Marino were stopped at a check barrier in Alexandria, arrested by Customs officers and turned over to the British military authorities.

All six men were awarded the Gold Medal for bravery, Italy's highest award for valour; by a nice turn of fortune, Captain Morgan who had commanded *Valiant* at the time of the attack, was present at the Investiture in March 1945 and accepted the Crown Prince of Italy's invitation to invest De La Penne with his medal.

Valiant and *Queen Elizabeth* were not sunk but both were too badly damaged to put to sea for some months, although the exact nature of the damage was concealed and shipboard life proceeded as normal, to mislead observers; daily ceremonial, hoisting and lowering of colours, parades and all the visible life of a great warship carried on, to suggest that neither ship was harmed. In fact, the attacks at Alexandria came at a particularly bad time for the Allies. The battleship *Barham* had been sunk by a U-boat the previous month, as had the aircraft carrier *Art Royal*. In the Far East, Japanese bombers and torpedo-planes had just sunk *Prince of Wales* and *Repulse*. The capital ship balance of power had swung markedly in the Axis' favour. In the Mediterranean, the Italian Navy now had an overwhelming superiority. That they made virtually no use of their advantage was not the fault of De La Penne and his crews.

By December 1941, the Japanese had made use of midget submarines as part of their forces for the attack on Pearl Harbour. The Japanese had pressed forward design and development and entered the war with large numbers of their *Ko-Hyoteki*, larger and faster than those of the 1930s. Two young naval officers (the Japanese equivalents of Tesei and Toschi), Lieutenants Naoji Iwasa and Keiu Matsuo, produced plans for using small submarines at the outbreak of a war. Admiral Yamamoto, C-in-C Combined Fleet, the chief architect of the Pearl Harbor plan, made what was in the light of subsequent Japanese tactics a significant objection: there seemed no feasible method of recovering the crews after the operation. But when recovery methods were worked out, Yamamoto reconsidered the idea and eventually it was approved.

The midgets, whose own endurance had been improved to about 16 hours, were taken to the scene of their operations by large orthodox submarines (rather in the Italian style) and launched off the enemy coast. A Special Naval Attack Unit was formed, of midget submarines, each 45-foot long, electrically propelled by batteries. The midgets had a crew of two, and were armed with two torpedoes, fired from tubes.

Five large 'I' class carrier submarines left Kure on 18 November 1941, and dropped their midgets off Pearl Harbor in the early hours of 7 December. The midgets' orders were to penetrate the harbour, fire on targets of opportunity, and rejoin their parent submarines at a rendezvous 7 miles to the west of Lania Island.

The first midget was detected by *Condor*, one of two minesweepers patrolling the entrance. *Condor* sighted a periscope at 3.42 am, summoned the duty destroyer *Ward*, while a Catalina flying-boat dropped smoke floats on the sighting position. *Ward* attacked with gunfire and depth-charges, after a search of some two hours, and sank the midget at 6.45. *Ward* reported this attack but the message was passed only very slowly (or possibly the main base might have been more ready when the air attack developed).

The anti-torpedo net which had been opened for *Condor* and the second minesweeper at 4.58 am remained open, by culpable negligence, until 8.40 am and at least one midget entered Pearl Harbor. At about 8.30 am this midget fired a torpedo at the seaplane tender *Curtiss*, which missed and hit a dock ashore in Pearl City. The destroyer *Monaghan* sighted the midget and prepared to ram. The midget fired its second torpedo, which also missed. *Monaghan* rammed at 8.34 am, passed over the target, returned and sank it with two depth-charges.

A third midget ran aground on a reef to the eastward of the channel, where it was spotted and fired on by the destroyer *Helm* at 8.17 am. It slipped off, submerged, and got away, but it had been damaged and was finally beached on the windward side of Oahu, opposite Bellows Field. Its captain, Ensign Kazuo Sakamaki, was captured. He was the only survivor. All the others (including Naoji Iwasa) were lost. The exact fate of the other two midgets is not known but very probably they were sunk in attacks carried out by *St Louis*, *Blue*, *Ramsay* and *Breese*.

None of the large carrier submarines sank any American ship entering or leaving Pearl Harbor and one of them, *I70*, was sunk by aircraft from *Enterprise* on 10 December. Thus the submarine Advance Expeditionary Force, as it called, lost all 5 midgets and 1 large submarine, and achieved nothing at all.

Matsuo had been disappointed at not being chosen for the Pearl Harbor attack (in which, like his friend Isawa, he would almost certainly have been killed) but he had his desire in the midget attack against Sydney harbour in May 1942. Four midgets were launched on the night of 31 May. They sank one old ferry-boat which was in use as a naval depot ship. They were all themselves sunk and none of the crews survived.

More successful was the attack the previous night in Madagascar. A midget, again carried by a large 'I' class went through the Oranjia Pass, the entrance to the harbour of Diego Suarez, in the northern tip of the island. The attack was made before the harbour could be rigged with nets or proper defences organised. The midget sank an oiler and put its other torpedo into the battleship *Ramillies*, which had to be docked at Durban later for repairs. The crew of two abandoned their craft and got ashore, but were rounded up by Commandos and shot themselves rather than surrender.

On 28 November 1942, during the later struggles by land and sea for the island of Guadalcanal in the Solomons, one midget submarine penetrated the destroyer screening off Lungga Point anchorage, where the transport *Alchiba* was unloading her cargo of petrol, bombs and ammunition, and hit her with one torpedo forward. *Alchiba* caught fire and had to be beached to prevent her sinking. It was 4 days before the fire was finally extinguished. There were reports of Japanese midget submarines at various times during the Guadalcanal campaign, threatening attacks or being used for transporting stores.

In May 1942 the Italians tried to repeat their great *coup* at Alexandria, but the method was not new and the attempt failed. Every action provokes an equal and opposite reaction and the Allied patrols became ever stronger and more numerous. When five swimmers made an attack on 14 September 1942, there were far fewer targets, they were wall anchored much further away, and the roadstead was more intensively patrolled. Only one small steamer was sunk. On 8 December three 'pigs' made another attack. Only one crewman returned. Three were killed and two made prisoners-of-war.

By December 1942, the Allies had landed in north Africa. On the 12th the submarine *Ambra* dispatched three 'pigs' and ten assault swimmers with explosives against Allied shipping in Algiers Bay. One unusual and ingenious device on this operation was a swimmer specially equipped with a telephone, to sight likely targets from the surface and con the submarine in towards them. All three 'pigs' were sunk and their crews captured on shore, and all the assault swimmers were also captured. However, some 20,000 tons of shipping was sunk or badly damaged which, once again, was a fair return for the losses in manpower.

The year 1942 ended with a similar exploit, but this time on the Allied side. The weapon and the training found their inspiration, as so often and in so many different navies, from one man, in this case a Royal Marine, Major J H C 'Blondie' Hasler. From his boyhood, Hasler had loved to mess about in boats and in 1941 he submitted a paper on methods of attacking enemy ships with swimmers and canoes. The paper was rejected but after the Italian success at Alexandria official opinions changed drastically almost overnight. Hasler was summoned to join Combined Operations Development Centre where he supervised the birth of a new unit, formed on 6 July 1942, known as the Royal Marine Boom Patrol Detachment.

As the name suggests, the Detachment were originally to have used Boom Patrol Boats, based on the Italian explosive motor-boat design. But while these were being developed the Marines tried out a number of different craft, canoes, assault boats, and inflatables of various types, including the 'Sleeping Beauty' or Motor Submersible Canoe designed by Quentin Reeves, which was an electrically propelled canoe, crewed by one man wearing protective underwater clothing and breathing gear, so that not much more than the crew's head appeared above water during an attack.

The craft in which Hasler and his Detachment actually went into action was the Folbot Mark II, which Hasler had partly designed himself. It was 16 feet long, $28\frac{1}{2}$ inches in the beam, weighed about 90 pounds, carried two men and about 150 pounds of explosives and equipment. The boat had a flat wooden bottom of $\frac{1}{8}$-inch plywood, with shallow bilge keels or runners, so that it could be dragged across mud or shingle. The sides were of canvas or rubberised fabric. The deck was plywood with rigid gunwales. The folbot was erected by eight hinged struts, and when collapsed, the sides folded in and the deck lay flat on the keel bottom. The crew sat in a central cockpit, covered by a waterproof cover. The crews' anoraks had elastic round the bottom of the tunic which fitted round the cockpit cover to make virtually a watertight seal. The craft, known as 'cockleshells', carried eight magnetic limpet mines.

The chosen objective was Bordeaux, on the river Garonne, at which Axis blockade runners were delivering priceless cargoes of rubber, tin, tungsten, and valuable mineral and vegetable oils for the German and Italian war effort.

Hasler's party started intensive training, using their folbots, at Southsea. A special method of launching the cockleshells was developed using a submarine's gun, with a fitted extension, as a derrick. The folbots would be dropped from a submarine off the Gironde estuary. The Marines would paddle the 70 miles up to Bordeaux, lying up by day, paddling by night. They would fix their limpets to the hulls of blockade runners in harbour and make their escape. They would not be able to return down-river to the submarine but would try to make their way back via the French escape and evasion route organised by the French Resistance.

Hasler first carried out a full-scale exercise in the Thames estuary, which proved a failure in almost every respect. Every single one of the folbots was sighted and none of them came within miles of its target. But, undismayed, and having learned from the lessons of the exercise, Hasler and his party embarked in the submarine *Tuna* on 30 November 1942, with six folbots.

Precise navigation was vital and Lieut Cdr Raikes, *Tuna*'s captain, had his task made much more difficult by an almost featureless coast-line and by the presence of an RAF-laid minefield offshore which could not have been more neatly placed to cause the maximum inconvenience to *Tuna*. But, at last, on 7 December, Raikes was satisfied *Tuna* was exactly in position and gave orders for the folbots to be brought up on deck. One folbot, *Cachalot* (they were all named), was too badly damaged to take part and only five folbots eventually made off, in the loom of German search-lights, looking for *Tuna* who was within German radar range (a calculated risk by Raikes).

The first hazard was a quite unexpectedly fierce tidal race in which *Coalfish* capsized. Her crew, Sergeant Samuel Wallace and Marine Robert Ewart swam ashore and were captured by the Germans who at once began an intense interrogation.

The four remaining folbots paddled on, only to meet an even more violent tidal race in which *Conger* capsized. Her crew, Corporal George Sheard and Marine David Moffat hung onto the gunwales of the others and were taken in tow. But they slowed the others down so much they had to be taken close inshore and dropped. Moffat's body was washed up on the beach 70 miles away long afterwards, but Sheard was never seen again.

There were now only three folbots and one of those, *Cuttlefish*, with Lieutenant Jack Mackinnon, Royal Marines and Marine James Conway were separated from the rest. *Cuttlefish* was holed and sank. Mackinnon and Conway were also captured.

The two folbots went on up river. The two were *Catfish*, with Hasler himself and Marine Ned Sparks, and *Crayfish*, crewed by Corporal Laver and Marine Mills. Both folbots made successful attacks, *Crayfish* on two vessels some way down river from Bordeaux itself, at Bassens South, while Hasler and Sparks succeeded in paddling right up the Garonne and into Bordeaux where, on the night of 11/12 December, they laid all eight mines, dividing them between a cargo ship, a tanker and a small warship.

Afterwards, both crews landed downriver and tried to escape across country. After many adventures, Hasler and Sparks crossed the Pyrenees and eventually reached Gibraltar. But they were the only 'cockleshell heroes' to survive. In his notorious Commando Order, Hitler had ordered all Commandos to be killed or hounded to death. When captured they were not to be given quarter or mercy. Thus, Wallace and Ewart were executed by shooting on the very night Hasler made his attack. Mackinnon, Conway, Laver and Mills were also shot, probably in March 1943.

In the end, the exploit achieved very little. The ex-French ship *Alabama* and the German *Portland*, at Bassens South, the *Dresden* and the *Tannefels*, in Bordeaux, were damaged by the limpets and settled on the bottom. But all were later pumped out and salvaged. The Allies had still not brought off an operation with a strategic value to rank with De La Penne and the other Italians in Alexandria. However, this was to come in 1943.

Above: A Welman craft on launchway with detachable warhead (left) being prepared for fitting. (Royal Navy Submarine Museum)

Below: A 'T' class submarine, with Mk I Chariots and two containers, mounted aft, alongside a depot ship. (Author's Collection)

Above: A British Mark I Chariot being hoisted out for trials. (Imperial War Museum)

Below: German explosive motor-boats found at Flushing, 1945. (Author's Collection)

CHAPTER 9

'Please report what is being done to emulate the exploits of the Italians in Alexandria harbour and similar methods of this kind,' Winston Churchill wrote to the Chiefs of Staff Committee. 'Is there are any reason why we should be incapable of the same kind of scientific aggressive action that the Italians have shown? One would have thought we should have been in the lead. Please state the exact position.'

The exact position, at the time when Churchill wrote that minute in January 1942, was that the Allied Navies were still examining the possibilities in the Italians' human torpedoes. There was no doubt they could have an effect on the war out of all proportion to the resources expended on them. A British 'chariot' was developed from an Italian model recovered in Gibraltar harbour. By April 1942 the first party of 10 charioteers had assembled for training at Fort Blockhouse, the submarine base at Gosport, using a dummy torpedo known as 'Cassidy'. After trials at Horsea, in Portsmouth harbour, an operational training base was set up with the depot ship *Titania* in Loch Erisort, on the island of Lewis in the Outer Hebrides.

The first chariot was ready in June 1942. It was the size of a normal 21-inch torpedo with a detachable head containing 600 pounds of explosive, driven by an electric battery giving a speed of 2.9 knots for 6 hours, with an operational range of about 18 miles. The crew of two sat astride the craft, which dived and surfaced by means of a ballast tank. The forward crewman worked the controls for diving and steering. Both men wore specially designed diving suits.

Throughout that summer the crews trained in the loch, learning how to survive, how to move, and then how to attack with their new weapon, practising diving, surfacing and manoeuvring underwater, graduating to exercises in net-cutting, escape and evasion. In September the whole flotilla moved to Loch Cairnbawn on the mainland, and a full scale attack was made on the new battleship *Howe*. Seven teams of charioteers attacked. Three were judged successful, four charges were laid. One chariot was judged 'destroyed'.

The obvious target for the flotilla was another great warship, the German battleship *Tirpitz*, lying in her Norwegian fastness where, as Churchill said, her mere presence influenced movements of Allied shipping all over the world. She was then at Trondheim, where Bomber Command had made four fruitless attempts to sink her that spring. Albacore torpedo-bombers from the carrier *Victorious* had also tried and failed during one of *Tirpitz*'s rare sorties to sea in March 1942. She could not be reached by other warships or by orthodox submarines. Perhaps the chariots could succeed where more orthodox methods had failed.

The problem of getting the chariots to the target was most ingeniously solved by using the converted Norwegian fishing boat *Arthur*, commanded by the notable Norwegian patriot Leif Larsen. The chariots were to be carried on deck, concealed under a cargo of peat. They would be hoisted out at some time during the approach voyage, and towed submerged to the slipping point.

Arthur was provided with a petrol generator, for charging the chariots' batteries, false papers (made out with the close co-operation of the Norwegian resistance), and a false bulkhead to conceal the charioteers and their equipment. There were six men in the party: Lieutenant W R Brewster RNVR and Able Seaman J Brown, Sergeant D Craig RE, with Able Seaman R Evans, and two dressers, Able Seamen M R Causer and W Tebb.

A successful trial of *Arthur*, the chariots and the gear was carried out against the battleship *Rodney* in mid-October and *Arthur* sailed on her venture on the 26th. She survived engine breakdowns, a defective petrol generator (which was thrown overboard), German examination, inquisitive Norwegian fishermen and by the evening of the 31st was making steady progress towards Trondheim, towing the chariots which had been launched the day before.

After dark that evening, a brisk easterly wind strengthened, kicking up a short, steep sea in the waters of the fjord, and *Arthur* began to pitch and plunge about in an ominous manner. Everybody hoped the storm would blow out, but soon they could hear the jarring noise of the chariots riding up and banging on *Arthur*'s hull. They were then only some 15 miles from the slipping point and the charioteers had actually begun to dress. Just after 10 pm there was what Brewster later called 'a loud, grinding, tearing noise' and *Arthur*'s hull began to shudder, as though the propeller was fouled. Fearing the worst, but still hoping for the best, Larsen put *Arthur* into sheltered water, where Evans went over the side. Both chariots had torn adrift. 'I don't think anyone has ever been so disappointed as we were that night,' said Brewster. 'We were within 10 miles of the pride of the German navy; all our obstacles were behind us; and we might as well have been at the North Pole. Looking back, I don't remember a single curse. We were all too unhappy for that.'

Arthur was still undetected but Brewster and Larsen decided that it was too risky, on *Arthur*'s unreliable engine, to attempt to return. Besides, the peat would have to be somehow sold to obtain the necessary papers. *Arthur* was scuttled and the crew landed in rafts, to set out for the Swedish frontier overland. They all reached the frontier but Evans was shot and captured during a skirmish at the border. Later, after he had recovered from his wound, he was shot as a spy.

In November 1942, a chariot party of 11 officers and 15 ratings went to Malta to operate with the Tenth Submarine Flotilla. Three submarines, *Thunderbolt*, *Trooper* and *P311* were fitted with the external containers to carry chariots. All three sailed early in January 1943 for chariot operations at Palermo in Sicily and La Maddelena in northern Sardinia.

Like the Italians, the Royal Navy had mixed success with chariots. *P311* was sunk (probably mined) on 8 January on the way to the operation at La Maddelena. Ten charioteers – 6 divers and 4 dressers – were lost in her. But by the late evening of 3 January, *Trooper* with three chariots and *Thunderbolt* (whose original objective had been Cagliari in southern Sardinia, changed *en route*) were both off Palermo.

From *Thunderbolt*, Lieutenant Richard Greenland RNVR, and Leading Seaman Alec Ferrier made a perfect chariot attack, penetrating two wire barriers and sinking the new cruiser *Ulpio Traiano*, which was undergoing trials on first commissioning, with their main charge, and also distributing four smaller charges amongst other shipping in the harbour. They then sank their chariot and got ashore, where they were made prisoners. The other chariot from *Thunderbolt*, crewed by Petty Officer Miln and Able Seaman W Simpson, suffered a battery explosion on the run in and went out of control. Simpson was drowned.

From *Trooper*, Sub Lieutenant R G Dove RNVR and Leading Seaman J Freel got inside the harbour and damaged the 8500-ton troop transport *Viminale*. After sinking their chariot, they were taken prisoner. Sub Lieutenant H L H Stevens RNVR and Leading Seaman Carter could not find the harbour, headed back out to sea and were later picked up the submarine *P46*. The third chariot from *Trooper*, crewed by Lieutenant H F Cook RNVR and Able Seaman Worthy, went out of control in rough water and had to be abandoned. Worthy swam ashore and was captured. But Cook was never seen again.

Despite the failures, the chariots had proved remarkably cost-effective. A light cruiser had been sunk and a trooper damaged, for the loss of 2 men, 6 made prisoners-or-war, and the expenditure of 6 chariots. On 18/19 January *Thunderbolt* tried again, this time at Tripoli, with two more chariots, crewed by Lieutenant G W J Larkin RNVR and Petty Officer Cook C L Berey, and Stevens (on his second operation) and Chief ERA S Buxton. Larkin's chariot would not dive properly. A surfaced attack was out of the question. They had been briefed to stay undetected, so as not to prejudice any remaining chariot attacks. They therefore set their chariot going straight out to sea, with its charge timed to explode later, while they took off their suits and sank them. Both men were eventually liberated by advancing Allied troops near Tripoli.

Stevens and Buxton also abandoned and sank their chariot. Ashore they were first imprisoned, and then released after the Italian armistice. Finally they were given sanctuary in the Vatican City until July 1944.

On 21 June 1944, there was a chariot attack on the heavy cruisers *Bolzano* and *Gorizia* at the Tenth Light Flotilla's old base at La Spezia. Through an irony of war, the operation was carried out jointly with the Italians. The Italian destroyer *Grecale* carried the attackers to the scene and three Italian Gamma Group swimmers also joined in the attack. There were two chariots, crewed by Causer (now promoted to Sub Lieutenant RNVR) and Able Seaman Harry Smith, and Berey (on his second operation) and Stoker Ken Lawrence.

MTB74 took the chariots in to within 3 miles of the harbour entrance. Her stern had been specially modified for launching chariots and both got away successfully. Berey's chariot had an air leak in its ballast chamber which made depth-keeping impossible and the attack had to be abandoned. But Causer and Smith penetrated the harbour and got underneath *Bolzano*. By 4.30 am they had fixed their charge securely. 'Having exchanged the "thumbs up" with a fair degree of swagger about the gesture, I turned the handle of the time-fuse setting until I felt two distinct clicks,' said Causer. 'Two clicks, two hours – so the balloon should go up as near as damn it at 0630.'

The balloon duly did go up and *Bolzano* sank alongside, becoming a total loss. The charioteers hoped to be picked up at a rendezvous the following evening but were unable to get clear of the harbour. They sank the chariot, cut up and dumped their suits. Later they met Berey and Lawrence and all four spent some weeks with the Italian partisans. Berey succeeded in crossing the enemy lines and rejoining British forces on the river Arno on 10 August. Lawrence was wounded by a German hand-grenade and captured. Causer and

Smith tried to cross next day, but were both captured.

The Italians had carried on with their own chariot operations almost to the day of the Armistice. They abandoned attempts to get inside Gibraltar harbour and concentrated instead upon shipping anchored in the roads outside. In two attacks, on 8 May and 3/4 August 1943 they sank another 50,000 tons of shipping. Attacks wera also made on Allied ships in the Turkish ports of Alexandretta and Mersina. When the war ended for the Italians in September 1943 they were planning further attacks at Gibraltar, and one at Freetown, Sierra Leone, with a midget submarine attack on New York in October. With the naval war in the Mediterranean almost at an end, attention turned to the Far East. The depot ship *Wolfe*, sailed for Trincomalee in May 1944, with improved Mark II chariots on board. The new models were faster, at $4\frac{1}{2}$ knots, had a longer range, of 30 miles, and an enlarged warhead of 1100 pounds. Seven chariot teams began training in the tropical waters of Trincomalee.

The only chariot operation in the Far East was a complete success and was the only occasion when all the charioteers were recovered. Two chariots, crewed by Sub Lieutenant A Eldridge RNVR and Petty Officer S Woollcott, and Petty Officer W S Smith and Steward A Brown, were dropped off the harbour of Phuket Island, on the west coast of Malaya by the submarine *Trenchant* on 27 October 1944. Their targets were (Eldridge) the 5000-ton merchantman *Sumatra*, which had recently been refloated and was about to be towed to Singapore, and (Smith) another merchantman, the 5272-ton *Volpi*, which was partly submerged, further in the harbour, and also being salved. Both chariots reached their targets, laid their charges and retreated out to sea, where the crews were picked up by *Trenchant* and the chariots sunk. Both charges exploded, destroying their targets, in due course. With *Sumatra* and *Volpi*, charioteering in World War Two came to an end.

One evening in October 1943 the Admiralty released a communique announcing 'a very gallant enterprise': *Tirpitz* had been badly damaged by midget submarines in her protected anchorage in a fjord in northern Norway.

This was the first time the existence of these weapons had been made public, but their design history went back some years. In the 1930s Commander Cromwell Varley, who had been a submarine officer in the 1914–18 war, experimented with midget submarines as a private venture. In 1940, when the energetic and forceful Admiral Sir Max Horton, then Admiral Submarines, heard that Varley was building a midget on the River Hamble, he went to see him and was immediately impressed with the potential of the weapon (which in many ways resembled with his own inventions before the war). The

159

project was given official sponsorship, design facilities and finance. In 1941 the first naval personnel were appointed.

The first midget submarine was launched on the Hamble River at 11 pm on 15 March 1942 and made her first dive on the 24th. She was called *X3* (because *X1* was a large cruiser-submarine of 3500 tons commissioned in 1929, and *X2* was the designation given to the Italian submarine *Galileo Galilei* which surrendered earlier in the war). The first volunteers for service in X-craft, as they were called, reported for training in May 1942. A training base was set up at Port Bannatyne, on the island of Bute, and *X3* herself travelled up to Scotland by train, in August. Another training base was established, using *X3* as training 'horse' at Loch Striven. In November a second prototype, *X4*, arrived. Six operational X-craft, built at Vickers in Barrow and numbered from 5 to 10 arrived at intervals in the early months of 1943. In April a special flotilla was formed, called the Twelfth Submarine Squadron in combination with the charioteers, with the depot ship *Bonaventure* in Loch Cairnbawn.

The X-craft were not chariots or converted torpedoes. Though very small, they were true submarines, 51 feet in length, weighing about 35 tons, with a full diving depth of 300 feet and an operational range of 1500 miles. They had a diesel engine for surface propulsion and batteries giving a maximum dived speed of about 5 knots. They had all the normal submarine equipment of hydroplanes, periscopes and compasses, with a special compartment, known as the 'wet and dry', which could be flooded and drained down to enable a diver to leave and rejoin the X-craft while dived. They had a crew first of three and then, after a fatal accident in a net-cutting exercise, four, with a specialist diver as net-cutter, usually drawn from the ranks of ex-charioteers. Each X-craft had two side-charges, one on each side, containing 2 tons of explosives, which could be detached from inside the X-craft whilst under the target.

Trials showed that the best way of getting the X-craft to their target areas was by towing them, while dived, by an orthodox submarine on the surface. The operational crew travelled in the parent submarine, whilst a 'passage crew' manned the X-craft during the tow. The two crews changed over on the eve of the attack.

The Twelfth Submarine Squadron trained hard through the summer of 1943, just as the charioteers had done the year before. Their target, as it had been for the charioteers, was still *Tirpitz*, now moved further north to Kaa Fjord, the furthest inland stretch of water in Alten Fjord, but still by her very presence throwing an ominous shadow across the convoy route to Russia and the North Atlantic as a whole. After a short trip to sea in September 1943, for a somewhat futile bombardment of shore installations at Spitzbergen,

Tirpitz returned to Kaa Fjord where photo-reconnaissance revealed her on 10 September.

The first towing submarine, *Truculent*, with *X6*, left Loch Cairnbawn at 4 pm on 11 September 1943. *Syrtis*, with *X9*, *Seanymph*, with *X8*, and *Stubborn* with *X7* left at 2-hourly intervals. *Sceptre*, with *X10*, sailed at 1 pm the next day. The X-craft were towed dived, surfacing to ventilate for 15 minutes every 6 hours. All the submarines were to make their way independently to a position 75 miles off the Shetlands and then to proceed on a parallel course, 20 miles apart, until they reached a point some 150 miles west of Alten Fjord. From there they would head for their various landfalls.

After photo-reconnaissance on the 14th had shown the latest positions of the German heavy warships, the X-craft were allocated targets as follows: *X5*, *X6*, and *X7*, would attack *Tirpitz*, in Kaa Fjord; *X9* and *X10*, the battlecruiser *Scharnhorst*, also in Kaa Fjord; and *X8*, *Lutzow*, in nearby Lange Fjord. All three capital ships were protected by a formidable array of nets, booms and patrols.

Passage to the Norwegian coast was full of incident. *X9* dived early in the morning of the 16th, when her tow-line parted almost immediately. It was some time before the break was discovered in *Syrtis*, who retraced her course to search. But nothing more was ever seen of *X9* and she was lost with all hands. Meanwhile, *X8* had been having difficulties with her tow-line and with her side cargoes, both of which leaked destroying the X-craft's stability. Her crew were eventually taken off on the evening of the 17th and *X8* was scuttled. Her charges, exploding unpleasantly near and with unexpected violence, did considerable damage to *X8* and also to *Syrtis*.

By dawn on 20 September the four remaining X-craft were all in their slipping areas, with their operational crews embarked. *Stubborn* and *X7* had had problems with the tow during the night. Just after 1 am Lieutenant Godfrey Place RN, the operational CO, had to get out on the casing and clear a mine mooring cable entangled in *X7*'s bows. It had one horn ominously broken, but Place successfully kicked it away. 'When I got below', he said, 'I thought a tot wouldn't do us any harm so we toasted the Geneva Convention and Minerva – the mine with the crumpled horn'.

Stubborn slipped *X7* at 8 pm that evening. By 2.30 am Place had identified Stjernsund, leading to Alten Fjord, and at 12.30 pm on the 21st *X7* entered Alten Fjord itself. Place surfaced at 7.45 pm to repair defects to the engine exhaust system and to charge up the battery. The charge was broken at 1 am on the 22nd and *X7* dived to make her way in to Kaa Fjord. At about 4 am Place sighted the gap in the anti-submarine nets in the fjord entrance. A minesweeper was luckily just coming out, so Place took *X7* in, at a depth of 40 feet. At periscope depth inside, *X7* ran into the anti-torpedo net which was *Tirpitz*'s close protection. It was made of thin wire, two thicknesses, of close mesh, and could be easily seen through the periscope in the clear water. 'It appeared', said Place, 'as the most formidable-looking underwater defence I had seen.'

For a time *X7* stuck in the net, but by thrashing to and fro, flooding and blowing main ballast tanks, and by going full astern and then full ahead, *X7* at last broke free, and sank to the bottom like a stone, about 2 tons heavy. Place first saw *Tirpitz* at about 6.40 am, range about a mile. 'My intention for the attack was to go deep at a range of 500 yards, pass under the anti-torpedo nets at 70 feet and run down the length of the target from bow to stern, letting go one charge under the bridge, the other well aft and altering to port to escape under the nets on the *Tirpitz*'s starboard side.'

But at 7.05 *X7* stuck first in the net at a depth of 70 feet and again when Place tried at 90 feet. At last, *X7* seemed to break clear and rose to the surface. 'I saw we were inside the close-net defences (how we got underneath I have no idea) about 30 yards from the *Tirpitz*'s port beam'.

'We actually hit the target's side obliquely at 20 feet and slid underneath, swinging our fore-and-aft line to the line of her keel. The first charge was let go – as I estimated, under the *Tirpitz*'s bridge – and *X7* was taken about 200 feet astern to drop the other charge under the after turrets. The time was 0720.' *X7* crossed under *Tirpitz*'s hull to the starboard side where Place tried for nearly $\frac{1}{4}$ of an hour to find a way out of the net.

He was still trying when at 8.12 the charges exploded – 'a continuous roar that seemed to last whole minutes'. *X7* lay on the bottom while Place considered their situation. Many gauges and instruments were broken. No pumps would work. There was hardly any compressed air left. *X7* surfaced, when her night periscope was hit by gunfire from *Tirpitz*, and sank to the bottom again.

The next time *X7* surfaced Place decided to abandon her. This time, *X7* fetched up beside a battle practice target about 500 yards from *Tirpitz*'s starboard side. Place stepped out on the target and began to wave a white sweater. Unfortunately, a small amount of water entered *X7*'s open hatch, just enough to sink her, taking the rest of her crew with her. Sub Lieutenant R Aitken RNVR escaped from the flooded submarine, semi-conscious, about an hour later. But Lieutenant L B Whittam RNVR and ERA W M Whitley were both drowned.

Place was taken on board *Tirpitz* feeling 'ridiculous walking on to the quarterdeck of a Fleet flagship wearing vest, pants, sea-boot stockings and army boots size twelve. When I was told that I would be shot if I did not state where I had laid my mines (this much, at least, they now knew by surmise) I stated I was an English naval officer and as such demanded the courtesy entitled to my rank.'

On board *Tirpitz*, Place joined Cameron and his crew who had already been captured. Lieutenant Donald Cameron RNR, the operational CO of *X6*, who had been one of the first men to serve in X-craft from the very early days, had had problems with a flooded periscope and a defective hoisting motor. Almost blind while dived, Cameron had taken the risk of following a small coasting vessel through the Kaa Fjord anti-submarine net on the surface. The gamble succeeded, and Cameron was equally lucky in finding a gap through the close anti-torpedo net. At about 7.12 am *X6* surfaced close alongside *Tirpitz*, too close for any of the battleship's gun to bear on her, but under intense rifle and machine-gun fire from the crew on deck.

Cameron decided to manoeuvre *X6* alongside *Tirpitz* and jettison both charges abreast 'B' turret. The crew destroyed secret papers, opened the kingston valves to scuttle the submarine and stepped out on to the casing, where a German picket-boat was actually trying to take *X6* in tow. But *X6* sank and Cameron and his crew were taken on board *Tirpitz*.

X5 was last sighted on the evening of the 20th, when Place exchanged shouts of good luck with her captain, Lieutenant H Henty-Creer RNVR. The subsequent fate of *X5* is not known but at 8.43 am on the 22nd a submarine, almost certainly *X5*, was sighted from *Tirpitz*, about 650 yards away, broad on the starboard bow, and close in to the shoreline. Heavy and light AA guns opened fire and some hits were claimed, before the submarine sank. Neither Henty-Creer nor his crew survived.

X10 had been plagued with defects of various kinds throughout her journey. Her crew were trying to make some of them good on the morning of the 22nd when they heard the side-charges exploding. Her operational CO Lieutenant K R Hudspeth RANVR, decided that it would be suicidal to go on against a thoroughly alerted enemy. The charges were set to safe and jettisoned, while *X10* withdrew to sea. Later, it transpired that *Scharnhorst*, *X10*'s target, was not in her berth, having gone to sea for gunnery exercises the day before. *X10* met *Stubborn* at a rendezvous off the coast in the early hours of the 28th and was taken in tow. Because of bad weather, the passage crew could not embark until the 29th. But with a gale forecast in the offing, *Stubborn* recovered the passage crew, let go the tow and *X10* was scuttled, on the orders of Admiral Submarines, at 8.45 on 3 October.

Tirpitz was very badly damaged. Her hull was split, the port rudder put out of action and the propeller shafts jammed. 'A' and 'X'

163

turrets jumped off their roller paths, much machinery was put out of action and there was no power for pumping or starting machinery for some time. The German naval staff decided on 25 September that *Tirpitz* could be repaired in a northern port but it was possible she might never again be operationally fully efficient. For the loss of 6 X-craft, the deaths of 2 complete crews and 2 men of *X7*, with 6 more made prisoners-of-war, the Allies had won a tremendous and far-reaching strategic victory. Place and Cameron were both awarded the Victoria Cross.

While the X-craft attack on *Tirpitz* has rightly become one of the naval legends of the Second World War, a very similar exploit in the same waters which demanded a great deal of its participants has lapsed into total oblivion. With X-craft and chariots, the Admiralty also developed a third design of small submersible. It was a one-man submarine, called the Welman after its designer Colonel Welman, developed and built under the auspices of the Inter-Services Research Bureau. The Welman was a true submersible, like the X-craft, with after hydroplanes, controls for steering and diving, a compass, and a detachable warhead. The Welmans were built at Welwyn Garden City and their drivers, British and Norwegian, trained with the Twelfth Submarine Squadron.

Originally the Welmans were intended to be used by Combined Operations for surveys of beach gradients and obstacles but they were later found to be unsuitable and were trained instead for harbour penetration. They had no net-cutting apparatus, relying on the skill of the driver and the manoeuvrability of the Welman to surmount obstacles.

Early in November 1943, preparations were made for six Welmans, driven by three British and three Norwegian officers, to attack shipping in Bergen, being carried to the launching position by MTBs. One MTB was unserviceable and in the end only four Welmans, driven by Lieutenant J F L Holmes RN, Lieutenant B M Harris RNVR, Lieutenant C A Johnson RN, and Second Lieutenant Pedersen of the Norwegian Army, left their base at Lunna Voe on 20 November in two MTBs and were dropped off the entrance to Solviksund, near Bergen, in the early hours of the 21st. By dawn the Welmans had reached a small bay, which was a summer resort normally deserted in winter, where they intended to lie up during the daytime.

Next day, to their consternation, the Welman drivers found the bay crammed with Norwegian fishermen, some of whom were curious enough to come over and inquire about the Welmans. Trusting to the patriotism of these fishermen, the Welman drivers decided to go on with their attack. They had little intelligence on targets inside Bergen and would have to attack any ships or docks they saw. Afterwards, they were to withdraw north of Bergen, scuttle their craft and walk overland to an appointed rendezvous, where an MTB was expected to pick them up.

The first Welman, driven by Pedersen, set off at about 6 pm followed at 15-minute intervals by the others. After 3 miles, when approaching Bergen, Pedersen's Welman fouled an unexpected net. Powerful search-lights were switched on and the Welman was damaged by fire from a patrol-boat. Pedersen tried to scuttle his craft but was captured, with his Welman, by the enemy. Meanwhile, the other three drivers tried to follow but were forced to dive again and again by the search-lights. All three eventually abandoned their attacks, scuttled their Welmans, and met at the rendezvous ashore. They spent some months with the Norwegian resistance and were finally picked up by an MTB on 5 February 1944. Pedersen survived interrogation by the Gestapo and finished the war as an ordinary prisoner-of-war.

But where the Welmans failed, an X-craft succeeded in the following year. Twelve new X-craft were delivered early in 1944, 6 training boats numbered *XT1* to *XT6*, and 6 operational, numbered *X20* to *X25*. In January preparations began for an attack on the Laksevaag floating dock, in Bergen. Originally, *X22* was to have made the attack but she was rammed and sunk with all her hands by her towing submarine *Syrtis* during a gale. The operation was taken over by *X24*, who left Loch Cairnbawn in tow of *Sceptre* on 9 April 1944, bound for Burra Forth in the Shetlands, where the operational crew under Lieutenant Max Shean RANVR, took over.

The submarines sailed on 11 April, *Sceptre* dropping *X24* in position on the night of the 13th/14th. Shean managed to run *X24* for some 25 miles on the surface up the fjord until he was forced to dive. There was a good deal of enemy shipping about, including one patrol-vessel, using her asdic, who actually had *X24* in contact for a time before Shean evaded her. By 7.45 am *X24* was inside Bergen harbour and Shean could see the floating dock, although she was indistinct in morning haze and partly obscured by a large merchantman beside her.

After one careful run, to check the position and length of the target, *X24* approached again and shortly after 9 am successfully laid her two charges. *X24* then withdrew, back up the fjord without being molested and was picked up again by *Sceptre* that night.

Shean had made an excellent, painstaking attack. Unfortunately he had mistaken his target and sunk the 7500-ton *Barenfels*, the merchantman which had been obscuring the floating dock. The job had to be done again, this time with a new captain, Lieutenant H P

165

Westmacott RN. Once again the towing submarine was *Sceptre*, who left Loch Cairnbawn with *X24* on the afternoon of 3 September, the fifth anniversary of the outbreak of war.

The two submarines reached Balta Sound in the Shetlands, where the operational crew took over, and sailed again on the 7th. The weather was atrocious, blowing a near full gale, and next day Sub Lieutenant D N Purdy RNZNVR was washed overboard and lost. He was replaced by Sub Lieutenant K St J J V Robinson RNVR, but the weather was so bad that the transfer could not be made until the next day.

The tow was slipped at 8pm on 10 September 1944. Although there was still a great deal of traffic in the water way and a bright moon overhead, Westmacott brought *X24* safely and unobserved to Puddefjord, in Bergen harbour, where he picked out the floating dock shortly after 7 am that morning. He also saw the mast of *Barenfels*, sticking out of the water, with the notice 'Langsam Fahren' (Go Slow) posted on it.

Westmacott released the port charge at 8.40 and the starboard 10 minutes later, and made his escape. After this model attack, which blew up both the dock and a small merchantman beside it, *X24* rejoined *Sceptre* at about 9 pm that evening.

Although various targets were talked about, *X24*'s was the last attack by an X-craft in an European harbour. The X-crafts' attention, like the charioteers' before them, now turned to the Far East.

The attack on *Tirpitz* had the same stimulating effect upon the German Navy as the attacks on *Queen Elizabeth* and *Valiant* had had on the Royal Navy. For the first time, the Kriegsmarine began to give serious attention to the possibilities in these small specialised assault craft and in January 1944 the first Commando unit was formed of the *Kleinkampfmittelverband*, literally 'small battle weapon force', known colloquially as the K-Force. They were not a suicide force but, as Admiral Helmuth Heye their commander later wrote, 'aimed at the ideal of "Nelson's band of brothers".' This, he added, was 'a concept that was not so easy to achieve in the last phase of the war when suitable leaders were at a premium and operational conditions increasingly severe'.

Time was always against the German K-Force. The Kriegsmarine had virtually no experience of these weapons. There had been preliminary consultations with the Italian Navy in the summer of 1942, but little had come of them, and the Germans knew nothing of their Japanese allies' experience. Dönitz gave Heye authority to approach manufacturers direct, and bypass the official naval procurements bureaucracy, but even so the weapons had to be designed from scratch and in haste, pressed into operational service without proper trials or development, and manned by crews who might have been brave and dedicated but were only part-trained.

'Our first intention,' said Heye, 'was to design and build midget submarines on the English pattern, for penetrating into enemy harbours and other special operations; also to train assault troops, which could be sent in small vessels and submarines to attack important points on the enemy coast, such as radar stations and gun-emplacements.' The first weapon was a one-man torpedo, code-named Neger ('Nigger'). It had a battery-propelled body, with a torpedo slung underneath it. It weighed, with the torpedo, 2.8 tons, had a maximum speed of $2\frac{1}{2}$ knots, and a range of 35 miles. It travelled awash, with the driver, wearing a special diving suit, looking out through a plexi-glass dome over his head. Later models, code-named Marder ('Marten'), were fitted with a small diving tank to make them capable of submerging to a depth of 30 metres. There was no suitable compass for the craft and the driver wore a wrist-compass. He also ran the considerable risk of asphyxiation from carbon dioxide, and special potash absorbent was provided.

The first 40 Neger were rushed across Europe by train to attack the Allied ships off Anzio. At dusk on 20 April 1944, 23 Neger were launched on their first mission. They had a journey of 18 miles (the nearest German-held suitable launching place to the Allied anchorage at Nettuno), which was not only long but dangerous. Several Neger grounded on shoals. Alerted by Allied intelligence, the anchorage defences were ready. Four Neger were sunk by depth-charges or gunfire. One was captured intact by the Allies, its driver dead under his dome, of carbon dioxide poisoning. Another was recovered by German troops, with its suffocated driver still inside. A handful of drivers abandoned their craft and made their way back, arriving over a period of several days. One driver, Midshipman Potthast, fired his torpedo at a patrol vessel but it probably detonated astern of its target. Potthast made his way back from behind Allied lines. No Allied vessels were sunk or damaged, and the existence of the Neger had been revealed.

Much more successful off Anzio than any midget craft were radio-controlled glider bombs, developed from weapons the Germans had first used off Salerno. The Allies had fitted ships with jamming equipment on the weapons' wave-lengths. In spite of this, a glider bomb hit and sank the light cruiser *Spartan* on 29 January, and a Liberty ship was also blown up and sunk.

In June 1944 the surviving Neger were once again transported across Europe by train, subjected to almost ceaseless air-raids, to Paris and thence to a small summer resort, Villers-sur-Mer, on the bay of the Seine, south of Tourville, where a base was set up hidden

167

in a wood. Special wooden runways were built by the sea, to launch the weapons quickly. The crews looked forward to attacking the great Allied armada lying off the invasion beaches of Normandy.

The first sortie, of 26 weapons, including the improved Marder, was on 5 July. Nine Marder were sunk by the guns of the protective screen of ships on the eastern edge of the beach assault area, and only 14 returned to base. They sank the minesweepers *Cato* and *Magic*. Two days later, another 21 Marder set out, but they were all destroyed by depth-charges, aircraft or gunfire. The exceptional Midshipman Potthast attacked several warships crossing his course. 'They appeared to be in quarter-line formation and I steered to attack the rear ship, which seemed larger than the others and had evidently slowed down to permit a redeployment of escorts. I was rapidly closing in on this ship; when the range was a bare 300 yards I pulled the firing lever, then turned the Neger hard round. It seemed ages before an explosion rent the air, and in that moment my Neger was almost hurled out of the water. A sheet of flame shot upwards from the stricken ship. Almost at once I was enveloped in thick smoke and I lost all sense of direction.'

After depth-charging, Potthast was run down by a corvette. 'Instinctively I tried to duck as the bullets rained on the Neger, shattering the dome and bringing the motor to a stop. Blood was pouring down my arm and I collapsed.' He was picked up and became a prisoner-of-war. His target had been the old cruiser *Dragon*, manned by the Polish Navy. She was so badly damaged she was later sunk as an extra block-ship off the coast. Another Marder sank the minesweeper *Pylades* the same night.

At the end of July, a K-Flotilla No 211 reached Seine Bay, equipped with a new weapon, the Linse ('Lentil'). These were 30-knot motor-boats which operated in units of three, with one control-boat, containing the unit commander and two control operators, following close behind two explosive-boats which each had one driver on board. When the explosive-boats neared their targets, the drivers jumped overboard, leaving the control operators following to con the boat into its target. The explosive-boat had a 600-pound main charge and a second charge in the bows which exploded on impact, sinking the boat. After a 7-second delay by which time the boat had sunk beneath its target, the main charge exploded. Clearly it was a device which showed its Italian origins.

The flotilla had 32 explosive- and 16 control-boats. After a serious premature explosion in harbour which delayed an operation for 29 July, the Linsen were ready for their first attack on the night of 2/3 August, with 20 explosive- and 12 control-boats. They also carried a number of airtight plexi-glass domes, with human heads painted inside them, to distribute about the anchorage and suggest a simultaneous Marder attack. (If pursued, some later designs of Linsen could also release a cloaking cloud of artificial fog, to cover their escape.)

But none of these ruses was of much avail that night. The Linsen were as roughly handled as the Marder had been. All the explosive-boats were destroyed and only 10 of the control-boats returned. However, they sank the destroyer *Quorn*, the trawler *Gairsay* and 1 Landing Craft (Gun), and damaged 2 transports. According to the Germans, Marder were never used in conjunction with Linsen. In the British accounts, 40 Marder were destroyed that night.

A second Linse attack, with 16 explosives and 12 controls, took place on the night of 8/9 August. All the explosive-boats, and 4 of the controls, were destroyed. On two nights afterwards, the Germans fired long-range pattern-running Dackel ('Dachshund') torpedoes into the anchorage. These had an initial straight-running range of 27,000 metres and could then run on for another 30,000 metres at a speed of 9 knots. If fired from Le Havre they could reach the Allied invasion beaches off the Orne and the naval bombarding ships off Courseulles, which were 18 and 24 miles away. These torpedoes damaged the old cruiser *Frobisher*, the repair ship *Albatross*, a minesweeper and a 5205-ton transport. The last Marder attack off Normandy was on the night of 16/17 August, by no less than 42 Marder. They sank a Landing Craft (Flak) but only 16 of them returned. Two attacked the old French battleship *Courbet*, one of the harbour blockships, without doing any damage.

The Marder, Linsen, and long-range Dackel certainly kept the Allied anchorage patrols alert, but it seemed that the results were hardly worth the effort. The German Navy, however, decided they were and when the Allied advance made further operations off the French coast impossible, the K-Force weapons were moved up to Holland. In the meantime, they were used against Allied shipping taking part in Operation Dragoon, the invasion of the south of France.

On the night of 4/5 September 1944, 4 out of 5 attacking Marder were sunk. Ten more Marder were lost on the 10th. On 26 September a new weapon appeared, the midget one-man submarine Molch ('Salamander'). Designed for submerged travel only, with batteries and electric motor, the Molch weighed $10\frac{1}{2}$ tons, was 35 feet long, could dive to 40 metres, and had a range of 43 miles at 5 knots. The weapons were two underslung torpedoes. Ten Molche were used in the first attack and only 2 returned. None of these craft had the slightest effect on Dragoon, but in December they were used again. Nine Marder were destroyed on the 19th and another 5 on 1 January 1945.

Below the Belt

From about September 1944 almost until the very end of the war in Europe, K-Force commandos, raiding parties and frogmen, using small ex-Italian one-man and two-man craft and occasionally even collapsible canoes, carried out raids on Zara, Ancona, and Split. They achieved little, and the K-Force themselves suffered serious setbacks. Three submarines, *Grongo*, *Morena* and *Sparide*, all specially converted to transport midgets, were all destroyed in an air raid on 4 September 1944. K-Force personnel were lost in several heavy air raids on their base at Pola in 1945. However, they attacked and damaged a French destroyer, *Trombe*, on 17 April 1945 and on the 24th carried out what was almost a suicide raid on Leghorn; only 2 out of 17 craft returned. But an air raid on the same day on their base at Brioni Island, in the entrance to Pola, destroyed virtually all their remaining craft and their war came to an end.

At the end of 1944, the Germans moved numbers of special assault craft to bases to Holland to operate against Allied shipping off the Dutch coast and especially against the mass of shipping passing to and from the great port of Antwerp. By 20 January 1945, their strength was 87 Linsen, 30 Molche (with another 120 Molche in reserve inland), 20 Biber, and 26 Seehunde.

The Biber ('Beaver') and Seehund ('Seal') were new weapons. The Biber was, as Admiral Neye said, a weapon born of active service experience. The first trials were held in March 1944, and a total of 324 were eventually built. It was a one-man midget submarine, $28\frac{1}{2}$ feet long, 3 feet in the beam, weighing 6 tons. For surface running, it had a Opel $2\frac{1}{2}$ litre petrol engine, giving about 7 knots for 13 hours. Dived, on batteries and electric motor, it could make as much as 6 knots, for $1\frac{1}{2}$ hours. It could carry two underslung torpedoes, or two mines. The first flotilla of them, No 261, arrived at Fécamp late in August 1944, and 18 Biber made a sortie on 29 August. They sank 2 ships that night, before being withdrawn to a base at Rotterdam, for operations in the New Year.

The Seehund was a two-man midget submarine, handy, quick-diving, the best and most successful special assault craft the German Navy built. Known also as U-boat Type XXVIIB, it superseded the unsuccessful Hecht ('Pike'), U-boat Type XXVII. It was 30 feet long, weighed 15 tons. For the surface, it had a Büssing 6-cylinder truck engine, giving 8 knots for 15 hours, or 5 knots for 54 hours. Dived, it could make 5 knots for 4 hours. Maximum diving depth was 50 metres. Some 250 Seehunde were built, first training starting at a base at Neustadt in the Baltic in September 1944.

Eighteen Seehunde made their first sortie on 1 January 1945 to attack convoys along the Belgian coast. They sank 1 trawler, for heavy losses amongst themselves. Escorts were known to sink 2

170

Seehunde but only 2 of the 18 returned to their base at Ijmuiden. The rest were stranded in heavy weather, or the crews died of cold or suffocation.

But the Seehunde improved with practice. Later in the year they began to patrol as far as the Kentish Coast and occasionally up the East Coast towards the Wash. On 22 and 24 February 1945, Seehunde sank *LST364*, the small cable ship *Alert* and, the Free French destroyer *La Combattante*.

This last success, by Sub Lieutenant Klaus Sparbrodt and Engineer Gunter Janke, was carried out at unusually long range. 'Estimating the range at 600 yards,' said Sparbrodt, 'I ordered "Port torpedo − fire!" and Janke pulled the lever; from the side of the Seehund came a scream and a roar as the torpedo revved up and sped on its way. Starting the stop-watch, I put the rudder hard-a-starboard, intending to turn through a complete circle and return to the same attacking position: 50, 60, 70 seconds elapsed with no detonation. I thought the torpedo had missed. However, I was determined to get off the second one. At last after 80 seconds there sounded through the water a sudden sharp crack − nothing more. This told me that the running range of the torpedo had been 850 yards.'

Meanwhile a Biber attack on Russian warships in Wajenga Bay, Murmansk had been planned for 8 January 1945. Six Biber were transported on the casings of three U-boats as far as the North Cape, before defects in the Biber caused the operation to be cancelled. But between December 1944 and February 1945, Biber made 110 sorties from Rotterdam. In this period Seehunde and E-boats sank 7 ships of 13,000 tons. But the Biber, Molche and Linsen sank nothing at all, and 14 Seehunde, 16 Biber and Molche and 10 Linsen were sunk.

But the Germans did not lose faith in the weapons. Their numbers were actually increased and the Seehunde made sortie after sortie in March. A Beaufighter sank one on the 10th, a frigate two more on the 11th and 13th, and others were dispatched by MLs and the corvette *Puffin*. The Seehunde did pick off the odd ship: the 2878-ton *Taber Park* on the 13th, the 1500-ton *Newlands* on the 26th and the 833-ton *Jim* on the 30th, in the East Coast waters between North Foreland and Orfordness. It was a determined effort by the Seehunde and only complete air superiority and alert escorts kept the losses down.

The K-Force suffered a major disaster on the night of 11/12 March, in the estuary of the Scheldte. Every available craft was thrown into action against Allied shipping but 13 Biber, 9 Molche and 16 Linsen were sunk. Not one Allied ship was hit. In the final analysis, between January and May 1945, Seehunde made 142 sorties, and lost 35 of their number. Their torpedoes sank 9 ships of 18,500 tons, and damaged 3 of 18,500 tons. Biber and Molche made 102 sorties, for casualties of 70 lost. Their mines sank 7 small ships, of under 500 tons, and damaged 2 of 15,000 tons. Linsen made 171 sorties and 54 of the Linsen were sunk. They themselves sank nothing at all.

Ironically, the last Seehunde sorties of the war, in April 1945, were with 'Butter torpedoes' − external cargoes of edible fats and other food for the beleaguered German garrison at Dunkirk. They also brought back the 'Seehund Post' − letters from the garrison to their families in Germany. Several Seehunde were lost in these missions.

By the end of the war in Europe, improved versions of the Biber and the Seehunde, with closed-cycle diesel engines, were under development. A prototype was actually built of the Seeteufel ('Sea Devil') a name and a weapon which would have delighted Jules Verne. It was a two-man midget submarine which could also crawl out on land on caterpillar tracks. It had two torpedoes for its *per mare* role; *per terram* it had a machine-gun and a flame-thrower.

A prototype was also built of the Schwertwal ('Grampus'), which was a miniature submarine powered by a 500 hp turbine driven by a Walter closed-cycle engine using hydrogen peroxide as fuel, and designed to achieve underwater speeds of 28 knots. German midget submarine design was moving towards the development of an Otto engine for the surface and Walter engine for underwater.

Then there were the grosse and kleine Delphine ('Big and Little Dolphins') The grosse Delphin had an Otto engine, two torpedoes or mines. The kleine Delphin was really a midget submarine bomb, carrying more than a ton of explosive, which the driver steered and set on its way to the target, before ejecting himself to safety, exactly as Herbert had envisioned for his Devastator. Both Delphine were lightly built, with no diving tanks. They were intended as 'underwater aircraft' ie they submerged, surfaced and changed depth by the pressure of water passing over the surfaces of their hydroplanes, and not by changing the submarine's bodily weight by pumping or flooding water to achieve positive or negative buoyancy.

A small speed-boat called the Wal ('Whale') reached line production. With a crew of four, it carried two torpedoes, two rocket projectors and a machine-gun, and was driven by a 600 hp engine. Sachsenberg, Tietgen and Zisch were three types of hydrofoil boats, carrying torpedoes or explosive at speeds of up to 55 knots. A variation was the Driesen Sea Kite which had two Hydra speed-boats, coupled by an aerofoil wing surface and powered by a turbo-jet. These were intended to spring out at enemy ships, fire their four torpedoes each, turn and disappear at very high speed.

Finally there was the simple Schlitten ('Sledge') consisting of four pressed steel 'skimming dishes' welded together, easy to mass-produce, with a 600 hp engine on a hydrofoil boat.

The K-Force devices and sorties never had more than a pin-prick effect on the war. The Allies always had enough surface and air escort in the right places to contain them, and it is arguable whether the Germans had value for money from these special assault craft. The chief limitations arose perhaps from the German national temperament and its philosophy towards sea power. These weapons were used too late and entirely defensively. A Seehunde developed 3 years earlier might have had an appreciable effect on the Battle of the Atlantic, used against Allied shipping in estuaries such as the Mersey or the Clyde, when large convoys were assembling, or against almost any port in southern England in the months before D-Day. After Prien, Scapa lay unmolested for the rest of the war, and there was never any German equivalent of the raid on St Nazaire.

Above: German 'Linse' explosive motor-boats in harbour. (Imperial War Museum)

Below: A German 'Neger' human torpedo being readied for action. (Conway Picture Library)

Above: Captured German 'Seehund' midget submarines in the bomb-proof factory where they were being built, 1945. (Author's Collection)

Below: German 'Biber' one-man midget submarine beached ashore. (Imperial War Museum)

Above: XE-craft midget submarine on the surface in Sydney Harbour, 1945. (Imperial War Museum)

Below: Two Japanese suicide motor-boats, captured by US Marines on Okinawa, April 1945. Chalked on the nearest boat is the warning: 'Danger. These boats are booby-trapped.' (Author's Collection

CHAPTER 10

'You're the little guys with a lotta guts!' the Americans told the fourteenth Submarine Flotilla in April 1945, when they arrived in Australia in *Bonaventure*, with 6 improved XE class midget submarines on board. But though the US Navy approved of midget submarines in theory, in practice they had no use for them, believing, quite rightly, that they had the beating of the Japanese with orthodox submarines. Japan had no *Tirpitz*, laid up in an otherwise impregnable lair. By the summer of 1945 most of Japan's ports were within range of naval and land-based air attack, and most of her waterways vulnerable to aerial or submarine mine-laying. Thus the Americans believed they had no targets for such weapons, which they had not used since the Civil War, while the British preserved their long tradition of messing about in such small boats. Midget submarines were in the Elizabethan tradition. As had been aptly remarked, they were the lineal descendants of the Elizabethan fireship.

In fact, there were suitable targets for X-craft all along the coastline of South-East Asia and China: Japanese shipping at Singapore, Hong Kong, Saigon, Camranh Bay, and, as the war rolled nearer Japan, in Japanese mainland harbours. Japanese naval and diplomatic codes had long been broken and the only secure messages were those passed by the submarine cables running from South-East Asia to Japan. After a long period of uncertainty, in which it seemed very likely that the flotilla would be disbanded, the XE-craft scrapped and *Bonaventure* converted into a store ship for the fleet train, it was suggested that the midget submarines attack these submarine cables.

In July 1945, *Bonaventure* arrived at Victoria Harbour, Labuan, by which time three operations were in preparation: FOIL, to cut the submarine cables in the Lamma Channel, off Hong Kong; SABRE, to do the same at Cap St Jacques, Saigon; and STRUGGLE, to make attacks similar to that on *Tirpitz* on two Japanese heavy cruisers, *Myoko* and *Takao*, then lying in the Johore Strait, at Singapore. Both ships had been badly damaged in earlier actions, but it was thought they could be made operational again.

The three operations began within a day of each other. *Stygian* and *Spark*, with *XE3* (Lieutenant I E Fraser RNR) and *XE1* (Lieutenant J E Smart RNVR) respectively in tow, sailed from Labuan for STRUGGLE on 26 July 1945. *Spearhead* with *XE4* sailed for SABRE a day later, *XE4*'s operational CO being Shean. *Selene*, towing *XE5* for FOIL, sailed from the depot ship *Maidstone*, at Subic Bay, in the Philippines, on the same day. *XE5*'s operational CO was Westmacott.

SABRE was a neat and quick operation, a thoroughly professional undertaking. *XE4* was slipped 40 miles off Saigon on the evening of 30 July. Next morning, Shean reconnoitred the coast-line before beginning a sweep with the grapnel. After an hour's sweeping, the grapnel snagged. The diver, Sub Lieutenant A K Bergius RNVR, left *XE4* to search the bottom and found two cables. He came back inboard with two pieces of cable, one cut from each, which were taken back, tied with pink ribbon, to *Bonaventure*. *XE4* was taken in tow by *Spearhead* that night and both returned in good order to Labuan on 3 August.

Westmacott, in FOIL, had a much more difficult time. The tow parted near *Selene*'s end in the early hours of the 30th and *XE5*, weighed down with over 300 feet of line hanging from her bows, began to plunge towards the bottom of the sea. Furiously blowing main ballast tanks and going full ahead with hydroplanes hard a rise, Westmacott managed to catch *XE5* at about 300 feet and slipped the towing line, whereupon *XE5* soared up to the surface like a giant cork. After such an experience, Westmacott decided to go on alone, and *XE5* reached the Lamma Channel on 31 July.

Hampered by poor visibility in the channel and bedevilled by dozens of junks, sampans and small craft, Westmacott began grappling on the morning of 1 August. When the grapnel fouled an obstruction, the diver Sub Lieutenant B G Clark RNVR, went out to examine the cable. But he was blinded by the deep mud on the bottom and badly injured his hand with the wire-cutter and had to come inboard again. The second diver, Sub Lieutenant D M Jarvis RNVR, took over but though *XE5* grappled to and fro all that day nothing was found. Westmacott retired to charge the battery that night and returned on 2/3 August, grappling without success. At last, Westmacott gave it up and *XE5* was taken in tow once again by *Selene* on 4 August, both submarines returning to Subic Bay on the 6th. When the Allies reoccupied Hong Kong, it was found that *XE5*'s activities had damaged the cables after all. Ironically, within a few weeks, the Allies were repairing the cables, which Shean and Westmacott had so coolly and skilfully attacked.

An even greater irony awaited the aftermath of *XE3*'s attack on

Takao, which was one of the bravest single exploits of the Second World War at sea. *XE3* slipped her tow from *Stygian* at 11 pm on 30 July, about 2½ miles from the Horsburgh Light, at the eastern end of the Singapore Channel. Fraser, the operational CO had to take his X-craft through an intricate and dangerous passage of some 40 miles, past shoals and wrecks, across minefields and beside listening posts, through a buoyed boom and surface patrols, first along the length of the Singapore channel and then north and west through the Johore Strait, which lay between Singapore island and the mainland. If there was any mishap, and Fraser and his crew fell into Japanese hands, they were likely to be tortured and then executed as spies.

XE3 made a steady 5 knots on the surface, to pass the Johore listening posts just after 2 am on 31 July. At 4.30 am, Fraser had to dive in a hurry to avoid a small tanker and her escort which loomed up out of the dark. *XE3* hit the bottom so hard she damaged the log from which Fraser measured speed and distance to work out his dead reckoning navigation. At 6 am Fraser and his crew took Benzedrine stimulant tablets. Just then, *XE3* was off the eastern point of Singapore island and looking to port through the periscope Fraser could see the grim towers and roofs of Changi Gaol – where thousands of Allied prisoners-of-war were incarcerated – with the Rising Sun flying overhead.

At 10.30 am Fraser managed to follow a small trawler through the boom and began to work *XE3* up the Strait at a depth of 40 feet. Leading Seaman Magennis, the diver, began to dress in his heavy rubber suit. The temperature inside *XE3* was over 85°F, with a very high humidity. Shortly before 1 pm Fraser sighted his target – *Takao*. 'Although she seemed to appear with the suddenness of an apparition,' he said, 'I had the feeling that I had been staring at her for a long time.' At 1.50 pm, when Fraser began his attack, *XE3*'s crew had been 9 hours dived and 19 without proper sleep. But now was the time for their supreme effort.

Takao was anchored with her stern only some 50 to 100 yards from the Singapore side of the Strait. She lay in shallow water, only between 11 and 17 feet deep, but her length was across a much deeper depression. Fraser had to slip *XE3* across the shallows and into the hole beneath *Takao*.

Fraser thought his first attack was too fine on the target's bow. He retired and at about 3 pm he tried again, this time sliding *XE3* neatly under *Takao*'s hull. Magennis went out through the 'wet and dry' compartment and fixed magnetic limpet mines to *Takao*'s side. Her plates were covered in marine growth and Magennis had to chip away for nearly half an hour before he could settle his mines properly on bare metal.

179

When Magennis came back, Fraser released the port charge, of 2 tons of Amatol. But the starboard charge stuck. So also did *XE3*, underneath *Takao*, and Fraser had to manoeuvre *XE3* frantically for several minutes before she came clear. But the starboard charge still refused to drop away. Magennis insisted that he was the ship's diver and climbed out again with a large spanner. In 5 minutes – the longest 5 minutes of everybody in *XE3*'s life, during which time a Japanese sailor could have looked down and seen the submarine clearly on the bottom – the charge at last fell clear and Magennis climbed back. Fraser wasted no time in taking *XE3* back down the Strait and out to sea, where he rendezvoused with *Stygian* and reached Labuan again on 4 August.

Fraser and Magennis were both awarded the Victoria Cross. On his way home, Fraser passed through Singapore and went on board the wreck of *Takao*. To his bitter disappointment he was told that the Japanese Navy had long since written the ship off. At the time of his attack, she was almost derelict, of no operational value, with only a skeleton crew on board.

Lieutenant Smart in *XE1* had had a frustrating time. He had been delayed by patrols and had been unable to reach *Myoko* which was much further up harbour. As the time for the detonation of Fraser's charges was running out, Smart had added his under *Takao* and retired, being picked up again by *Spark*.

The Japanese for their part designed and built numbers of special attack craft: fast motor-boats, midget submarines and human torpedoes. But for all the Imperial Japanese Navy's great offensive tradition, these were defensive devices, which had only the slightest pin-prick effect on the war before their construction and deployment were swept aside and swamped by the tide of events.

By September 1944 the Japanese had 759 'Shinyo' motor-boats (actually only half the number planned) for the defence of the Philippines. They were some 18 feet long, made of light plywood, carrying two 260-pound depth-charges, a light machine-gun, a few hand-grenades and a crew of two or three. Their tactic was to approach their target from astern, heave overboard the depth-charges and retire at full speed. On the night of 9/10 January 1945, 70 Shinyo manned by the Japanese army sallied out from nearby Port Saul to attack Allied landing craft in Lingayen Gulf. In a confused situation, where targets were sighted all over the harbour, and firing went on for some time after the attacks were over, the Shinyo sank 2 landing craft and damaged 8 other ships. All 70 of them were lost, to gunfire, or explosions, or from running aground, or were simply abandoned.

On the last night of January, more Shinyo from Mariveles, outside Manila Bay, made an attack on Allied shipping across the nearest stretch of water at Nasugbu. In another wild and confused night for the defenders, a submarine-chaser was sunk and a few other ships damaged. When troops landed at Mariveles in mid-February, 30 Shinyo were dispatched from Corregidor to attack them and sank 3 landing support craft.

On Iwo Jima the same month, the fierce resistance put up by the Japanese garrison meant that Allied ships had to stay in the waters nearby for much longer than was planned or safe. Japanese submarines missed a great opportunity to attack the invasion ships off shore. Two midget submarines were sunk off Iwo Jima on 26 and 27 February. A third returned to Japan after being kept down by destroyers for 48 hours – surely a record for this size of submarine. Two more midgets left Japan on 1 March but returned without having achieved anything.

The Japanese had been experimenting with midget submarines for much of the war and by 1945 had two types in service. The larger, the Type D, Koryu ('Dragon with scales'), was built as a prototype in June 1944 and completed in January 1945. It was some 85 feet long, weighed 60 tons, had a diesel generator giving 8 knots on the surface, and batteries giving a maximum of 16 knots dived. Its endurance was 1000 miles on the surface, but only 40 minutes at full dived speed. Its safe diving depth was 300 feet, and it was armed with two 18-inch torpedoes in tubes. With a complement of three, it could be built and manned in 60 days and the Japanese planned to build 580 of them, at a rate of 180 a month, after September 1945. But because of intense bombing of Japanese shipyards, only about 110 Koryus were actually built.

A smaller type, the S-Kanamono (literally, 'S-Metal Fitting') was built as a prototype at Kobe in 1943. Later a much modified version went into production (it could be built in 30 days) as the Kairyu 'Dragon in the sea' at Yokosuka in 1944. The two-man Kairyu was 56 feet long, weighed about 20 tons dived, had two 18-inch torpedoes in tubes, or two 600 kg, mines. The range was 450 miles at 5 knots on the surface, 36 miles at 3 knots submerged.

The Koryu and Kairyu crews had a fair expectation of return to base. The Kaiten ('Tremendous') were pure suicide weapons, the naval equivalent of the kamikaze bomber. The Kaiten was a mounted one-man torpedo, oxygen-powered to give speeds of up to 30 knots, with a range of 25,000 yards (85,000 at a lower speed such as 12 knots) carrying a warhead of $1\frac{1}{2}$ tons of explosive. Later Kaitens were powered by hydrogen peroxide motors to give speeds of 40 knots and were much larger (19 tons as opposed to the earlier $8\frac{1}{2}$). The Kaitens were carried to their targets on the casings of larger submarines and saw a good deal of service off the Philippines, Guam and Okinawa, from 1944 onwards.

Below the Belt

When the Allies invaded the Kerama Retto, a small group of islands lying south-east of Okinawa, in March 1945, as a preliminary to the main invasion of the island on 1 April, they captured some 350 suicide motor-boats. These were three out of seven 'sea raiding battalions' of Shinyo intended for the defence of Okinawa. But neither they nor the Shinyo on Okinawa played any part in the campaign. By July 1945 the Japanese had 3294 special attack craft (2850 Shinyo, 73 Koryu, 252 Kairyu, 119 Kaiten) for the defence of metropolitan Japan, disposed in 8 squadrons along the coasts of Kyushu and Honshu. But none of these played any part before the end. When the Allies reoccupied Hong Kong at the end of August, suicide motor-boats were sighted in the Lamma Channel, appearing to be getting under way. They were attacked and destroyed by aircraft from the carrier *Indomitable*.

Had the Allies gone on to carry out Operation OLYMPIC, the planned landing on Kyushu in November 1945, they would have been opposed by one of the most macabre Japanese suicide weapons, the Fukuryu ('Hidden Dragon'). These were human underwater weapons, men in rubber suits and breathing apparatus who literally walked on the sea floor, patrolling off Japanese coasts from dawn to dusk. In one trial, a Fukuryu officer marched on the sea bottom, 27 feet deep, at 1 mile an hour for 8 hours. The Fukuryu had vacuum flasks of hot soup incorporated in their suits which they drank through rubber tubes.

Each Fukuryu had a long pole with a contact mine fixed to the end of it. He was a human spar torpedo carrier, in a throw-back to the weaponry of eighteenth and nineteenth century navies. Any Fukuryu who succeeded in banging his mine against the hull of a landing craft would blow himself and his target to pieces. But he would also kill nearby Fukuryu who might not yet have achieved their own personal consummation through immolation. So, with gruesome compassion, the Japanese constructed underwater bomb-shelters for those Fukuryu who had not yet made their attacks. It was generally a weapon which reverted to the days of the ancient Greeks, employed in a way which would have disgusted the Greeks themselves.

There were in World War Two several adventures in places and with weapons which would have been familiar to seamen of previous ages. There were, for instance, schemes to flood coastal waters off southern England, such as the Solent, with a covering of inflammable materials, so as to envelop any invading force in flames, and, in September and October 1940, actual attempts to send fire-ships against the German invasion fleets assembling at Calais and Boulogne.

The best opinion in the Navy was that the Germans would not be able to make a successful invasion anyway, but fire-ship schemes were prepared and Captain Agar VC was given charge of them. The plan codenamed Operation LUCID originally was for four old First World War tankers to have their tanks filled with 'Agar's mixture' of roughly 50% heavy oil fuel, 25% diesel oil and 25% petrol, with sheaves and bunches of old loose cordite tied together and scattered here and there. A number of depth-charges were also placed in the holds, with a quantity of gun-cotton. The charges were to be detonated electrically, after a timed delay, to allow the volunteer crews to escape by boat.

Some of the volunteers were somewhat reluctant. The two tankers from Portsmouth were commanded by Lieut Cdr, later Captain, 'Tiny' Fell, a notable figure in the submarine world, who commanded the charioteer and Welman depot ship *Titania*, and the XE-craft depot ship *Bonaventure*, later in the war. Fell, when he heard of the scheme, 'was so horror-struck by the idea that I could not find any words to say that I was absolutely terrified at the thought'.

The fire-ships were to be escorted by minesweepers and motor torpedo-boats, and accompanied by a diversionary air raid by the RAF. Even so, Fell calculated that they would be sighted at least a mile off the harbour and would be under fire from the guns on the breakwater for some 6 minutes before they could light the fuses. In the event, on the night chosen, 26/27 September 1940, only two fire-ships sailed, *War Nawab*, commanded by Fell, and *War Nizam*, commanded by Lieut Cdr Stratford Dennis, from Sheerness. Fell and his crew of 10 were slightly reassured by the presence of two launches, one of them brand new, provided for their escape. They had to be hoisted in improvised fashion, on davits that did not fit them, but at least they were on board.

War Nizam started her attempt but by 10 pm a red glow from her funnel showed that something was wrong and she turned round. Fell, in *War Nawab*, had actually got to within 8 miles of Boulogne when the wind backed and freshened from the south, meaning that oil released on the water would be blown out of Boulogne harbour. Even so Fell was preparing to go on when the message 'Operation abandoned – return to base' was flashed from the minesweeper astern of him. 'Unlike Nelson,' wrote Fell, 'I felt only pure relief at being spared, and without any qualms I ordered "hard-a-starboard" and returned back towards England.'

Meanwhile, in *War Nawab*'s engine room, men were beginning to pass out because of petrol fumes from the fuel escaping through her rusty old bulkheads. Later, when Fell and his men wanted to leave, one launch's engine stopped dead after 200 yards, and the other, the new boat, had a flat battery. It was as well they discovered this off Sheerness instead of inside Boulogne. Other attempts at LUCID were made on three nights early in October but each time, bad weather or mishaps to the escorts, caused it to be cancelled. By the end of the month, the risk of invasion had, realistically, faded almost completely. So the fire-ship schemes came to nothing, (as did an earlier venture with a familiar ring to it: a plan in the spring of 1940 to disrupt German river traffic by floating delayed action mines down the Rhine).

But the greatest theatre of the Second World War, in which many old principles and examples of tactics and weaponry were demonstrated once again, was the Atlantic – which, as Churchill said, was a 'war of groping and drowning, of ambuscade and stratagem, of science and seamanship'. It was a battle which the Allies had to win; if it were lost, all else would be lost. It was the longest battle of the war, lasting from 3 September 1939 until 8 May 1945.

The U-boats, led by a most able commander in Dönitz, were formidable opponents. They began their first tentative experiments in 'wolf-pack' tactics as early as January 1940 and, when they took to attacking on the surface by night, they soon showed that pre-war confidence in the efficiency of asdic equipment was almost completely misplaced. On the surface, each U-boat became a torpedo-boat, impossible to detect by asdic and, with its very low surface profile, almost as difficult to sight visually. Even when a U-boat was sighted, the early, slow convoy escorts were unable to overtake the 17-knot submarines.

But each move in the Atlantic had a counter-move. Pre-war flares were too dim and dropped too quickly. Brighter, slow-dropping illuminants such as 'snow-flake' were developed. Aircraft were fitted with intensely bright, downward-shining searchlights, known as Leigh lights, after their inventor Squadron Leader H de V Leigh. Radar sets were fitted in aircraft and some escorts from January 1941 onwards. An aircraft could track its target from long range on radar and illuminate suddenly when it was overhead.

Against radar, the U-boats' hulls were coated with rubber, which was believed to absorb the beams, or released decoys, which were often buoys sprayed with metallic paint, left bobbing about on the surface after the submarine had dived. Dived, a U-boat might release oil, or even specially prepared 'debris', to suggest that it was sunk, while in fact it was making good its escape. Later in the war, U-boats discharged 'Pillenwerfers', canisters generating a stream of bubbles which counterfeited the asdic 'echo' of a genuine submarine hull.

For submarines that went deep, depth-charges were designed to explode at greater depths, and their patterns were increased from 5 charges to 14. For submarines which stayed on the surface, to fight it out with gun-power, depth-charges were designed with pistols detonating at depths as little as 20 feet. The dead period, between the moment a U-boat passed out of the asdic beam ahead of the escort, and the time the escort took to run over the target and release depth-charges astern, was removed by ahead-throwing weapons, first the Hedgehog and then the Squid, so that a U-boat could be held in the asdic beam while it was being attacked.

The standard torpedo used by the U-boats was the Type G-7e: battery-powered, it carried 660 pounds of explosive at 30 knots to a range of 5500 yards. Later the Germans introduced the Gnat acoustic torpedo and the Lut zig-zag running torpedo. The escorts countered with the 'Foxer' a noise-generating paravane towed astern to attract the torpedo's attention. The Americans developed Fido, a 21-inch acoustic airborne torpedo and as the war progressed, shore-based Liberators, Catalinas, Wellingtons and Beaufighters, and carrier-borne Avengers, Swordfish, Albacores, Barracudas and Martlets, were possessed of a formidable armoury of depth-charges, rockets and acoustic torpedoes.

Eventually, more escorts, more aircraft, better weapons, closer co-operation between the Admiralty and Coastal Command and above all, brilliant decoding of German signals, won the Battle in the Atlantic. Just as the U-boats had their aces, so the escorts had their maestros, one of the very best being Captain F J Walker RN. The ships in 'Johnnie Walkers's' escort groups were highly trained, drilled to perform as team, perfectly skilled in 'passing the ball' from one ship to another, one taking up the attack as another relinquished it, to keep the U-boat under constant pressure.

One of Walker's most successful tactics was the 'creeping barrage'. When a U-boat had been detected it was held in the asdic beams of two escorts, steaming one on either quarter and keeping pace with it. The 'tocking' of the asdic on the hull reminded the U-boat captain of the escorts' presence. Meanwhile another escort, not using her asdic, steamed quietly ahead along the U-boat's track, until he was far enough ahead. At the correct estimated distance, the attacking ship ahead would begin to drop depth-charges, normally 26 charges in pairs at 9 second intervals, set to explode at depths between 500 and 740 feet. A deadly carpet of charges was thus laid in front of the unsuspecting and advancing U-boat, which was still steering directly into it. The first (and last) intimation of the depth-charges the U-boat had was their detonation all around. If a U-boat tried to take evasive action, then Walker would use more than one escort ahead, to lay creeping barrages across a wide sector.

For the U-boats, one of the best offensive and defensive weapons was speed, and the Germans made endless attempts to increase submarine speed, using Type XXI U-boats with increased battery capacity, capable of reaching underwater speeds of 17 knots in short bursts. These boats never saw operational service. Nor did another potentially brilliant weapon, the Walter-engined submarine, driven by burning diesel fuel in hydrogen peroxide. Experimental boats did run successfully, proving that the method was correct, but luckily for the Allies the war ended before the Walter U-boats could put to sea.

The Germans did, however, make use of the schnorkel breathing tube in U-boats from July 1944 onwards. This was originally a Dutch invention, evolved as early as 1927. Four Dutch boats with incomplete schnorkel sets escaped from Holland and joined the Royal Navy in 1940. But the Navy could see no use for the devices and they were removed. But after the success of centimetric radar in detecting submarines, the Germans turned to schnorkels, which at once enabled U-boats to charge their batteries without surfacing, and enabled them to operate again in areas which radar surveillance had closed to them for some time. Schnorkel-fitted U-boats were operating until the very end of the war in Europe and it is true to say that they posed a problem which was not fully solved by the escorts.

So many ships were sunk in the Atlantic in two wars, so many lives were lost on both sides, that it might have been thought that all susceptibilities were dulled; any tactic was permissible, any behaviour condoned. But there were limits, even at the end (although it is arguable that those limits were set by those who won the war).

Shortly after 7 pm on the evening of 13 March 1944, the 8800-ton tramp steamer *Peleus* was steaming alone, bound from Freetown to the Plate in ballast, a few miles south of the Equator and about 300 miles from the nearest coast of Africa. She was unescorted, but defensively armed with a gun on her poop. Suddenly, without warning, the tracks of two torpedoes were seen on the port beam. Both torpedoes hit and exploded. *Peleus* sank within 2 minutes.

Despite the suddenness of the attack, some of *Peleus'* crew survived. (She was Greek owned, under charter to the British Ministry of War Transport, and her crew of 35 included, curiously, British, Greek, Egyptian, Chinese, Chilean, Russian, Polish, and one man from Aden.) The survivors were 300 miles from land, in shark-infested waters, with little food or water and no protection from the tropical sun. But in addition to these dangers, the U-boat herself appeared, on the surface, and the Third Officer and a Russian seaman were taken on board for questioning. They were asked the name of the ship, where bound and where from, questions about convoy routine about warships in Sierra Leone and, significantly, whether those warships included an aircraft carrier. After the interrogation, the Third Officer was deprived of his life-jacket, and he and the Russian seaman were put back on a raft.

By then, some of the survivors had managed to bring two larger pieces of wreckage together to form another makeshift raft. They were hailed from the U-boat and ordered to come closer. A signalling lamp shone out from the U-boat's bridge, to illuminate the targets, and in its light the survivors, the *uberrest*, (or remnant) were machine-gunned and fired on with pistols by the men on the U-boat's bridge. Hand-grenades were also thrown, to further break up the wreckage.

The U-boat cruised in and out of the *uberrest*, firing machine-guns and pistols intermittently, for nearly 5 hours. Then, apparently satisfied that all the *uberrest* had been destroyed, the U-boat sheered off on the surface, just before dawn broke. Many of *Peleus'* crew had been killed by the torpedoes' explosions, and many more were killed on the rafts.

But not all. The Greek First Officer, Antonios Liossis, the Third Officer, another Greek, Agis Kefalas, a British greaser, Rocco Said, and a Greek seaman, Dimitrios Argiros, though all wounded, survived. Kefalas was badly wounded in the right arm and died after 25 days on the raft. But the other three all lived and were picked up on 20 April by a Portuguese steamer, *Alexandre Silva*, after 38 days on the raft.

Meanwhile, the U-boat continued her patrol, operating off Cape Town for a time, where she sank a steamer, *Dahomian*, on 1 April, before heading up the east coast of Africa, to operate in the Indian Ocean. On 2 May 1944, off the coast of Italian Somaliland, the U-boat was attacked and sunk by two aircraft of 621 Squadron RAF. Five officers and 54 petty officers and men were made prisoner of war.

The U-boat was *U852*, a Type XI D2, of 1200 tons, armed with four bow and two stern 21-inch torpedo tubes, carrying 21 torpedoes on board, and one 37-mm and two 20-mm guns. She was a new boat and had sailed on this, her first and last war patrol, from Kiel on 18 January 1944. Her commanding officer, Kapitan Leutnant Heinz Eck, had been in the German Navy since 1934 and in submarines since 1942. He was 29 years old, and *U852* was his first command.

U852's log was not destroyed and from it, and from the sworn depositions of *Peleus'* survivors, the facts of the sinking were reconstructed. At Hamburg on 17 October 1945, Eck was charged by a War Crimes court with 'committing a war crime in that you in the Atlantic Ocean on the night of 13/14 March 1944, when Captain of Unterseeboot 852 which had sunk the steamship *Peleus* in violation of the laws and usages of war were concerned in the killing of members of the crew of the said steamship, Allied nationals, by firing and throwing grenades at them.' Also accused with Eck of taking part that night were the First Lieutenant, Leutnant-zur-See August Hoffmann, the Engineer Officer, Kapitan Leutnant (Ing) Hans Richards Lenz, the doctor, Marine Oberstabsarzt Walter Weisspfennig, and one petty officer, Matrosen-Obergefreiter Wolfgang Schwender.

The President of the Court was a Brigadier and the six members were senior Navy and Army officers, including two officers from the Royal Hellenic Navy. The prosecutor was a colonel from the Judge Advocate General's Office. The Judge Advocate was Major Melford Stevenson, KC. All five accused were ably and vigorously defended by German lawyers, who, naturally, attempted to upset the premises which formed the basis of the charges. For Eck in particular it was argued that he acted from 'operational necessity'. He had been specifically warned against the dangers of air attack at his briefings before sailing. Four other U-boats, sister ships of *U852*, had disappeared without trace (actually sunk by aircraft) in those very waters during the previous 9 months. At that stage of the war at sea, any sinking by a U-boat almost anywhere in the Atlantic almost always brought down swift retribution from aircraft, using the stricken vessel's SOS signal, or oil traces or debris, or survivors if any, as a datum point. So Eck was entitled to destroy such evidence, to protect his U-boat and his crew. For the other defendants, the plea of 'superior orders' was put forward. They had to obey, even if they disapproved (as Lenz did, but fired just the same). In Schwender's case, it was argued that he had only fired at wreckage, not survivors. There was also a good deal of discussion from the defence side, of what constituted a war crime, and the authority of that Court to try the defendants at all.

The prosecution contended, and produced another U-boat commander to give evidence that if Eck had really wished to safeguard his submarine he would have put as much distance as possible between himself and the sinking, and as quickly as possible. He would not have lingered for 5 hours, shooting up harmless survivors floating on rafts or in the sea. By that stage in the war the U-boat arm had lost hundreds of boats and thousands of men. Service in U-boats was hard, uncomfortable and dangerous. Life was lived under constant strain and fear of attack. What could be more natural, the prosecution suggested, than for Eck and his officers to take at least some form of revenge on the Allies, in the shape of these hapless seamen, while they had the chance?

As for the doctor, Weisspfennig, he had special status under the

Geneva Convention and was absolved from the necessity to carry weapons. He had profaned his calling by firing upon the *uberrest*. His had been a crime against humanity and the medical profession. Hoffman had aided and abetted his captain. Relations between the two were not good, but Hoffman had obeyed to the limit and it was he who had hurled the hand-grenades. Lenz might have expressed his disgust but he had fired just the same. Further he had taken a gun out of Schwender's hands and used it himself, giving the incomprehensible reason that he did not think Schwender a fit person to fire upon the *uberrest*.

The prosecutor recalled the case of a similar outrage by a U-boat, against the *Llandovery Castle* during the First World War, in which it was held that, just as the killing of unarmed persons was unlawful in land warfare, so it was not permissible to kill shipwrecked persons who had taken refuge in lifeboats. As for the plea of 'superior orders', this went to the heart of what was and was not a war crime. Certain acts were unlawful whether or not there had been orders to carry them out, and whether there was or not any rule of law in force on the spot at the time.

Evidence was given of orders relating to the rescue of survivors, issued from the headquarters of Dönitz (who was himself under trial as a war criminal) on 17 September 1942. 'No attempt of any kind must be made at rescuing members of ships sunk, and this includes picking up persons in the water and putting them in lifeboats, righting capsized lifeboats and handing over food and water ... Be harsh, having in mind that the enemy takes no regard of women and children in his bombing attacks on German cities.'

In its own way the *Peleus* trial, as it was called, was an admirable paradigm of the state of the law as regards war crimes at sea, in which the difference between German and British law, and between municipal and international law, the conflict between conscience and command, and the various definitions of war crimes at sea, were all thoroughly aired and explored.

The Court was not impressed by any of the defence submissions and, although the Judge Advocate reminded the Court he was there in an advisory capacity, his summing-up clearly foreshadowed the verdicts. All five defendants were found guilty as charged. Eck, Hoffmann and Weisspfennig were sentenced to death; the sentences were later confirmed and all three executed by shooting. Lenz was sentenced to imprisonment for life, Schwender to 15 years.

Fear of air attack had been the main motive behind Eck's action. Air power, by means of very long range shore-based, or carrier-borne, aircraft was the key to the winning of the battle of the Atlantic. In the latter days every convoy carried its own air power, by means of a 'Woolworth' escort carrier, or a tanker or grain-ship, converted to operate aircraft, actually steaming in the convoy's ranks. But until enough of these ships were available, the search for possible deployments of aircraft at sea sometimes took some strange bypaths.

There was, for instance, the Battle-Carrier, which was a hybrid vessel, half battlecruiser, half aircraft carrier, similar to the Japanese battleship/carriers *Ise* and *Hyuga*. In theory, the battle-carrier would have half the battlecruiser's gun power and half the carriers air power. In practice, it was inefficient in both roles. Further study showed that two inefficient battle-carriers would consume as much men, materials and effort as one proper battlecruiser and one proper carrier. So the scheme was dropped.

Another more durable scheme, which originated in September 1942, with the strong support of Mr Churchill was code-named Habakkuk. It was nothing less than a proposal to construct a floating self-propelling island aircraft carrier made of ice. Although the idea seemed fantastic to the stupefied layman, work was actually put in hand to build Habakkuk of blocks, welded or frozen together, of Pykrete which was a mixture of 86% ice to 14% wood pulp, named after its inventor Mr Geoffrey Pyke, Director of Programmes at Combined Operations Headquarters. The final craft was to have been 2000 feet long, 200 feet deep, 300 feet wide, weighing approximately 2,000,000 tons, covered with an insulating skin, kept permanently frozen by its own refrigerating machinery and propelled by 26 electric motors, each mounted in its own submerged nacelle, thirteen nacelles on each side. A trial model, 60 feet by 30 feet, was actually ordered and work on it began at Lake Patricia, Jaspar, Alberta.

Habakkuk was intended to be on station somewhere in mid-Atlantic, operating aircraft with the wing spans of Wellingtons and Mosquitoes. Unfortunately, it was one of those ideas which, like the Holy Grail, was always just out of reach. However hard its designers tried, Habakkuk never became feasible. It always 'almost worked'. Every time its designers believed they had broken through to success, another serious snag was discovered. The scheme was dropped in December 1943.

Much later in the war, the concepts of the Battle-Carrier and Habakkuk were turned over to Naval Intelligence Division, Section 17M. It was suggested that there might be some value in convincing the enemy (who was, by then, Japan only) that the Allies were developing such weapons. But the atomic bomb was dropped on Hiroshima and the war came to an end before either scheme could be properly evolved.

Led by Lieutenant Commander Ewen Montagu RNVR, 17M had been one of the most successful Admiralty 'dirty tricks' departments since 1941. With the advantages of ULTRA, the Allied code-breaking, which enabled the Section to read enemy signals, and of German spies in the United Kingdom, every one of whom had been discovered and 'turned round' so as to work in some way for the Allies, Montagu's section emitted a stream of facts, information and rumour which were false, half-false, or not-quite-true, to confuse, perplex, deceive and dismay the enemy.

Their great *coup*, appropriately gruesomely code-named MINCEMEAT, was 'The Man Who Never Was': the deception plan in which the body of an Allied officer was put overboard from a submarine in such a position that it would float to the Spanish shore and fall into Axis hands. The body carried misleading but convincing information about the choice of the next Allied landing (in this case, Sicily). But this was just one high point in what amounted to a great campaign of deception, which extended through the war years like a vast web, composed of dummy minefields and public house tittle-tattle, phantom ship movements and cocktail party gossip, holiday snaps and non-existent secret weapons, designed to convince the enemy, for instance, that the Allies had more ships of a particular kind (such as Woolworth carriers) than they actually had, or weapons (such as rocket-powered depth-charges, or torpedo-tubes in *King George V* class battleships) which they did not actually have, or that the enemy's own devices (such as the schnorkel) were less effective than they actually were.

Some of the Section's schemes would have been greatly approved of by the ancient Greeks. In particular, Montagu showed a fine Greek hand in a plan, codenamed IAGO, to remove from operational existence a spectacularly successful U-boat commander, who was based at Bordeaux. It was 1942 and morale in the U-boat arm was still as high as their sinking rate. This man was an ace, with a huge score to his credit of thousands of tons of Allied shipping sunk and hundreds of Allied seamen's lives lost, and he was becoming a national hero back home in Germany.

The scheme was for the British Secret Intelligence Service, known as 'C', to send to this U-boat captain a 'pin-up' calendar, with pages of sexy pictures of girls, which he would be likely to hang up in his cabin. (But it was not important whether he used the calendar or not; it could be traced to him.) On the back of the calendar was a message, in invisible ink which had been developed and allowed to fade again, thanking him for his latest report on U-boat sailings and changes in U-boat strategy and weaponry.

Another message would then be sent to one of 'C's' agents in France who was known to have been discovered by the Germans. Anything sent to this agent would certainly be read by the Gestapo.

The agent would be instructed to send the U-boat captain his money, and also a scarf impregnated with invisible ink of the same kind as had been used on the calendar. (An agent then soaked the scarf, to melt the crystals dried on it, and squeezed the resulting liquid into a bottle for use.)

The Gestapo would now certainly begin enquiries and would inevitably arrest the U-boat captain, even if he had given the calendar to someone else. Useless for the U-boat commander to protest his innocence. The calendar, the messages from the agent, the invisible ink of the same type, would be irrefutable proof of guilt. To clinch the matter, 'C' would send another message through the same source, thanking the U-boat captain for his valuable information of U-boat routes through the German defensive minefields off Bordeaux, and asking for further information on some details. It would be unlikely that the U-boat captain would escape execution as a traitor.

But IAGO was turned down. It was 'not cricket'. Montagu was told 'We don't assassinate people'. The ethics of this case occupied Montagu's mind for some time. If the scheme had been to assassinate *Hitler*, then surely there would have been no qualms? The death of that one man would undoubtedly save many lives. Many lives (although admittedly fewer than if Hitler were killed) would be saved by the death of this U-boat captain. But was the plan inadmissible because fewer lives would be saved? If that was so, then at what number of lives did such a plan become admissible? If a hundred, five hundred, several thousand, Allied lives could be saved, could IAGO then proceed? In Montagu's own account, the problem should be seen in its contemporary context: in 1942 the United Kingdom was fighting for its very existence, for the preservation of freedom in the world, and was still very close to being beaten. Perhaps unconsciously, Montagu was contributing to the debate which had continued since the Greeks, of precisely what is and what is not, 'below the belt' in war at sea.